The
Mormon
Corporate
Empire

The Mormon Corporate Empire

John Heinerman
Anson Shupe

Beacon Press   *Boston*

Beacon Press
25 Beacon Street
Boston, Massachusetts 02108

Beacon Press books are published under the auspices
of the Unitarian Universalist Association
of Congregations in North America.

92 91 90 89 88 87 86 85   8 7 6 5 4 3 2 1

Library of Congress Cataloging in Publication Data

Heinerman, John.
   The Mormon corporate empire.

   Includes bibliographies and index.
   1. Church of Jesus Christ of Latter-day Saints—
Controversial literature.   2. Mormon Church—
Controversial literature.   3. Church of Jesus Christ of
Latter-day Saints—Finance.   4. Mormon Church—Finance.
5. Church of Jesus Christ of Latter-day Saints—
Political activity.   6. Mormon Church—Political
activity. I. Shupe, Anson D.   II. Title.
BX8645.H45   1985   289.3'32   85-47527
ISBN 0-8070-0406-5

To Dean R. Brimhall, a steadfast public servant
and tireless observer of Mormonism

Contents

Preface

Research on a religion is rarely considered "objective" by devout followers if it is not to some degree apologetic. Moreover, insiders to the faith tend to indulge their group's shortcomings, even discounting them altogether — an attitude that nonmembers and those marginal to the group do not always share. This book may offend and even infuriate the faithful of one particular religious organization, the Church of Jesus Christ of Latter-day Saints, popularly known as the Mormons. We hope that it will also inform and sensitize them as well as readers in the "Gentile" (non-Mormon) public. Our premise — that the Mormon financial/political enterprise is not simply an American success story but rather an ongoing crusade to reshape our society and its democratic traditions — will inevitably prompt accusations of bigotry.

We are also aware that this book will not satisfy many academic scholars. Historians and social scientists, both Mormon and non-Mormon, disagree about how Mormonism should be interpreted. According to the largely optimistic academic "pitch" now current, earlier "hard-line" millennial Mormonism has now mellowed and accommodated itself to middle-class America. Our project may seem to many a return to the anti-Mormon muckraking of the past.

Our aim, however, is neither to muckrake nor to pursue a vendetta. As academic researchers (one of us is an anthropologist, the other a sociologist, Mormon and Methodist respectively), we propose to interpret the patterns we document in this book. That the public is so little aware of these patterns testifies to the effectiveness of the Utah Saints' Church in managing its public image.

There is, to our minds, nothing antireligious or antidemocratic in undertaking such an examination of one American church's financial and political involvement in the wider society. We argue that the American pluralistic religious system cannot afford to ignore a rising, authoritarian, powerful group like the Latter-day Saints Church, particularly if its actions influence national events and help shape government policies that affect many people, Mormons and non-Mormons alike. If controversy arises over our interpretation of the vast wealth and secular ambitions of the Mormons, let it rage. We believe that such a debate is in the long-range interests of American religious freedom, and therefore of us all.

ACKNOWLEDGMENTS

Research for this book entailed several years of effort and thousands of miles of travel throughout the United States. Some of the information obtained was already available to the public in courthouses, public utility stock reports, and libraries. An important part of it, however, came from hundreds of interviews with persons both inside and outside the Church of Jesus Christ of Latter-day Saints (LDS). To those Church members who graciously talked with us, we reiterated our commitment not to deprecate the characters of either LDS founder Joseph Smith, Jr., nor any present Church leader and not to deprecate the *Book of Mormon* in any way. Such attacks have been standard anti-Mormon fare for years and were not our intent. Under such conditions most of the people we contacted were cooperative and open. We cannot and will not name them all, for the corporate entity we describe in this book is jealous of its good image and intolerant of member-critics. Nevertheless, we express our deep appreciation to all those anonymous informants otherwise uncited in the following pages. We are particularly grateful to several anonymous faculty members at Brigham Young University for their assistance and moral support.

Significant Dates in the History of the Church of Jesus Christ of Latter-day Saints

1820   Joseph Smith receives a vision from God and Jesus Christ announcing the Second Coming of Christ and Smith's post-millennial role as prophet.

1823   The angel Moroni first appears to Joseph Smith, telling of Christianity's "lost" heritage in North America.

1827   Joseph Smith begins translation of the *Book of Mormon*.

1829   Translation of the *Book of Mormon* is completed and a first edition printed.

1830   Joseph Smith founds the Church of Jesus Christ of Latter-day Saints in Fayette, New York.

1831   The Church moves its members and center to Kirtland, Ohio.

1832–   Mormons settle in various Missouri counties, seeking to
1839   escape persecution and establish Zion.

1839   Nauvoo (Commerce), Illinois, becomes the new Zion.

1844   Joseph Smith campaigns for the presidency of the United States. He and his brother Hyrum are shot and killed in cold blood by a mob at Carthage, Illinois. Brigham Young assumes the presidency of the Council of the Twelve.

1845   Plans and preparations for western migration begin as persecution in the Midwest worsens.

1847   Mormon pioneers begin establishing a permanent settlement in the Great Salt Basin, Utah.

1849   The provisional State of Deseret is organized.

1850   Utah is admitted to the Union only as a territory.

1857   United States troops "invade" Utah.

1869   The Union Pacific and Central Pacific railroads are joined at Ogden, Utah.

1882   The Edmunds Act is passed by Congress, outlawing polygamy as a felony.

1887   As anti-Mormon sentiment increases, the Edmunds-Tucker Act is passed by Congress, legally disenfranchising the LDS Church corporation.

1890   LDS Church President Wilford Woodruff issues the Manifesto, ending plural marriage for Church members.

1896   Utah is admitted to the Union as a state.

1903   Reed Smoot becomes the first Mormon member of the U.S. Senate.

1918– The LDS Church experiences rapid financial growth and
1945   attains a membership of almost one million during the presidency of Heber J. Grant.

1953   Ezra Taft Benson becomes secretary of agriculture to President Dwight D. Eisenhower.

1968   George Romney (two-term governor of Michigan) becomes the first modern Mormon candidate for president in the Republican primary.

1978   LDS President Spencer W. Kimball announces the decision to open the Church priesthood to blacks.

1

The Emerging Kingdom of the Saints

E veryone knows the Mormons. Mormons are the splendid white-robed Mormon Tabernacle Choir heard worldwide through records, radio appearances, and concerts. They are the clean-cut, conservatively dressed pairs of young men on foot or on bicycles who trek door-to-door witnessing for their faith. They are the late screen stars Dean Jagger and Tyrone Power heroically battling bigotry, Indians, and locusts in the prewar Hollywood epic *Brigham Young*. They proudly lead daily tours through their impressive complex of temple and buildings in the heart of Salt Lake City for tens of thousands of non-Mormon tourists each year. If a traveler staying in a hotel of the nationwide Marriott chain searches in the dresser drawer for the usual Gideon Bible, he or she instead finds the touch of the Mormons — in the form of a paperback copy of the *Book of Mormon*.

Yet most people do not know the real Church of Jesus Christ of Latter-day Saints (the formal name of the Mormons' organization) as it exists in modern-day America. They may have heard about some of the Church's more exotic aspects, such as its now extinct practice of polygyny (marriage of one man simultaneously to more than one wife), its taboos against tobacco, alcohol, and caffeine, its preoccupation with genealogy, or its belief that American Indians are really the descendants of ancient Lamanites (fallen Jews who immigrated by ship to this continent in 600 B.C.).

But most people, including many social scientists who study either the Church's family style or its activities on behalf of certain causes (such as lobbying against the Equal Rights Amendment), have largely missed seeing the greater extent of Mormon influence. The real character, style, and purpose of the corporate Church of Jesus Christ of Latter-day Saints (LDS) are usually left unexamined and undiscussed. In most analyses the Mormons are portrayed as an American success story in the marketplace of competing Protestant Christian sects. Homegrown in this country, they have reached out through extensive missionary efforts, both national and international, to become one of the fastest-growing Christian groups on the North American continent and now rival the expanding Jehovah's Witnesses in South America, Africa, and other Third World regions. Once persecuted and driven out of fertile farmlands in the Midwest, the Mormons endured a long ordeal to end up in a forsaken salt basin in Utah, which they converted, through hard work and ingenuity, into the prosperous seat of an important western state. Once considered a threat to society, they now register enviably low rates of many current social ills that plague American families, such as divorce, alcoholism, and juvenile delinquency.

But the Mormons are more than the well-scrubbed face they present to the world. They represent a movement and a crusade — not just another wealthy denomination that has made its peace with America's plurality of religions. Moreover, their Church's leadership is still guided by fervent inspiration and (ultimately) a sense of superiority over all other groups. The Mormons, in their own eyes, are the "true Israel," the makers of a new Zion, the select Children of God so designated by the Deity through His most recent prophet, Joseph Smith, and appointed to establish a national theocracy. Their mission is not simply to coexist with other religions in American society (though that was the most pragmatic goal they struggled for in the beginning) but rather to supersede them. Like most groups convinced of their elite character, they can be distinctly contemptuous of those who oppose them. Church elder Orson Pratt, an early Church "apostle," more than a century ago wrote a catechism formulating the Mormon attitude as succinctly as any Church official has ventured to do in public:

Q. What does the Lord require of the people of the United States?

A. He requires them to repent of all their sins and embrace the message of salvation, contained in the Book of Mormon, and be baptized into THIS church, and prepare themselves for the coming of the Lord.

Q. What will be the consequence if they do not embrace the Book of Mormon as a divine revelation?

A. They will BE DESTROYED from the land and SENT DOWN TO HELL, like all other generations who have rejected a divine message![1]

This is not merely the hyperbole of a first-generation firebrand whose descendants toned down their beliefs as they found middle-class affluence and acceptance. Rather, as we will show, such sentiments still dominate the outlook of many members of the corporate hierarchy that directs the LDS empire and still motivate its members' decision making. In this book we document that the Mormon belief that God's providence is that they assume political and economic control of the United States is still alive and well in the late twentieth century. More important, this goal is being actualized to a much greater extent than most people realize.

The nineteenth-century Mormon rhetoric calling for a new Zion on the North American continent was filled with belligerence toward Gentiles and spoke explicitly of eventually controlling this nation's political structure, subduing its economy, and eliminating religious pluralism. Theocracy, not democracy, and communalism, not capitalism, were its ideals. Willing to use the protection guaranteed by the First Amendment to establish themselves, Mormon leaders did not necessarily intend to extend such protection to other groups if given the power to decide. Persecution by other Christian groups had left Mormons with few illusions about the reality of "freedom of religion" and public tolerance in America. Thus Mormon leaders like Elder Pratt were once open in their denunciation of the forces they perceived to be aligned against them. Mormon cynicism and ill will toward the outside world were understandable in light of the hostile cultural context within which they fought for survival.

But times have changed. Non-Mormons seldom hear such bold language today. More than 150 years after the founding of their church, many Mormons — from politicians Orrin Hatch, Morris Udall, and George Romney to entertainers Donny and Marie Osmond to columnist Jack Anderson to people in the offices of the Federal Bureau of Investigation, the Central Intelligence Agency and the Department of Defense — stand in the front ranks of various powerful professions. The Church is no longer small. Worldwide its members number over five million. Its current wealth, measured in stocks and property ownership alone, hovers around eight billion dollars by conservative estimates.[2] Except in fundamentalist Christian tracts that still denounce Mormons as a "cult," the LDS is rarely defamed. Indeed, as we will see, Mormons currently receive equal, if not preferential, treatment by government recruiters for certain influential positions. At the federal level their conservative views are appreciated. Ronald Reagan's administration has employed more Mormons, particularly in policy-relevant positions, than any other president's.[3]

At the same time — and this is our critical thesis — the LDS Church's goals have not mellowed or narrowed, even late into this century. The Church is still engaged in a crusade to bring about theocracy in the United States. It still rejects religious pluralism as a desirable condition. The LDS style has merely changed. From the standpoint of church-state relations and religious liberty in American society, the new style — corporate, polished, and public-relations conscious — is perhaps more disturbing because it is less noticeable. Unlike the policies of mainline organizations such as the National Council of Churches or the World Council of Churches, Mormon ambitions do not usually enter public debate. Yet the new LDS Church is much more effective in gaining influence than were its abrasive first-generation apostles.

Why do the Mormons want to remake the United States of America in their own image? What explains their desire to accumulate not just larger financial holdings, radio and television stations, and massive insurance interests, but also crucial political power? To understand the LDS's aggressive empire building, we need first to look at what Mormons say their church is about and how it began.

MORMON MILLENNIALISM

The thrust of Mormon theology is unquestionably millennial. That is, it is closely tied to the millennial (or millenarian) expectation that Jesus Christ will soon return to earth, combat and vanquish Satan and his followers, judge the good and the wicked, and begin a thousand-year reign (or millennium) before time as we ordinarily perceive it ceases to exist. Scholars of religion distinguish two types of millennialists. *Pre-millennialists* anticipate a sudden return of Christ, without warning. His return will be prefaced by wars, misery, chaos, and widespread social breakdown. Since He will come "as a thief in the night," Christians must live their lives daily as if His arrival could occur at any minute. But besides keeping the faith and converting as many others as possible, true Christians have little to do with bringing the Second Coming about. Among the ranks of pre-millennialists are many well-known fundamentalists such as Billy Graham, Jerry Falwell (founder of the right-wing Moral Majority, Inc.), and Falwell's fellow "televangelist," recording star Jimmy Swaggart.

The Mormons, however, are *post-millennialists*.[4] Like pre-millennialists, post-millennialists believe that Christ is soon to return and that they are living in the last days of the world as we know it (thus the designation *Latter*-day Saints). But they hold to the idea that they must actively prepare the way for the Second Coming. As philosopher Joe E. Barnhart describes it, post-millennialism is

roughly the position that through the increasingly influential work of the Holy Spirit in the lives of Christian believers and the activity of the churches on Earth, the Kingdom of God will in fact gradually and steadily settle in, spreading around the globe, triumphing over evil and disease with a spiritual and moral power hitherto unknown in the world.

Particularly important for an understanding of the LDS Church's drive to accumulate financial and political influence is this belief that human beings must achieve certain preconditions before Christ's return is possible. Barnhart adds:

The millennium will come, not apocalyptically or with cataclysmic eruption, but with gentle persuasion and works of mercy and righteousness. In short, God will usher in his Kingdom through the mediation of human cooperation. After (post) the millennium,

Christ will himself return to Earth. In some versions of post-millennialism, Israel will be restored to unparalleled prosperity and influence for good, thus allowing God to fulfill literally his promises to Abraham and his descendants.[5]

In the Mormon view, the Church's members are Abraham's true descendants, and the "Israel" to which Jesus Christ will address himself is presently headquartered in Salt Lake City. Mormons certainly interpret their church's worldly success as part of this divine post-millennial scheme. The post-millennial agenda underlies the Mormons' phenomenal success, for individuals and groups will always risk more, work harder, and sacrifice more willingly when they are asked to do so not for profit but for a cause.

THE MORMON CHALLENGE

Mormonism began in an area of upper New York State that scholars of American religion refer to as the "burned-over" district. It has been so-called because in the early 1800s that part of the country seethed with the ferment of intense religious revivals and millennial sects, all frantically engaged in gathering souls.

Around 1820 in Palmyra, New York, a teenager named Joseph Smith experienced a vision in which God and Jesus Christ appeared, revealing to him several important things: that Smith was forgiven his personal sins by the grace of Christ's death and resurrection, that God was simultaneously angry at the ungodliness and hypocrisy of most of Smith's contemporaries, and that Jesus Christ was soon to return to earth as the Bible had prophesied. Furthermore, before this Second Coming, Smith would become a key figure in helping restore the true Church of Christ on earth. The legitimate succession from Israel's King David, in which Jesus had shared through his earthly family's lineage, had been corrupted by the sun-worshiping Roman Emperor Constantine when, by official edict, he made Christianity the imperial religion in the early-fourth-century Roman Empire. Joseph Smith was charged with restoring the legacy of the true Israelites.

Later visitations by the original apostles Peter, James, John, and, most important, the angel-prophet Moroni elaborated the initial message for young Smith. These visions filled in the details and revealed a fantastic, forgotten history of the Americas. In about 600 B.C. a band of inspired Hebrews had left Jerusalem shortly before the Babylonian army overran the city. These Hebrew refugees sailed west across the Atlantic and founded a mighty civilization in both the North and South American continents, where Jesus Christ manifested himself several times again to supplement His Middle Eastern visitations. Moroni, the last prophet of one warring Jewish faction called the Nephites and son of Mormon, the Nephites' final historian, led Joseph Smith to ancient gold plates on which the account of these events was written. Fourteen centuries earlier, Moroni had hidden the plates beneath a large rock on a hillside near Smith's house after the Lamanites (who became the root stock from which American Indians sprang) wiped out the Nephites. The Lamanites advanced civilization then deteriorated into barbarism. Smith was appointed to translate the golden texts, creating from them a third biblical testament, the *Book of Mormon*, which would establish the legitimacy of the new Zion in North America and complete the books of the Bible.

A growing, cohesive group grew around "the prophet" Smith, and in 1831, after more than a decade of continuous persecution in New York, he led his band of followers to Kirtland, Ohio. But they were eventually pushed out, and from 1832 to 1839 they tried to establish a base for Zion in a number of different counties in Missouri. Finally, they created their Mormon stronghold in Nauvoo (Commerce), Illinois. At each location along their way, they were pursued by angry mobs, denounced by the local newspapers and clergy, and spied on by suspicious politicians. It also seems clear that law enforcement officials consistently looked the other way when Mormon rights were violated. Mormon historians Leonard J. Arrington and Davis Bitton summed up the most frequent public reaction to the Saints: "Except for the small minority who greeted Mormonism as the answer to unmet spiritual needs, most felt that its beliefs were superstitious, disgusting, repellent."[6]

In its first fourteen years the Church gathered approximately 35,000 members. Since Joseph Smith had repeatedly issued the call for all Saints to gather at Zion (that is, Nauvoo) in expectation of the millennium, they began to cluster in southern Illinois. By 1844 Nauvoo's population had reached 10,000, making it the second-largest city in Illinois (only Chicago was larger).[7] Nauvoo had been incorporated under a charter granted by the state and had also been given considerable autonomy. Not only did the Mormons establish a model theocracy there, bolstered by economic monopolies, but their militia, the Nauvoo Legion, numbering between 4,000 and 5,000 men, became the second-largest standing army on the continent, next to the United States military. Bold talk about the corruptness of American society, the coming downfall of its government, and the important social role that the Mormons would play in "rescuing" the nation, combined with the obvious signs of the Church's growing economic and political power, made many outsiders wary, particularly in Illinois but also wherever large pockets of Mormons thrived.

In retrospect it is difficult to imagine the viciousness with which the LDS members were hounded, just as the brutal treatment of nineteenth-century Irish Catholics and mob lynchings of Jehovah's Witnesses in this century seem almost unbelievable to those raised on the myth of America as the cradle of religious liberty. The Mormons, however, demonstrated a number of "odd" characteristics that created threats to virtually every settled community they encountered, threats that ensured that they would never be allowed to coexist until they removed themselves to some remote frontier beyond the prejudiced reach of their Gentile neighbors. A brief look at the most important of these "odd" characteristics and the reasons they aroused such ire will heighten our understanding of the defensiveness that became a permanent part of the Mormon outlook.

MORMON BELIEFS

That Mormonism was a religious or theological threat to traditional Christianity has often been noted. Certainly Mormon beliefs were and continue to be a major concern for their enemies, as the numerous anti-Mormon tracts still in circulation in evangelical bookstores attest. Not only did Mormons claim to possess a third (or Newer) Testament to complete the Bible, special rituals kept secret from other Christians, and a special status or covenant with God that made them His new Chosen People, but they also held that in time each member could literally become a god and ruler of the planets just as the biblical Jehovah had become in this corner of

the universe. This last belief amounted to blasphemy as well as poly-
theism in the eyes of most outsiders and called down on the
Mormons the condemnation of other Christian clergy.

By their aggressive style of proclaiming this new message, the
Mormons often did little to avert Gentile outrage and in fact often
fanned the fires. Religious historian Edwin Scott Gaustad reminds
us that "[religious] dissent as live action rather than as safe replay
can be, and generally is, irritating, unnerving, pig-headed, noisy,
and brash."[8] The Mormons, in the eyes of their neighbors, were
all that and more. Convinced of the special purpose of their church
as restored Christianity, Mormon preachers and apostles literally
consigned the mainstream American religion that rejected them
"TO HELL!"[9] One account of a speech made by Mormon leader
Brigham Young during the great trek of Mormon refugees to Utah
in the mid-1840s illustrates the hostility that Mormons returned to
those who had forced them out of homes and farms in Illinois,
Missouri, and elsewhere:

> He [Young] called upon the Lord to bless this place [winter
> quarters in Council Bluffs, Iowa] for the good of the Saints and
> curse every Gentile who should attempt to settle here, with
> sickness, rottenness and death. Also to curse the land of Missouri
> that it might cease to bring forth grain or fruit of any kind to its
> inhabitants, and that they might be cursed [with] sickness, rot-
> tenness and death; that their flesh might consume away on their
> bones. And their blood be turned into maggots, and that their tor-
> ments never cease, but increase until they leave the land and it
> be blessed for possession of the Saints.[10]

But the issue above all others that infuriated non-Mormons and
that became the symbol of all they despised in the Church was
polygamy (or, more correctly, polygyny, the practice whereby one
man is married to more than one woman at the same time). Since
the early 1850s, when Mormon leaders began to advocate the sacrament of plural marriage for male members, polygamy became the
rallying cry of Gentile critics. They roared against supposed Mormon
immorality and licentiousness, the existence of harems, the practice
of female bondage, and other fantasies that plural marriages suggested to Victorian Protestant minds.[11] Predictably, ex-Mormon
women published lurid exposés of their lives as "slave-brides," and

evangelical "analysts" were quick to link the practice and these apostates' claims with false religion.

Yet in the face of this uproar, no more than one Mormon in five (men and women) ever lived polygamously while such marriage was a Church-approved custom. It was, obviously, more frequent among the well-to-do members than among the poor (which also made it more visible to journalists and other sensation-mongers). Though plural marriage caused many Mormons to defect or separate and begin their own churches, it was for Gentiles that Mormon polygamy became an obsession that overshadowed every other characteristic, controversial or ordinary, of the Saints. Whatever the facts, polygamy was a definite liability for the Church's public image. It eventually was formally banned among Mormons by the Manifesto of 1890, announced after a "revelation" by LDS President Wilford Woodruff.

THE MORMON ECONOMIC AND POLITICAL CHALLENGE

The first-generation Mormons believed in self-reliance and sacrifice, in addition to investment, for the common good. Since they identified themselves as special people possessing a special covenant with God, they believed they had good reason to avoid becoming entangled in the worldly affairs of outsiders. While this philosophy has become modified in modern times — always, however, with an eye to the Church's best advantage — it posed a blatant challenge to nineteenth-century American society.

Early Mormon economics were communitarian. Mormons founded, operated, and supported Mormon businesses as Church policy. Whenever possible, they established "vertical" Mormon industries in which all stages of production, from purchasing raw materials to merchandising, were supervised by the same company or owners. In regions of the country where increasing proportions of the population became Mormon owing to conversions and immigration, this pattern became more than an irritation to Gentiles — it presented a genuine economic threat. The Mormon threat to local economic success was an important source of persecution in Missouri, Illinois, and eventually Utah.

Just as the LDS Church began to tighten its ranks in establishing a separate Mormon economy, it also appeared as a serious political threat to outsiders. Its religious antipluralism was matched by a political agenda that seemed to bode ill for American democracy. Early Mormons expected an imminent millennium, and, according to Joseph Smith, shortly before it occurred the United States would suffer crises that only the Mormons would be able to resolve (presumably by taking over leadership of the nation). Indeed, a literal doomsday was predicted, with the Mormons cast as saviors of the Republic, rewarded by favored political positions in the aftermath.

MORMONISM AND POPULAR NATIVISM

Beginning with the immigration of large numbers of Irish fleeing adverse economic and political conditions in their homeland, America saw the rise of nativism in the 1830s and 1840s on a scale never before experienced. Nativism — a pro-white, pro–Anglo-Saxon Protestant, essentially antiforeign prejudice — has always been one of the uglier faces of American popular culture. Nativists argued that anyone deviating from a narrow range of acceptable racial, religious, and ethnic characteristics was inherently inferior and ought to be kept out of the country.

The Mormons offended nativist sentiments in a number of ways, adding to the sense of threat among non-Mormons. As early as the late 1830s Joseph Smith had sent missionaries to Europe, and their early results were impressive. Thousands of British converts soon began embarking from Liverpool to "gather" in Zion via Boston, New York, and New Orleans. During the first ten years of what was called the British Mission (1837–1846), missionaries converted an estimated 17,849 persons, about a third of whom headed for Utah. In 1850 the Church established the Perpetual Emigrating Company, known generally as the Perpetual Emigration Fund, to help pay their expenses. Missionary efforts were intensified in England as well as in Scandinavia and other European countries. By 1887 more than 85,000 Mormons had made their way across the Atlantic and migrated from the port cities to Utah on foot, by covered wagon, or on the transcontinental railroad.[12]

Many Americans reacted to this immigration with fear. The Mormons' message had appealed to many poor Europeans who saw in Mormonism, among other things, a chance for a fresh start to better their lives. These were often the same poor non-Mormons about whom middle-class nativists had been raising an alarm for years. Thus anti-Mormonism and nativism conveniently overlapped. It is no accident that a key provision in the Edmunds-Tucker Act of 1887, which sought to disenfranchise the LDS Church as a corporation, dissolved the Perpetual Emigrating Company.

Race entered into the Mormon threat in other ways. Before the Civil War the largely groundless accusation arose, particularly in Missouri, that Mormons intended to help runaway slaves and encourage abolition. The Mormons were also accused of stirring up Indians in Missouri, Illinois, and Iowa. It is true that Mormons had a special interest in native Americans: the *Book of Mormon* pointed to them as Lamanites, part of the original Palestinian immigration to North America in Old Testament days. Mormons believed the Lamanites were destined to regain their biblical heritage and shed their inferior status. Many accounts show that the Mormons tried to deal fairly with the Indian tribes they encountered, particularly the Shoshone[13] and others in Utah.[14] And the Mormons were quick to portray themselves to the Indians as qualitatively different from (that is, more honest than) other whites, especially agents of the United States government. This engendered within the Indians a kind of special "love Mormons but hate whites" sentiment, as illustrated in an incident that occurred in a Mormon meetinghouse in the late nineteenth century:

> One Indian chief who came to a Mormon testimony meeting stood up and bore his testimony: "Mormon bueno, Mormon tick-a-boo (friend). Make-em water-ditch. Plant-em grain. Feed-em Indians. Mormon tick-a-boo. White Man, SON-OF-A-BITCH."[15]

More than many whites of their time, the Mormons managed to coexist successfully with native Americans, perhaps because both groups were so unpopular with other whites. In fact, the Mormons made their own peace treaties with different tribes independent of federal authorities. For these reasons the Mormons were regarded by Gentiles as troublemakers in Indian affairs, adding to their bad reputation in many frontier areas. Since the days of Joseph Smith, it has been a part of Mormon doctrine that the Lamanites (American Indians) will play a special retaliatory role in defending the Latter-

day Saints in the immediate future when the Mormons are sur-
rounded on every side by their enemies.[16] This idea lives on today
in the minds of some of the Church hierarchy.

THE GARRISON MENTALITY

Persecution and intolerance by outsiders, generated by challenges to the established order, had profound effects on the nineteenth-century LDS Church. One result was an authoritarian control
over Church members. Like soldiers under fire, they had to be committed, obedient, and disciplined to a hierarchy of command. During
the massive migration westward after they abandoned Nauvoo in
1845, Mormon wagon trains were organized into units resembling
military squads. Mormon leaders oversaw the daily routines of camp
life down to such details as when to rise, when to go to sleep, where
to make camp and start fires, when to douse them, and even where
to tie the family dogs at night. Then, as now, the authority of leaders
was believed to flow ultimately from the president and prophet.
The daily demands made by leaders also created a tradition of obedience and conformity that was to survive in later generations.

The Mormons endured and eventually prospered because they
could never simply exist. A condition of "optimum maladjustment"
to outside pressure kept them on the offensive, persevering through
troubles and never resting complacently. The persecution that cost
the lives of many hundreds of early members ironically built and
saved the movement. In the words of two Mormon historians, "It
was a refiner's fire from which emerged tougher Saints."[17]

Persecution provided the stuff that creates legends and martyrs.
Stimulated by persecution, too, was the belligerent confidence in
the Church's special destiny that still motivates its leaders today.
The trauma that anti-Mormon hostility caused early leaders has left
ineradicable marks on their successors and still flavors some
Mormon leaders' rhetoric of a "kingdom of God on earth" with
a more concrete emphasis than most Christians, premillennialist
or otherwise, ordinarily conceive. Not only are most upper-level
Church leaders only second- or third-generation Mormons, but
many of them are direct descendants of those original apostles.
Names like Kimball, Young, Grant, Benson, Richards, and others

that fill the Mormon history books have also occupied corridors of power within the Church hierarchy in modern times. And for them, neither the millennialism nor the siege mentality of early Mormonism is passé. Like the Protestant colonists who fled Europe, the Mormons fought other whites, native Americans, and the natural elements for a foothold on the North American continent, developing a sense of manifest destiny that justified (and continues to justify) economic and political expansionism not only in this country but in foreign nations as well.[18]

In a larger sense, persecution of the Mormons produced a militarist counterchallenge to the outside world. The "garrison mentality" that was adopted by the members and particularly the leaders had been growing along with the escalating harassment of Mormons by their neighbors and with official hostility during the 1830s and 1840s. Indeed, the event that precipitated the Smiths' arrest and eventual murder by a mob in an Illinois jail could be seen as growing out of the Mormons' fear and isolation: Joseph Smith had instructed followers to wreck the print shop of a newspaper critical of the Church. This is the sort of Mormon retaliation that further threatened the neighboring Gentiles, who in turn increased pressures on the Mormons to leave the area. There is little doubt, moreover, that much of the mob violence directed at Mormons in Missouri and Illinois was deliberately ignored, minimized, or even aided by public officials. Once in Utah and more confident in their isolation, the Mormons reinstituted the Nauvoo Legion as a permanent militia, partly to deal with some hostile Indians among the Snake and Shoshone tribes and also, undoubtedly, as a gesture to Gentiles that here they would dig in to make a permanent stand.

The Mormons' garrison mentality, in fact, became more pronounced rather than abating in Utah. In 1848 Brigham Young formed a provisional government for the State of Deseret (an area roughly encompassing modern Utah, named after an ancient word for honey bee mentioned in the *Book of Mormon*). Soon after, Mormon leaders were lobbying for admission to the Union. But officials in Washington were less than eager to make the Utah Territory a state. Both northern and southern members of Congress feared that admitting the Utah Territory as a state would upset the delicate balance of slave and free states that was established by the

Compromise of 1850 to preserve a pre–Civil War harmony between the two regions of the country.

To Mormons, however, their five separate appeals for statehood during the 1850s were frustrating, and exacerbated their sense of Gentile rejection. Meanwhile, relations between the official territorial government appointed by Washington and the real governors of the Utah Territory — the LDS leaders — steadily deteriorated. Many of the men sent by Washington as territorial governors were suspicious of and unsympathetic toward the Mormons, and their accurate perception that they had very little control over affairs in Utah caused them frustration. They repeatedly reported their feelings until, in Washington and elsewhere, people began to speak of "the Mormon problem" in Utah. The so-called Mormon problem was in part political, in part religious, and in part focused on polygamy, but it kept mutual distrust and hatred alive between Mormons and Gentiles. It was one reason for the Utah War of 1857, which began when an army of 1800 federal soldiers was dispatched to support a new non-Mormon governor and give new strength to federal control of the territory. The Mormons reacted to this invasion by blocking or fortifying mountain passes, sabotaging bridges and interrupting the troops' supply trains, and establishing a "scorched-earth" policy organized with military efficiency. The orders were given in Salt Lake City and passed down through local stakes and wards (a stake was a Mormon region, similar to a parish, made up of wards). There were never major outright confrontations (and in the end the U.S. army withdrew), but the garrison mentality gained credibility for a new second generation of Church members.

An extreme example of the garrison mentality was the Mountain Meadows Massacre in the summer of 1857. To understand this event it is useful to consider first the doctrine of *blood atonement.* According to the *Doctrine and Covenants* (one of the four standard works of the LDS Church, which contains what members believe to be the inspired revelations of God to Joseph Smith and his successors), the "innocent blood" of Joseph and Hyrum Smith is still on the state seal of Illinois and continues to stain both the American flag and the Constitution. This martyrs' blood "will cry unto the Lord of Hosts till He avenges that blood on the earth."[19] Once the Mormons had completed their sacred temple in Nauvoo, Illinois, after the Smiths' death, a "blood oath of vengeance" was apparently demanded of all worthy Church members as part of the official temple Endowment Ceremony. From various accounts we have clear indications that an oath of vengeance based on the doctrine of blood atonement became an integral part of the Mormon perspective in the nineteenth century. There is also evidence that it survived well into this century as a doctrine and practice in temple ceremonies and among Church leaders.[20] For example, Joseph Fielding Smith, tenth president of the Church (1970–1972), firmly believed and taught many of the same doctrines that his great-uncle Joseph Smith introduced into Mormonism, including blood atonement. The later Smith described this belief:

> Joseph Smith taught that there were certain signs so grievous that many may commit, that they will place the transgressors beyond the power of the atonement of Christ. If these offenses are committed, then the blood of Christ will not cleanse them from their sins even though they repent. Therefore, their only hope is to have their blood shed to atone, as far as possible, in their behalf.

Blood atonement was unquestionably an important factor in the Mountain Meadows Massacre. In August 1857, a train of emigrants, the Fancher party, from Missouri and Arkansas passed through Mormon territory bound for California. In Parowan, Utah, the emigrants were not permitted to go through the town but were forced to take a longer route around it. In Cedar City, the next community and last sizable settlement in which they could obtain provisions, the travelers met with more hostility from Mormon residents. Most important, the Mormons refused to sell the Fancher party food and supplies they needed to continue their trip. The frustrated Gentiles responded with a good deal of name-calling. Some boasted of having participated in anti-Mormon mobs back home, and one bold member of the party even claimed "that he had the gun that killed Old Joe Smith."[21]

Whether or not this last claim was true, the Fancher party with its Missouri background knew how to outrage the Mormons. After the Fancher train of wagons turned south and moved on, local Church authorities met quickly and decided to take revenge on the emigrants. Their plan was to exterminate every man, woman, and child in the party, sparing only those too young to recount the massacre. The aid of about one hundred local native Americans was enlisted so as to make it appear to be an Indian raid. When John D. Lee, a Mormon farmer, caught up with the Fancher party, he carried a white flag of peace. Apologizing for Cedar City's rude treatment of the emigrants, he invited them back to secure necessary provisions. The emigrants fell into the trap. The Mormons killed all the men in the emigrant company, and the Indians murdered all the women and older children. Only seventeen or eighteen small children and infants were spared, most of them later adopted into Mormon families. John D. Lee became the official Church scapegoat for the massacre and was eventually executed by firing squad.[22]

Less sensational but revealing traces of the garrison mentality were evident in the Mormon subculture and folklore that rapidly grew with the Church. For example, some Mormon hymns written in the nineteenth century show a militaristic spirit and contempt for Mormon enemies, a spirit absent in other Christian sacred music.[23] The Church even created its own flag — the Flag of the Kingdom of God. One early attempt to insulate future Church members from Gentile "contamination" was the development of a special Mormon alphabet consisting of thirty-eight phonetic characters for Church members to use to communicate with each other. (It was also intended as a phonetic alphabet to help immigrants learn English.) In 1855 some Church members proposed to Brigham Young that the Church institute such an alphabet. With Young's approval, the Utah legislature appropriated $2,500 to buy the type to begin printing in the "Deseret alphabet." In 1868 the Utah legislature appropriated another $10,000 to purchase books printed in the alphabet. The plan was overambitious, but before it was abandoned in the early 1870s $20,000 had been spent on 20,000 first- and second-grade readers as well as 8,000 copies of part 1 of the *Book of Mormon*.

When Mormons had the opportunity, as they did in Utah and earlier in Illinois, they held no reservations about trying to set up Church monopolies and drive out Gentile competition. This practice was bitterly resented by their non-Mormon neighbors. One major issue in mid-nineteenth-century Utah was the influx of non-Mormon merchants who saw prospering communities full of potential consumers. The ability of many Gentile merchants to undersell Mormon merchants, at least initially, caused great concern among Church leaders. To counter this growing influence, Church leaders actively encouraged members to buy and shop Mormon exclusively. In the Mormon Schools of the Prophets (an indoctrination program in the late 1860s providing catechism classes and religious education in every Utah town), Church President Brigham Young opposed trading with any non-Mormon merchants. According to one member in the audience, after speaking harshly to the American Fork School in 1868, Young demanded an accounting of "all men who had bought goods of our enemies of late; he told them to leave the School of the Prophets and not come to the communion table any more, for we do not fellowship you." Young further condemned trade with Gentile merchants when he said that "he had tried to control the [Gentile] merchants, but could not do it. They would go to hell if they did not turn a sharp corner."[24]

With warnings not to trade or socialize with Gentiles, the practice of polygamy, the celebration of special Mormon holidays, and the prohibitions against alcohol, tobacco, and caffeine, Mormon lifestyles were kept distinct from those of other Americans. But there was also a unique folk tradition of visions and other supernatural events created by the Saints, much of which has been forgotten, discarded, or never learned by many modern members. The folk tradition is important because it fits with Mormons' self-image as a special people. Much of it reflects the Mormon emphasis on the active role of divine revelation and intervention in current affairs just as these occurred in the Old Testament. A few examples give a sense of what to outsiders may seem bizarre, dubious, or downright preposterous practices but to Mormons represent evidence of a supernatural realm active in the affairs of this world.

One Saint, Zeke Johnson, claimed to have uncovered an Indian burial site while plowing his cornfield and witnessed the literal resurrection of a young Lamanite girl; flesh, marrow, muscles, skin, hair, and even clothing all gradually returned and coalesced as he watched.[25] This is similar to another resurrection account told by a modern Church official, Elder George P. Lee of the First Council of Seventy. Lee said that when he was a youth his heart had stopped and he was pronounced dead. "My father made a casket and lowered me into the grave," he stated, but when the casket hit the bottom, "I came to."[26]

Other accounts are uniquely Mormon. Cain, the slayer of his

brother Abel in Genesis, figures in a number of them. According to numerous reliable Saints (among them several Church leaders) who independently encountered him over a number of years, Cain resembles an intelligent but despondent "big-foot" character, doomed to roam the earth like a wandering Jew.[27] There are also legends of the Three Nephites who cross this continent performing miracles, of Brigham Young rebuking a destructive wind to keep it from further harming Mormon homes and property, various resurrections of dead Mormons, and so forth.[28]

Such anecdotes testify to the dynamic aspect of Mormonism. They illustrate its charismatic emphasis on the ever-possible revelation that can drastically alter what is and what will be expected of Mormon believers.

THE ONCE AND FUTURE THEOCRACY

The second chapter of the Book of Daniel relates how the Babylonian king Nebuchadnezzar called the prophet Daniel and ordered him to interpret a dream. In this dream the king saw the total destruction of mighty nations and governments by a special power mysteriously associated with a *great mountain.* That passage has always held special meaning for Mormons. Traditionally Church leaders have interpreted the "great mountain" reference to mean the Church of Jesus Christ of Latter-day Saints, headquartered within the granite bulwark of the Rocky Mountains. For them the prophecy says that the Mormon people and the resources of their corporate empire will be the prime movers in a millennial overthrow of the United States government.[29]

Mormon leaders, beginning with Joseph Smith, tried to establish the roots of this theocracy in Nauvoo, Illinois, during the early 1840s. Smith's 1844 campaign for the U.S. presidency was nothing less than an attempt to hurry the millennium by preparing the kingdom of Christ on earth. In fact, Smith and his earliest apostles envisioned a one-world Mormon government long before the Church settled in Nauvoo. Sidney Rigdon, an intimate friend and counselor of Smith (though Rigdon eventually left the Church), once related how these leaders met as early as 1830 to discuss their theocratic ambitions:

The time has now come to tell why we held secret meetings. We were maturing plans fourteen years ago which we can now tell . . . When God sets up a system of salvation, he sets up a system of government. When I speak of a government, I mean what I say. I mean a government that shall rule over temporal and spiritual affairs.[30]

By 1844 the Mormon Church had grown considerably from its early days. Smith preached that the millennium was at hand and called for all Saints to gather at Nauvoo, where he was actively setting up the Mormon theocracy. One significant step in the direction of the theocracy was Smith's creation of the Council of Fifty, a group of specially chosen men to serve as God's political regents on earth. Surviving members operated openly within Mormonism with aspects of that goal in mind as late as 1945. Notable elements characterizing this early Council, such as extreme adoration of Church heads in political as well as religious matters, continue today, although somewhat modified.[31] Members of the Council chose Joseph Smith, in the words of one participant, "as our prophet, Priest and King by Hosannas."[32] Recognizing the LDS President as king of the earthly kingdom of God on earth, Zion, became a tradition in the Church. Mormon presidents after Smith were also named king of this theocracy in special temple ceremonies. Brigham Young followed Smith's practice, calling for the apostles and leaders to ratify his kingship. The third Church president, John Taylor, had himself anointed with olive oil during his coronation or "sealing" as king of the Mormon commonwealth. The fourth and fifth presidents, Wilford Woodruff and Lorenzo Snow, also were declared king by the Council of Fifty. Though the ceremony of coronation continues to this day, it is not publicized outside the Church. Conducted privately with only a few members of the Church hierarchy permitted to attend, it is nevertheless an explicit recognition that the kingdom of God is to be a political and spiritual reality.

The political, or temporal, reality is reflected in the organization of Church members into a pyramidal hierarchy established by the first-generation Church leaders. At the lowest level is the *ward* (approximately 400–500 people), the equivalent of a small congregation. The ward is overseen by a bishop (a nonprofessional clergyman) and his two counselors. The *stake*, equivalent to a Roman

Catholic diocese, is composed of five to seven wards (or approximately 3,500 people). The stake president (also a nonprofessional clergyman) has not only two counselors but also a stake high council made up of twelve councilmen to help him administer the wards under his jurisdiction. Stakes are in turn parts of *regions* (administered by representatives), supervised by the First Council of the Seventy. Above the Council of the Seventy is the Council (or Quorum) of the Twelve Apostles and the First Presidency (the president and his two counselors, each of whom carries the title President). The structure was designed to permit an efficient downward flow of information and directives, for the early Mormon leaders anticipated an imminent social upheaval in American society before Christ's Second Coming that would leave the Church an island of solidarity in a sea of chaos.

As persecution continued to reinforce Mormon defensiveness, millennial expectations that some major catastrophe was about to shake the foundations of the American Republic continued to build. Brigham Young was quite open about what he expected to see happen to America in the near future as the Civil War unfolded:

> We are called the State Legislature [of Utah], but when the time comes, we shall be called the Kingdom of God. Our government is going to pieces, and it will be like water that is spilt upon the ground that cannot be gathered. For the time will come when we will give laws to the nations of the earth. Joseph Smith organized this government before, in Nauvoo, and he said if we did our duty, we shall prevail over all our enemies. We should get all things ready, and when the time comes, we should let the water on to the wheel and start the machine in motion.[33]

Rhetoric such as this, whether simply inserted in speeches and sermons to boost morale or intended to be taken literally, frightened outsiders:

> Such a state of affairs means no more or less than the complete overthrow of the nation, and not only of this nation, but the nations of Europe.[34]

Such visions and expectations have always been an important part of Mormonism, and numerous Saints have continued the tradition of doomsday prophecy since Smith's martyrdom.

The theme of the annihilation of America and its ultimate dependence on the LDS Church for survival is still popular among modern Latter-day Saints. One of the best-selling Mormon doomsday books (over 200,000 copies sold) is *Prophecy: Key to the Future* by Duane S. Crowther, published in 1967. Two entire chapters are devoted to predicted catastrophes and the eventual Mormon takeover of the United States. Crowther, a Mormon businessman, has summarized the tenor of such words and visions by Church patriarchs:

> Latter-day Saint prophets have made many prophecies concerning a series of internal wars which will bring about the collapse of the government and dominion of the United States. [These] wars will cause the complete collapse of national and state governments in the United States![35]

It is easy to dismiss such predictions as transparent fantasies of revenge against Gentiles or morale-building rhetoric used to "whip up the troops." Certainly the nineteenth-century Mormon garrison mentality and the very real anti-Mormon hostility made such prophecies attractive to most Church members. But hasn't modern Church leadership "matured" beyond such fire-breathing now that persecution is at an all-time low? It appears not. A spiritual and political kingdom of God, established and administered by Mormons, has always been an integral part of Church goals and continues even in modern Mormonism, although in a somewhat lower key.

The retreat from the angry militancy of early Mormonism to a more conciliatory approach has been a modern public relations strategy. As Klaus Hansen concludes:

> In an attempt to live in the world, the Mormons were forced to modify their ideas of a political kingdom and to relegate them to the uncertain period of a future millennium, a context in which aspirations of world government would cause little alarm to suspicious Gentiles. In a logical attempt not to arouse the already excited non-Mormon world further, Church leaders thought it wise to publicize their true aims regarding the political Kingdom of God as little as possible. At times, the leaders felt it necessary to flatly negate political aspirations.[36]

However, the theocratic, millennial tradition persists, if only discussed for Mormon audiences, and its most outspoken champion is apostle Ezra Taft Benson, next in line to succeed current President Spencer W. Kimball upon his death. Benson's right-wing extremist views and his penchant for speaking openly about an imminent millennium have at times been an embarrassment to modern Mormons who prefer to downplay talk of a coming theocracy. In 1980 Benson, the oldest member of the Council of the Twelve Apostles, told a Mormon audience:

> Youth of Zion, do you realize you are living in the days of the fulfillment of these signs and wonders? You are among those who will see many of these prophecies fulfilled. Just as certain as was the destruction of the temple at Jerusalem and the scattering of the Jews, so shall these words of the Savior be certain to your generation. . . You will live in the midst of economic, political and spiritual instability. When you see these signs — unmistakable evidences that His coming is nigh — *be not troubled*, but, "stand. . . in holy places. . ." These holy places consist of our temples, our chapels, our homes and the stakes of Zion, which are, as the Lord declares, "for a defense, and for a refuge from the storm, and from the wrath when it shall be poured out without mixture upon the whole earth". . .We have every confidence that you, "the rising generation," will not falter. I repeat: You were valiant spirits reserved for this exceptional time. You have but one choice: To rise to the task of history's most significant hour![37]

In fact, theocracy is still a fundamental goal of Mormonism and a subject of Mormon education. A prominent Mormon scholar, Hyrum L. Andrus, who has served a distinguished career in the Church as a missionary, a stake mission president, a high counselor, and a bishop has written on this theme often and has taught it in religion classes at Brigham Young University for years. In his third volume of the "Foundations of the Millennial Kingdom of Christ" series, entitled *Doctrines of the Kingdom*, Andrus discusses "the idea and the principles of the government of God — the divine political system which would prevail in the Millennium."[38] He informs modern Church members in considerable detail about the original militant doctrine that Joseph Smith and the nineteenth-century Church leaders preached. For example, in a chapter entitled "The

Nature of the Kingdom," Andrus elaborates on what the term "Government of God" means. Joseph Smith, Andrus explains, had a political kingdom as well as a spiritual one in mind when he referred to the Church: this kingdom of God is supposed to obtain civil power and will soon have an enlarged political importance, eventually replacing all state governments when the nation has been "broken and destroyed." The role of the LDS Church until this time, Andrus explains, is to "precede the divine political organ to establish a foundation of union upon which the latter organization could rest and by which it could function properly."[39]

Andrus is just one Mormon educator who holds such views. He alone has taught them to thousands of students at Brigham Young University and at various youth fireside gatherings held throughout the Church. Several years ago one of us attended such a gathering and heard Andrus tell his young listeners that Joseph Smith was such a dynamic leader because "the Prophet taught POWER doctrine." "POWER doctrine," he repeated, driving his right fist into the open palm of his left hand. "This is what the Church thrives on! And this is what will help us to bring about the political part of God's kingdom on earth!"

How can we discern the goals of modern Mormonism? One way is to study the speeches, sermons, and writings of Mormon leaders published in official Church documents, where theocratic ambitions are spelled out. Their message is clear. In the expectation that Jesus Christ will return in the near future to rule over the kingdom of God on earth, the LDS Church must be prepared to take charge of a deteriorating American government and economy. It must be prepared to carry this coup beyond this nation to others. It must build a membership as large as possible to provide soldiers for the struggle. It must remain strong, in order to provide an island of faith and order during the coming time of troubles.

In the end, such sources say, there will be no place for religious pluralism as we know it. Constitutional guarantees of religious freedom will give way just as the American Republic itself will be overthrown. As both former Church President John Taylor and apostle Orson Pratt stated publicly at various times, "The Constitution of the United States was not a perfect instrument; it was one of those stepping stones to a future development," one with "a higher law, more noble principles, ideas that are more elevated and expansive" that constitute a kingdom "disunited from all forms of government, both civil and ecclesiastical...a kingdom with a separate form of government [that] shall be given to the Saints of the Most High."[40] Accompanying this expectation and hope is a defensiveness among Mormon leaders barely mellowed by the passage of time. The late apostle Bruce R. McConkie told several million Latter-day Saints worldwide by television and radio during the Church's 1980 General Conference that "the way ahead is dark and dreary and dreadful" for the Mormon people and that "there will yet be martyrs" in the tradition of the Smiths' murder in 1844 in Carthage, Illinois.[41]

The record of history shows that Mormon leaders beginning with Joseph Smith tried to establish a theocracy in the Midwest during the early 1840s. Brigham Young and his successors tried again decades later, but anti-Mormon prejudice and federal power curtailed the growing Utah theocracy. In modern times we know that the stated goals of the Mormon movement have not changed appreciably. But is the quest for theocracy abandoned or alive? John Taylor, third president of the Church, seemed to feel that it would continue, but in a somewhat different form. "Now the Kingdom of God," he predicted in the mid nineteenth century, "is assuming another phase to what it has done." "And what shall we do?" he queried his large audience in the great Salt Lake City Tabernacle. His answer: "Seek to carry out the designs of the Almighty and his representatives upon the earth. And if we do *these things*, in the name of Israel's God we shall arise and flourish, and Zion will become a terror to all nations."[42]

Another way to know the goals of Mormonism — less direct than studying the actual words of LDS Church leaders, but perhaps more meaningful because it deals with actions and trends, not just rhetoric — is to examine Mormon influence in the corporate world, in communications and the media, in politics, in the military, and in the international community. The rhetoric of both past and present Church leaders may indeed be hollow. Likewise, worldly success alone is not conclusive proof of a crusade to undermine religious pluralism, alter the conditions of economic power, or reshape the status quo of the American political system. Diligence and other virtues of individual Mormons, including their well-known generosity in tithing to their Church, may account for much of the Church's apparent financial and political influence. The circumstantial evidence for systematic Mormon efforts to transform power and influence in various important spheres that affect all Americans must link actions to stated Church goals.

MORMONISM AND RELIGIOUS PLURALISM

The First Amendment of the U.S. Constitution reads, "Congress shall make no law respecting an establishment of religion, or prohibiting the free exercise thereof." Thus all religious groups, from the most bizarre cults and backwater sects to respectable mainline denominations, are equal before the law. As legal experts Wilber G. Katz and Harold G. Southerland put it:

A religiously pluralistic society . . . is one in which the principal religious groups not only claim freedom for themselves, but affirm equal freedom for others, whatever their beliefs may be. In such a society, these groups have also an internal freedom which is reflected in toleration of criticism and openness to new insights. Individuals are free to doubt and to believe. This freedom is affirmed because of a realization of the need for dialogue, because groups and individuals have a stake — a religious stake — in the freedom of others.[43]

But to be truly pluralistic, a society may have to tolerate groups that reject pluralism and seek to control their own members in an authoritarian, nondemocratic manner. Society will have to extend full rights and protection even to groups that, given the power, would set themselves above all other groups or even eliminate pluralism altogether. Many American religious groups regard their counterparts not merely as rivals or as well-intentioned persons lost in error but as satanic. They do not respect the integrity of other faiths, nor do they refrain from persuading those with political power to promote their own unique claims to truth. Yet a pluralistic system must allow such antipluralists their intolerance and even their declared purpose to eliminate the pluralistic system. This irony is similar to that facing civil libertarians who support the First Amendment's guarantee of free speech even for groups such as the

Nazis, who oppose free speech and who would deny it to the rest of us if they gained power.

At some point, however, even a totally open society has to review the practical limits of such freedom. As Katz and Southerland note, there are some reasonable boundaries to this toleration in the ideal pluralistic society:

> Such a society need not embody perfection; it may contain groups that do not believe in or practice religious freedom. But a society can approximate the model pluralism if such groups are not a great threat to freedom, if a trust in the common commitment to religious freedom prevails among the principal groups.[44]

The emerging Mormon empire sets up a dilemma for the polity. As long as groups that reject the pluralistic ideal remain relatively marginal or powerless, the system has no trouble accommodating them, for they cannot upset the balance and affect others' freedom. Consider, for example, the Unification Church of Korean evangelist Sun Myung Moon, one of the best publicized and most controversial modern religions. The post-millennial theology of the Unification Church resembles that of the Mormons: the "Moonies" also dream of uniting all religions and nations into a worldwide theocracy. Were they to obtain real political power, they would permit little diversity of religious belief and tolerate little science, art, or literature that did not conform to unificationist thought. But the Unification Church's resources and membership in this country are pitifully small compared with those of the Mormons, and its clumsy attempts to influence Congress during the mid-1970s won it more negative publicity than results. The Unification Church seems destined to remain a minority sect for the foreseeable future, whatever its own hopes and the fears of its opponents.[45] American pluralism, in short, is "big enough" to absorb this antipluralistic, antidemocratic group precisely because it poses no real threat.

But when there are clear signs that a group of considerable power and membership not only rejects the values of religious pluralism but also intends to influence national and international policy, in part through its enormous wealth, then there is an obligation to assess the possible implications for democracy. In 1949 journalist Paul Blanshard wrote, not of the Mormons but of the Roman Catholic Church in the United States:

The policy of mutual silence about religious differences is a reasonable policy in matters of personal faith; but when it comes to matters of political, medical, and educational principle, silence may be directly contrary to public welfare. When a church enters the arena of controversial social policy and attempts to control the judgement of its own people (and of other people) on foreign affairs, social hygiene, public education, and modern science, it must be reckoned with as an organization of political and cultural power.[46]

The Mormons, we maintain, represent such a group. They constitute a formidable economic force in late-twentieth-century America. Important owners of public utilities and mass communications, they also exercise corporate strength as a powerful lobbying force in the nation's capital. While such smaller groups as the Unification Church, the Hare Krishnas, and the Moral Majority continue to dominate the headlines, Mormons are making important strides behind the scenes toward fulfilling the promise of post-millennialism. Their success is directly related to general public ignorance about their methods and ends.

The following chapters document the various facets of the emerging Mormon empire. Chapter 2 explores the modern Church's investments in mass communications, particularly in radio and television stations: its holdings, in fact, are unequaled in size by any other religious organization in the world, including the Roman Catholic Church. Chapter 3 describes the Mormons' corporate empire, its interlocking directorates and networks, and its pattern of investment, particularly in agribusiness, public utilities, government stocks and bonds, energy/minerals/oil, and land. Chapter 4 considers the military/political dimension of the Mormon empire. Rising Mormon influence in the armed services, the U.S. Congress, and the intelligence community has the potential for significantly affecting policymaking — such as the placing of MX missiles, the fate of the Equal Rights Amendment, and legal decisions regarding abortion. The reality behind the public image of the LDS Church is the theme of Chapter 5 — the actual extent of the much-publicized Mormon welfare effort, for example, as well as other instances in which the Church is not all that its public relations would have the larger world believe.

2

From Telegraph to Satellite

C ommunications represents one of the linchpins in the Mormons' post-millennial plan for the kingdom of God on earth. A strong foothold in the communications industry is therefore a goal that the LDS Church is aggressively pursuing. Some of the current Church activities are essentially the same as they were in the days of the earliest Saints, such as missionizing and distributing the *Book of Mormon*. Other enterprises, particularly the Church's extensive investments in radio, television, and space satellites, are unique to the twentieth century. Indeed, the modern Mormon communications conglomerate has mushroomed so much in recent years that Nicholas Johnson, a commissioner of the Federal Communications Commission, once called the LDS Church "a media baron of substantial proportions."[1]

Mormon influence in communications touches virtually every person in the United States and, increasingly, millions of people beyond North America. It is a good beginning point for our investigation into modern Mormon influence and intentions.

An aggressive, comprehensive plan to communicate newly revealed truths was built into the foundations of Mormonism. As dedicated post-millennialists, Mormons believe they must gather converts and prepare a theocracy on earth for Jesus Christ to rule after the Second Coming (the Millennium). The result of this belief, seen throughout the history of Mormonism, has been an enormous 29 effort devoted to missionary work to spread the Church's doctrines.

The practice of individual missionizing by members has become one of the hallmarks of the LDS enterprise. The cost of this mission work, conducted worldwide in two-year stints by volunteers, are still born by the families of the young missionaries. As of 1982 the costs averaged $300 per month for each of the 32,000 Mormons in the field, or more than $100 million total.[2] However, the strategy is surprisingly ineffective. One estimate of missionary success from canvassing residential areas was as low as "only nine doors out of a thousand [opening] to missionaries."[3] The remaining 991 doors are not answered, are not opened beyond the length of the chain lock, or are slammed in Mormon faces. In reality, the two-year missionary experience is a sort of rite of passage for pre-college Mormon men (increasingly women are going on missions as well), a tour of duty in the unsympathetic world of the unbelievers that reinforces Mormons' differences from Gentiles.

In recent years Mormon field missions have come under criticism. For example, it is a common suspicion among Mormons that some foreign female converts are merely seeking mates among the male missionaries so they can immigrate to the United States. Many of the missionaries, fresh out of high school and with fairly provincial attitudes, merely memorize pat phrases in a foreign language without ever knowing much about the cultures they encounter. (One of us had the interesting opportunity to observe a pair of hapless teenage missionaries in rural Japan who energetically, but unsuccessfully, preached to Japanese housewives about the evils of drinking tea. The missionaries did not know that Japanese green tea (ōcha) contains no caffeine.) Moreover, almost half of the young missionaries reportedly become "Jack-Mormons" (inactive or backsliding members) after they return.[4] The Church does not encourage speculation about yet another controversial aspect of mission work: throwing pairs of young men aged nineteen to twenty-one into virtually monastic, celibate living conditions for long periods of time at the height of naturally strong sexual drives has fostered rumors of homosexual incidents.[5]

Yet, ironically, despite the visibility of the door-to-door ritual, the field mission is not particularly successful, and the more effective strategy of Mormon conversion remains unknown to the general population. This is the Church's home mission program.

The Mormon Church is the fastest-growing Christian sect in the United States. It swelled from 2,614,340 members to 4,180,000 between 1967 and 1978, and its home mission program helps explain why. Sociologists Rodney Stark and William Sims Bainbridge recently analyzed the subtle strategy of the home mission program in these terms:

> [Door-to-door] missionaries do not serve as the primary instrument of recruitment to the Mormon faith. Instead, recruitment is accomplished primarily by the rank and file of the church as they construct intimate interpersonal ties with non-Mormons and thus link them into a Mormon social network.[6]

Stark and Bainbridge examined the June 1974 issue of the Church magazine *Ensign*, which in one how-to article on conversion (written by Ernest Eberhard, then president of the Oregon mission) offered a thirteen-step method by which Mormons can gradually ingratiate themselves with their neighbors (doing minor favors such as babysitting, running errands, and lending tools), selectively reveal bits of Mormon lifestyle and faith, and eventually build friendship bonds with prospective converts long before proselytizing becomes overt. Eberhard urges that targeted Gentiles be wooed, cautiously engaged in conversations that involve moral subjects, incrementally exposed to testimonies of Mormon happiness, and ultimately indoctrinated in Mormon beliefs. Stark and Bainbridge concluded that "the important thing about the instructions is that they are directed toward building close personal ties and at many points specifically admonish Mormons to avoid or downplay discussion of religion."[7]

This strategy is well understood by sociologists who have studied conversion routines among contemporary religious movements such as the Unification Church.[8] Personal relations have always been used effectively by people trying to convert others, however deceptive the method may seem to outsiders. Just as this method helped transform the Unification Church from an obscure oriental Christian sect into a household word during the 1970s, it has likewise produced significant results for the Mormons. Using LDS Church statistics from the state of Washington for one year (1976–77), Stark and Bainbridge found that while the success rate for door-to-door conversions was a dismal one-tenth of one percent, the home mission conversion method succeeded *fifty percent* of the time. The Church goal for home missions is that each member bring one new person into the Church each year. Mormons can be working on various neighbors and acquaintances at different stages of the conversion process at any given time, and when adults join they frequently bring their mates and children with them. Thus, the Church unquestionably possesses a constant, effective method of increasing the New Zion's population. Certainly the home mission program succeeds beyond the relatively symbolic door-to-door efforts and is second only to the high Mormon birthrate (the Church discourages birth control) as a source of new members.

MORMON PUBLISHING

Publication and dissemination of the *Book of Mormon* was the first Mormon missionary effort, and it continues today. The first printing of 5,000 copies in 1830 (an enormous quantity by the standards of that time) cost $3,000, in large part subsidized by devout members such as the Palmyra, New York, farmer Martin Harris, who sold part of his farm to cover the printer's bill (an act that caused his wife to leave him).[9] The *Book of Mormon* quickly caused a sensation. However, despite angry denunciations by local clergy (one contemporary pastor claimed that the *Book of Mormon* "is from hell, from the bottomless pit, of the devil; and those who believe in it ought to go to hell!"),[10] this Newer Testament spread in a short time throughout nineteenth-century New England and the Midwest. Social scientists, including archaeologists, generally rejected the purported "revealed history" described in the book, including its "Jewish-Indian" theory of pre-Columbian native civilizations in North and South America. One anthropologist in 1899 termed the Mormon scripture "a grotesque monstrosity, born of deceit and bred in falsehood . . . a melange of plagiarisms from the Old and New Testaments." Not long after, a psychologist attacked Mormon founder Joseph Smith as "an ignorant conscious fraud."[11] More recent mainstream scientific criticism has usually been gentler but just as firm in denying credibility to the Mormons' unique views of American history.[12]

Nevertheless, following the post-millennial imperative of the early days, the Church still turns out huge printings of the *Book of Mormon*, currently as many as three million copies a year in languages as diverse as Polish, Norwegian, Samoan, and Korean. Along with the Bible, the *Book of Mormon* is undoubtedly one of the most widely published and distributed books in history. One Church publication reported:

> The Book of Mormon has been reprinted so many times that printers quit numbering editions years ago. No one knows exactly how many copies have been issued since 1830, but an educated guess puts the total somewhere near 21 million.[13]

After Mormonism's founder and prophet produced a unique body of scripture in the *Book of Mormon* and conversions began to occur by the thousands both in this country and overseas, it was natural for the LDS Church to embark on a series of publishing ventures. Many of these were newspapers, journals, and magazines aimed almost exclusively at Church members. Some others had a wider prospective audience. Not only did publishing give the Church its first means of tailoring its private and public images on a broad scale, but, as we will show, it also provided the Church with the opportunity to influence the non-Mormon communications industry.

The Early Days

Mormons started their own newspapers almost as soon as there was an organized Church. In 1832 the first of these, the *Evening and Morning Star*, was published in Jackson County, Missouri. Two years later some members began the *Latter-day Saints' Messenger and Advocate* in Kirtland, Ohio. The latter lasted until 1837, when another magazine, the *Elders' Journal*, succeeded it for another year. As Nauvoo, Illinois, became the major center of American Mormonism, these publications folded and the Nauvoo *Times and Seasons* became the major Mormon mouthpiece from 1839 until 1846 when the Church made its great evacuation westward. Meanwhile, a major foreign paper, the *Latter-day Saints' Millennial Star*, began in Liverpool, England, in 1840 and remained in operation until 1970.

The contents of these early publications reveal much about the embryonic LDS Church and how it has evolved. They were, of course, filled with local Church news and explicit religious doctrines. They also presented numerous, colorful faith-promoting stories of "miracles" recently experienced or witnessed by Church

members. Some seem extreme or overdramatic by modern standards. A typical sample of religious articles from the 1830s and early
1840s includes a story about nine-year-old James G. Marsh, who
reported he had spoken face-to-face with God and many of the
ancient prophets; an essay on archaeological evidence for the
argument that the serpent in the Garden of Eden walked upright;
and the Mormon claim that the ancient Jaredites (the original pre-
Hebrew migrants to North America from Babel) had created the
American prairies by extensive cultivation.[14]

These early publications also reveal a struggling new religion
experimenting with rituals and beliefs, constructing its faith as it
went along. They illustrate the growth of the modern Church out
of "primitive" Mormonism and the process the Church underwent
of selecting out some original elements for survival and rejecting
others. Sometimes these publications stirred up persecution and
could even help shape what would become Church policy as the
group attempted to accommodate to a hostile culture. A prime
example is the Church's pre–Civil War policy toward black
Americans. In July 1833, the *Evening and the Morning Star* extended
an open invitation to "free Negroes and mullatoes [sic] from other
States to become Mormons" and join the rest of the Church in the
"Promised Land" of Jackson County, Missouri.[15] Later that same
month an angry mob of 400 to 500 white Missourians completely
demolished the *Evening and the Morning Star*'s office in retaliation.
They were spurred on by incidents such as a Presbyterian minister's
claim that one of his slaves had been told by a Mormon that "he
[the slave] had waited upon his master long enough." The Mormons
denied that they had meant to cause the slaves to revolt against their
masters or to run away. W. W. Phelps, editor of the *Evening and
the Morning Star* and author of the offending article, wrote another
article in the hope of placating the Missourians by "insisting his
original intent had been to *keep* Negroes *from coming* to Missouri
and *from becoming* Mormons." This sudden about-face in the
aftermath of white outrage, according to one historian, "was
complete when Joseph Smith began to defend slavery."[16]

Joseph Smith had never before taken this position on blacks.
Though he reverted to opposing slavery before he died, his successor as Church president, Brigham Young, adopted the same
accommodationist pro-slavery views that editor Phelps was pres-

sured to endorse because of Gentile public opinion. These views became the basis for later discriminatory Church policy toward blacks (they could join the Church but were denied admittance to the priesthood) that lasted into the late twentieth century and earned for this otherwise public relations–conscious organization the embarrassing label "racist." Looking back over all the controversy that this emerging racial policy caused the Church during the past 130-odd years, Sterling McMurrin, a professor of philosophy at the University of Utah and a "liberal" Mormon, has commented:

> The Saints would have been so much better off if they had never gone near Missouri because they . . . compromised their position by adopting an idea that already prevailed . . . that "Negroes are cursed with a black skin and that they are intended as the curse of Noah on Canaan goes, to be 'servants of servants.'"[17]

Over time the Mormons became more adept at dealing with their Gentile neighbors through the printed media. Their best-known effort, the Salt Lake City newspaper the *Deseret News*, deserves to be examined separately not only because its operation reflects the Mormon view of how to use mass communications but also because it has served as the link to more sophisticated forms of influence.

The Deseret News

The *Deseret News*, founded on June 15, 1850, was the first newspaper west of the Mississippi. Typical of many early Mormon projects, it faced an uphill struggle to survive for many years. The most immediate problem was not public demand but the scarcity of paper. While the Mormons began transporting paper machines from St Louis and constructing one of the first paper mills in the Mountain West, they also started a mammoth campaign to collect rags for making their own paper. Rag drives became frequent events across Utah throughout the 1850s and 1860s. Church members could even donate clothing as part of their required tithe to the Church. In 1861, after a ten-month drive, one Church official had gathered 20,000 pounds of rags for the paper campaign. After three years he estimated that he had collected more than 100,000 pounds of rags![18]

Other troubles faced the new publishing venture. Type for printing presses was often in short supply, and Gentile competitors continually moved their unfriendly presses into the territory. Yet the *Deseret News* survived these challenges, and by the end of the century it had outlasted most of its rivals. In the early 1950s it even merged production facilities with the competing non-Mormon *Salt Lake Tribune*.

But the real importance of the modern *Deseret News* lies in what it can tell us about how the LDS Church has used such a public information medium. The *Deseret News* should be viewed as a forum for Church views and policy as well as a news organ. Though it would like to become a Rocky Mountain version of the *Christian Science Monitor*, it more closely resembles the Vatican's *L'Osservatore Romano*. (The former publication has built a solid reputation for fine journalism independent of the religious sect that founded it. The latter, Roman Catholic newspaper unabashedly reflects its sponsor's theocratic concerns.)

The highest levels of the Mormon Church hierarchy regularly screen the newspaper's editorials before they are printed. One journalist who was a *Deseret News* staff writer for twelve years wrote, "The *Deseret News* continues to routinely send all editorials to LDS Church headquarters at 50 E. North Temples before publication, where they are usually seen by Elder Gordon B. Hinkley, member of the Council of the Twelve, and president of the Deseret News Publishing Company, and by President N. Eldon Tanner of the First Presidency."[19]

That few editorials need major censoring or rewriting, however, comes as no surprise when one considers the links between Church leadership and those who control the newspaper's editorial policy. For example, Elder Mark E. Petersen, an apostle in the Council of the Twelve (recently deceased), was for years editor and general manager of the *Deseret News* before becoming president of Deseret News Publishing Company and chairman of the Church's public relations program. Thomas S. Monson, another apostle, left the *Deseret News* to become general manager of the Deseret Press and later president of the Deseret News Publishing Company. Elder Gordon B. Hinkley, an apostle and later one of the Church's "screeners" of editorials, has long been associated with media work for the Church as director of KIRO television and radio in Seattle, Washington, and secretary of the Church's Radio, Publicity, and Literature Committee.

The current editor and general manager of the *Deseret News*, William B. Smart, has been known in the past for his "progressive" editorial stands (such as on civil rights during the 1960s), but he toes the mark when it comes to Church approval of how the newspaper deals with certain issues. One *Utah Holiday* profile of him recalled:

> While the buck stops at Smart's desk for most important policies that affect the *News*, including most editorials, in the public eye he is often regarded as merely an extension of the Church. And in one of the most highly significant editorial crises of recent years at the *News*, that appears to have been precisely the case. During the next-to-last days of Watergate, the *News* drank the bitter dregs of the Nixon Administration's culpability and corruption with scarcely a complaint. Friends say Smart festered under advice of LDS Church President Harold B. Lee to give Nixon the ultimate benefit of a doubt before writing off his administration. As a result, the *Deseret News* was one of the last major dailies in the nation to take a strong editorial stand on Watergate.[20]

The Church does more than simply exert pressure to slant editorials in a conservative direction. For example, political candidates looked upon favorably by the Church hierarchy are treated kindly by the *News*. Others are not. In 1956 (before Smart's tenure) J. Bracken Lee ran for a third term as governor of Utah. In the eyes of Mormon leadership Lee had lost his usefulness for promoting Zion's interests. Both a Gentile and a Mason (Mormonism could suffer a Gentile governor but currently abhors Freemasonry), Lee had angered Church leaders for several reasons. Two years earlier he had vetoed a Church-inspired Sunday-closing "blue law" for retailers; he had failed to help the Church have some land adjacent to Brigham Young University condemned (so that the Church-owned university could take it over cheaply); and he had denied the Sons of Utah Pioneers (a largely Mormon group) an abandoned state penitentiary that they wanted to transform into a park-museum complex. During a close primary runoff the *Deseret News* ran a series of articles damaging to Lee and helpful to his Mormon opponent. The articles included coverage of alleged casualness by the state's Liquor Control Commission in keeping liquor out of minors' hands and of the fact that state employees were contributing heavily to

Lee's reelection campaign. Lee lost the race.[21]

Church attempts to influence *Deseret News* readers have some-times backfired. During the 1936 presidential campaign, Church President Heber J. Grant (who detested the Democrats' New Deal policies) had another member of the Church's First Presidency write an unsigned editorial accusing Franklin D. Roosevelt of "knowingly promoting unconstitutional laws and . . . advocating communism," among other things. The editorial outraged Mormon voters. Many saw the conservative hand of the Church presidency in the editorial; over seventy percent of the letters sent to the First Presidency of-fice soon after its publication condemned the editorial. One his-torian has noted that over 1,200 Latter-day Saints canceled their subscriptions to the *Deseret News* because of the editorial. It had clearly caused a backlash, and a few days after its publication, 69.3 percent of Utah's votes went for Franklin D. Roosevelt and the New Deal.[22]

Perhaps more important than slanted editorials is the Church's influence in determining what doesn't find its way onto the pages of the *Deseret News*. There have been several recent examples of solid investigative reporting by *Deseret News* staff members whose stories were killed because they would have proved embarrassing to the Church leadership. One prominent case involved the now virtually defunct Pinpoint Team of the *Deseret News*.

The Pinpoint Team was initially a crew of five young, ambi-tious reporters selected in 1975 by a *Deseret News* city editor to probe a scandal in which some deputy sheriffs in Salt Lake County were "judge-shopping" (that is, directing persons accused of traffic offenses and other minor infractions onto the dockets of certain courts where justices were paid a commission per case). A former staff writer for the newspaper recalled how publication of the re-sulting articles had "immediate and long-range impact." The judge-shopping practice quickly dwindled in the glare of publicity as justices of the peace were placed on fixed salaries instead of being paid per case. Two justices eventually were charged with mal-feasance in office. Administrative procedures were changed so that sheriffs could not arbitrarily target accused persons into specific courts for trial.[23]

The judge-shopping series received a special certificate of merit from the American Bar Association and was nominated for a Pulitzer

Prize. Locally it was nominated for the general excellence prize for print media awarded by the Utah Society for Professional Journalists (Sigma Chi Delta). Ironically, the Utah prize went to a series by a pair of Associated Press reporters that dealt with the finances of the LDS Church. The *Deseret News* had not printed the Associated Press articles, and nor had the *Salt Lake Tribune* with which it shares production facilities. In fact, Utah newspapers generally ignored the highly praised series.

The Pinpoint Team had a promising beginning, and during the next several years it covered other local and regional stories in a similarly thorough manner. These included reporting of insurance scams, Salt Lake City police problems, and zoning violations. The team tackled not only the stories considered "safe" for a Mormon-owned newspaper, such as pornography and liquor law violations, but also more delicate ones, such as the largely Mormon flock of assistants that isolated millionaire recluse Howard Hughes from the world.

But any investigative team faces problems in working for a sectarian newspaper, and two journalists explain the particular frustrations faced by the Pinpoint Team:

> It is hard to investigate in Utah without turning up a Mormon connection. The Church either owns, or has substantial influence in, banks, department stores, insurance, real estate, agribusiness, and energy and utility companies.
>
> The Pinpoint Team looked into real estate scams and Howard Hughes' Mormon aides without causing a ruckus in the church. The . . . [in 1978] . . . reporters took on a story that sparked a strong reaction. First, a Pinpoint Team special described a secret attempt by Mountain Fuel Supply, a local utility with strong church connections, to tape record a meeting held by a consumer group; then a column reported that Mountain Fuel had attempted to create a non-regulated subsidiary for the company's oil holdings, a scheme that would have allowed the company to pass on drilling costs to utility rate payers. Both articles appeared while Church officials who oversee the *News* were out of town. ("Whenever I'm onto something controversial," says one reporter, "it's crucial that I get it in before anybody can react.")[24]

Church leaders and the *Deseret News* publisher heard loud complaints over these articles from vested interests, and the complaints in turn led to pressures to "put a leash" on the Pinpoint Team. At the same time other stories became equally unpopular with the powers that be. Bob Mullins, an original member of the Pinpoint Team and an earlier Pulitzer Prize winner, talked in the spring of 1982 about the Church disfavor that eventually discouraged further investigations:

> When I did a series on the Central Utah [water] Project [CUP], it was killed by my editors and publisher because some of the brethren in the Church apparently felt it could be potentially damaging to future [federal] government funding.

Mullins suspected that the Church had played an important role in the newspaper's decision not to run his stories. "It's even more interesting," he reflected, "when you consider that in a year of budgetary cutbacks and belt-tightening by the current administration, President Reagan saw fit to substantially increase federal support of CUP with a little encouragement from [Utah LDS] Senators Garn and Hatch."[25]

When asked to confirm the Church's influence in not printing Bob Mullins's articles, editor William B. Smart responded: "I don't think any explanation needs to be given on that. The management and myself made an editorial decision that it would be best for the paper and everyone concerned not to have his material appear as he originally submitted it. But some of it, in fact, much of it, was used in a different form later."[26]

Another story on which Church influence apparently came to bear was the Pinpoint Team's investigation of the Johnson brothers. In a background study of Snellen M. and Lyle E. Johnson, entrepreneurs who made a $650,000 down payment to purchase the Utah Stars, a professional basketball team, in the mid-1970s, the reporters found that Snellen Johnson had been previously charged in U.S. District Court with conspiracy and violation of the Federal Securities Act. Both brothers, it turned out, had a decade-long abysmal credit rating and a history of lawsuits.[27] Yet the Pinpoint Team's findings about the Johnson brothers' affairs never made it into print, and only many months later was the matter even briefly noted by the *Deseret News*. The reason is that a high-level Church official telephoned the newspaper and vouched for the Johnsons' credibility and integrity.

The Johnsons, their lawyers, the Pinpoint Team, and editor William B. Smart met. Smart met again with the Johnsons and their lawyers, this time without the investigative reporters. "At this point," as Paul Swenson in *Dialogue* puts it, "the *News* lost confidence in the series and backed off from further disclosures." Not long afterward, the Johnsons were found to have written bad checks totaling $160,000 (while their basketball team went out of business).[28]

The Pinpoint Team never regained momentum after this. Five years later, Bob Mullins, the last reporter from the original Pinpoint Team still working at the *Deseret News*, summed it up:

A few years ago [in the late 1970s] we had five reporters working at different times on the Pinpoint investigative team. Everyone of them left, though, for better jobs elsewhere. I'm the lone hold-out now in this department. I don't know why the *News* hasn't put some more reporters in this department. There's certainly enough stories around to cover.[29]

Other stories ignored or minimized by the *Deseret News* have had national significance, such as the incident of the Dugway, Utah, sheep killed by U.S. Army experimental nerve gas in the late 1960s. Other issues have been more prosaic, such as the case of the Coalville, Utah, tabernacle, a beautiful nineteenth-century example of Mormon architecture listed in the Utah State Register of Historical Sites. In 1971 Church officials were determined to tear it down, historical nostalgia and the wishes of its congregation notwithstanding, to build a more functional, though unexciting, church building. Members of the congregation who petitioned and visited the First Presidency office were assured that due process would be taken for any decision on demolition. The *Deseret News* did report on the controversy, but only to publish the Church's official statements, which announced a guarantee of a "cooling off" period before any decision on the tabernacle would be made. In fact, the tabernacle was razed before the public could react.

The *Deseret News* made no direct mention of the tabernacle's demolition until after it was a *fait accompli*, despite the fact that the rival *Salt Lake Tribune* and other newspapers as well as local television stations covered the furor extensively.[30] Even non-Mormons in Coalville had become involved, petitioning the Church to save the historical building. Editor Smart described his dilemma in this situation:

> Being the editor of a Church-owned newspaper has not always been easy for me. The hardest thing I believe I've ever encountered was the reporting of the destruction of the Coalville tabernacle by the Church. I found it hard to report it like it should really have been reported. I mean, here is the uncalled-for destruction of an old and historic structure by the same people who own the newspaper I edit. What am I supposed to do?[31]

From a journalistic viewpoint, the situation is worse at the *Church News*, a weekly supplement to the *Deseret News*. There the articles on Church affairs are exclusively upbeat. News items that cast the Church in a favorable light usually get printed; those that could be considered critical or negative have slimmer odds of ever reaching *Deseret News* readers. This situation is understandable, for the Church can hardly be expected to air its own dirty linen in public. But at the same time the *Deseret News* aspires to be more than an apologetic Mormon tabloid. As yet the dilemma between reporting news fully, no matter how painful to Church mullahs, and projecting the Church's preferred self-image to the larger world has yet to be resolved. One strategy that the newspaper uses to avoid self-deprecating news has been referred to as "Afghanistanism," that is, concentrating on abstract moral problems far away (or on mundane local issues) while ignoring less pleasant major facts closer to home. Thus, in the early 1970s the *Deseret News* was more likely to carry a Church leader's tirade against mustaches and long sideburns on Mormon men or the evils of rock music than to provide readers with a serious look at the Watergate scandal.[32]

It might be expected that over time the LDS Church will grow out of its sensitivity to criticism and give the editors of the *Deseret News* the professional autonomy they do not yet fully have. Certainly the newspaper is no longer plagued by some of the problems it endured earlier in this century, when Church leaders filled the choicest editorial positions with their relatives and used the newspaper generally as a dumping ground for otherwise unemployable kin. Partly simple nepotism, the practice also served to insure the Church leadership against critical journalism, but the reputation it created of an inferior daily church newspaper still haunts the *Deseret News*.[33]

There are many other Mormon publishing outlets besides the *Deseret News*, and often their histories are linked to the newspaper's growth. The Deseret Book Company, for example, traces its roots to 1866 when Elder George Q. Cannon began publishing the magazine *Instructor* for young Saints. After his death in 1901, Cannon's business was sold to the Church, which operated it as the Deseret News Bookstore. In 1919 the Deseret Book Company was created through a merger of the *Deseret News* and Mormon (Deseret) Sunday School bookstores. The modern Deseret Book Company ranks as one of the largest religious book publishing houses in the Rocky Mountain region. It manages twelve stores in three western states as well as numerous outlets worldwide. Its twelve American stores operate in predominantly Mormon areas, employing several hundred people and enjoying gross sales of some $30 million annually. Most of the books sold are predictably Church related and faith-promoting.

Yet there is more to the *Deseret News* than just its links to other Mormon publications. One interesting aspect is its expansion into the ownership of other newspapers. In 1965 the *News* acquired about 300,000 shares of Times-Mirror Corporation common stock. At that time the Church's stock made up 5.5 percent of the total Times-Mirror stock in circulation (valued at $28 million in 1978), making the Church the second-largest controlling shareholder in the corporation. (Since then the stock has split. A market value of $52 million can be assigned to the Church-owned stock, which, while representing slightly less than 2 percent of the total circulating stock, still makes the LDS Church the corporation's second major stockholder.)[34] While a little less than 6 percent or 2 percent (depending on the year) of stock ownership might seem small, in the world of highly diffused stock ownership it can carry significant influence in a corporation. This fact becomes especially telling in light of Times-Mirror's ownership of some of the largest newspapers in the United States, principally the following:

Los Angeles (Calif.) *Times*
Orange Coast Daily Pilot (Costa Mesa, Calif.)
Newsday (Long Island, New York)

Dallas (Texas) *Times Herald* (Dallas, Texas)
The Hartford (Ct.) *Courant*
The Advocate (Stamford, Ct.)
Greenwich (Ct.) *Times*
The Sporting News (St. Louis, Mo.)
Denver (Colo.) *Post*

The Church has not been eager to share information about its
stock ownership. Repeated attempts to learn if the Church's stock
holdings in Times-Mirror had increased or declined in the last few
years met with silence from both Times-Mirror's attorneys and
Deseret News owners until such facts were reported in the *Los
Angeles Times* by an investigative reporter. Much of this stock
involves partial ownership of such major newspapers as the *Dallas
Times Herald*, the *Denver Post*, and the *Los Angeles Times*, which
is the West Coast equivalent of the *New York Times*. One Merrill
Lynch broker in Salt Lake City quipped to one of us, "Next thing
you know they'll be owning half of L.A. itself."

Thus, in an important sense, the *Deseret News* has served as
a stepping-stone for the Church to enter a communications network
that reaches beyond the community of Utah Saints to non-Mormon
audiences nationwide and even worldwide. The *News* has also been
a departure point from which the Church has shifted emphasis and
investments, moving into the sophisticated electronics field.[35]

THE MORMON ELECTRONIC CHURCH

Journalists as well as scholars of religion have recognized the
powerful blend of religion and electronic broadcasting that coalesced
in the late 1970s and 1980s. Through television and radio, evangelists like Robert Schuller, Jerry Falwell, Oral Roberts, and Jimmy
Swaggart, along with born-again Christian talk-show hosts like the
700 Club's Pat Robertson and *Praise the Lord*'s Jim Bakker, have
employed sophisticated technology, including space satellites, to
spread their versions of biblical gospel. American religion has been
accused of being faddish; if it is, then what has been called the
"electronic church" is its latest rage.[36]

Yet, fundamentalist Christians hold no monopoly on the latest
high-tech communications. They only command the most publicized

presence. The Mormons, too, have made impressive inroads into the electronic media. In fact, they have done so on a scale that dwarfs competitors' use of the media. Consistent with their millennial goals, they are using this latest medium both to propagate their faith and to protect it from outside scrutiny. LDS Church leaders have shrewdly evaluated the electronic media's enormous potential. Arch L. Madsen, former president of Bonneville International (an LDS communications holding company), recently reminded the faithful: "God in His wisdom has given us television and radio to assist Him in His great purposes. May we be blessed and ever diligent in the use of all communications media to hasten the day of His kingdom."[37]

The Church became involved in electronics early. In 1861 the first transcontinental telegraph line in the United States was completed, and soon the Mormons began developing their own version. Through local wards and stakes the Church collected tithes, volunteer labor, and raw materials to establish the first comprehensive regional electronic communications system in the country. By 1880 there were 1,130 miles of telegraph wire in Utah alone and 68 local telegraph offices. The entire system was connected to the outside world from Salt Lake City and extended from southern Idaho to northern Arizona and most of the mining districts in Utah and southeastern Nevada. It was a tremendous effort, undertaken by Mormons principally for Mormons. It improved Church communications, thereby strengthening the control of Church administration by linking even remote settlements to the Salt Lake City headquarters. In the 1880s it even served as an early warning system to alert polygamist Church officials on the run from federal agents.[38]

The Church sold its telegraph company to Western Union in 1900 but not long after moved into a more significant branch of electronic media. In 1922, only one year after the world's first commercial radio broadcast was delivered in Pittsburgh, Pennsylvania, Melvin R. Ballard, then circulation manager of the *Deseret News*, convinced the newspaper's management to allow him to build a ramshackle cabin to house a radio transmitter on the publication's roof. The newspaper invested $1,000, and the transmitter was built and managed by *Deseret News* staff members. Ballard originally directed his broadcasts at Boy Scouts, who meanwhile were building receiver sets for their local churches. This first station, KZN, operated for two years before the *Deseret News* sold it. Several owners later, the LDS Church again assumed ownership and changed the station's call letters to KSL. By 1929 KSL had become an affiliate station of the National Broadcasting Company (NBC) and later switched affiliation to the Columbia Broadcasting System (CBS). An important early KSL program that later became an invaluable public relations feature of the Church was the now-famous Mormon Tabernacle Choir, which appeared on the "Music and the Spoken Word" program. Fred C. Esplin, a Mormon and the director of information at the Public Television Network in Hershey, Pennsylvania, notes that

> *Music and the Spoken Word*...has the distinction of being the oldest continuously broadcast network program in America. It is significant too because it cast the mold for subsequent efforts at creating a favorable image for the Church. Church programs have largely been low key, with less emphasis on doctrine than on good taste and common appeal. It has never been the Church's style to attack other faiths or to use the hard sell common to many religious broadcasts. In fact, *Music and the Spoken Word* is not even classified as a religious program under FCC rulings.[39]

Today Bonneville International, the broadcast arm of the LDS Church created in 1962, is a powerful, lucrative, and fast-growing communications conglomerate. Linked directly to the Church's Corporation of the President through the Deseret Management Corporation, Bonneville in turn controls nine other Church-owned corporations all in one way or another expanding Church influence, managing its image, and tactfully promoting its post-millennial message. Besides owning two large commercial television stations and twelve radio stations in heavily populated and lucrative markets around the country, Bonneville owns a number of other thriving businesses that include a movie production studio in Hollywood, a full-time Washington, D.C., news bureau, and growing cable/satellite and radio data systems. We briefly mention the more important of these investments.

Mormon Radio and Television

The LDS Church actually owns three television stations: two commercial stations plus an educational outlet, KBYU-TV, at Brigham Young University. KSL-TV in Salt Lake City is a sister station to the original Mormon-owned radio station. It probably reaches more people in a wider area than any other television station in the United States because it consists of 121 translator stations scattered throughout the Mountain West. When the U.S. Justice Department opposed the station's petition in 1974 for license renewal with the Federal Communications Commission (on the grounds that the Mormon Church had created a communications monopoly in the region), it noted that "KSL-TV possesses the largest Area of Dominant Influence (ADI) of any station in the continental United States."[40] The Church's other commercial station, KIRO-TV in Seattle, Washington, also reaches an enormous audience by national standards.

Like its radio stations, the Church's television stations have two purposes. As investments they are supposed to generate profits that the Church can use for other projects. This they do. They are also intended to help promote Mormonism before mostly Gentile audiences. However, the airwaves technically belong to the public and thus are government-supervised. FCC regulations prohibit both KSL-TV and KIRO-TV from mixing Mormon theology with programming and from enforcing editorial policies like those of the *Deseret News*. As Fred C. Esplin explains:

> [These stations are limited] to indirectly portraying a positive image of the Church. Because the Bonneville stations cannot be used to proselyte, the Church has made a substantial effort to enlist non-Church stations through use of public service announcements.[41]

Millions of Americans have seen these LDS public service spots on television or heard them on radio as part of what is called the "Homefront Series." Most deal with basic family issues such as encouraging parents to spend more time with their children or spouses and to become more considerate of one another's feelings. They can be subtly anti-feminist: one spot aired nationally in the summer of 1983 showed a frazzled mother at a job and at night school but clearly finding her true fulfillment in being a parent. The spots are short, well-edited, professionally produced, and generally upbeat with only a brief mention of their sponsors at the end. Quintessentially middle class, they are confident (but not smug), benevolent, and low key — all the qualities in the modern Mormon image that the LDS Church wishes to project.

According to the Federal Communications Commission, Bonneville International currently owns twelve commercial radio stations in the United States:[42]

STATION	CITY	DATE OF PURCHASE
KSL-AM	Salt Lake City	1925
KIRO-AM/KSEA-FM	Seattle	1963
WRFM-FM	New York City	1966
KMBZ-AM/KMBR-FM	Kansas City, Mo.	1967
KBIG-FM	Los Angeles	1968
WCLR-FM	Chicago	1969
KAAM-AM/KAFM-FM	Dallas	1977
KOIT-AM/KOIT-FM	San Francisco	1975, 1983

This list of Church-owned radio stations illustrates several trends consistent with the picture of a sectarian religious organization vigorously pursuing mass media access to widest possible audiences. Since Bonneville International's creation in 1962, the Church has gathered considerable corporate momentum and purchased seven FM and five AM radio stations. Moreover, these outlets are located in cities with the nation's largest markets. For example, the two Dallas radio stations most recently purchased serve a metropolitan area consisting of Dallas, Fort Worth, and a dozen smaller cities that have a combined population of approximately four million — larger than the entire population of either Mississippi or Louisiana.

In addition, Bonneville International operates its own Washington news bureau in the nation's capital (three blocks from the White House) at an annual cost of approximately $250,000. The staff is modest: only half a dozen persons altogether. Its function is not just to report news but also to syndicate news, mostly to Bonneville radio and television stations, with profits paid to the news bureau circulated back to Church headquarters.

Besides those stations and the Washington news media directly owned by Bonneville International, the LDS Church has made other important electronic investments in the form of Times-Mirror Corporation stock. The growing Times-Mirror Cablevision, for example, has more than 500,000 subscribers nationwide after spending over $40 million in 1981 alone to expand its system. In the near future Times-Mirror plans to compete with Home Box

Office (HBO), the nation's largest subscription television service, with its own version called Spotlight.[43] In addition, the Times-Mirror Corporation owns the following television stations:

WVTM-TV   Birmingham, Ala.
KTV-TV   St. Louis, Mo.
WETM-TV   Elmira, N.Y.
WSTM-TV   Syracuse, N.Y.
WHTM-TV   Harrisburg, Pa.
KTBC-TV   Austin, Tex.
KDFW-TV   Dallas, Tex.

Though until 1984 (when the broadcast industry was deregulated) FCC regulations prohibited any owner from having more than seven television, seven AM, and seven FM stations at any time, the Mormon Church's critical mass of Times-Mirror stock actually gives it a significant investment and potential voice in the affairs of ten television, five AM, and seven FM stations, not counting cable operations.

One other factor must be mentioned. The Marriott family of hotel fame is active in electronic media ownership under their logo First Media. Currently the Marriotts own ten AM and FM radio stations, most in large metropolitan areas. There are a number of circumstantial links between the Marriotts and Mormon leadership and/or media property. J. Willard Marriott, the family patriarch, once served on the board of directors of the International Educational Broadcasting Corporation (a wholly owned subsidiary of the Church's Corporation of the First Presidency). Indeed, former Church President David O. McKay requested that Marriott serve. The late Nathan Eldon Tanner, a key figure in Church business operations and once the First Counselor to Church President Spencer W. Kimball, was also "closely advised by J. Willard Marriott."[44] Moreover, half the stations of Marriott's First Media Corporation currently employ Torbet Radio to sell air time to advertisers. Torbet Radio was until recently a subsidiary of Bonneville International and handled all the Church's directly owned radio and television stations' advertising.[45]

The Marriotts have always been loyal Mormons, even down to such fine points as furnishing copies of the *Book of Mormon* instead of Gideon Bibles in their hotel rooms. Church informants who know them portrayed them as favoring the use of the media whenever feasible to further the Church's interests. Seven of the family's AM and FM stations have recently been purchased in cities where the Church has built temples but as yet does not own any broadcast properties. While the Marriott radio stations and similar holdings by other individual Church members cannot be counted as part of the Church's own electronic investments, neither can they be considered irrelevant to the Mormon electronic church.

In the meantime, Church officials and members have managed to pave the way for Mormon media purchases more than once within the governing Federal Communications Commission. For example, in 1968 Bonneville International acquired KBIG-AM and KBIG-FM in Los Angeles and nearby Avalon, California, for $2 million paid up front and an estimated additional half million dollars for a long-term lease of equipment and real estate. One year later one of its license applications was strongly opposed by three of the seven FCC commissioners, who felt that the Mormon Church already possessed too much influence in the broadcast industry through its numerous holdings. Yet despite repeated efforts none of the members was able to initiate an official full-scale investigation, or even public hearings, into the financial affairs and cross-ownerships of the LDS organization. One reason is that FCC Chairman Rosel H. Hyde and Commissioner H. Rex Lee, both devout Mormons, were able to persuade several other commissioners to see things their way and overrule the dissenting votes.[46]

Commissioner Nicholas Johnson, who during his years on the FCC had a reputation for opposing media monopolies, stated the case for investigating growing Mormon power before granting the Church any further licenses:

Bonneville International Corporation receives approval today from this Commission to add to its stable of industrial and mass media properties an AM radio station, and an FM radio station, in the second largest market in the United States: Los Angeles — a city in which it already has a $20 million interest in the prestigious and dominant Los Angeles Times.

This action is taken without a public discussion of the principal issues raised by this case: the conflicts with the public interest in granting ever-increasing mass media power — with all its economic, political, and social implications — to large industrial conglomerate corporations in the United States, in this case an industrial conglomerate that is inexorably intertwined with a religious sect, the Mormon Church.[47]

Commissioner Johnson criticized the commission's perfunctory handling of the Church's license applications, particularly its failure to consider the implications of ignoring past Mormon acquisitions. After a lengthy listing of the Church's media and other business holdings (including his own well-known reference to the Mormon Church as a "media baron of substantial proportions"), Johnson concluded:

> This combination of media and other economic power raises a final issue — the domination of a city, State, and region by a particular religious sect. The issue is subtle — it is not occasioned simply by church ownership of property or a media outlet — rather the question arises because of the accumulation of power by the Mormon Church, and the increase of that power by actions of this Commission.[48]

Another case is the Bonneville International purchase of WRFM-FM in 1966 for $850,000, at that time the largest price ever asked for an FM radio station. The New York region the station serves has the largest, most concentrated potential listening audience in the nation. FCC Commissioner Robert T. Bartley disapproved of the purchase, calling for an investigation. His request was over-ridden by the FCC board, and Mormon interests pressed ahead.[49]

Favoritism toward the Mormon Church within the FCC, an organization that in principle serves the public as a watchdog against partisan influence, has surfaced more than once. In spring 1962 the FCC received a petition jointly filed by the Salt Lake City Broadcasting Company and the Granite District Broadcasting Company (both owned by non-Mormons) to obtain rights to the sole remaining FM radio channel in Salt Lake City. A decision on the petition was continually postponed and delayed by lengthy hearings, the latter ostensibly called to determine if the two companies should be awarded this last FM channel. Meanwhile, an official FCC report issued during the waiting period observed in a footnote: "Another party filed for this new [FM channel] assignment and was granted a construction permit, leaving Salt Lake and Granite still in a hearing situation." This other party, which had apparently managed to bypass ordinary red tape, was, in fact, KSL, Inc., the Mormon-owned Salt Lake City broadcasting stalwart.[50]

The Mormon-owned media conglomerate, Bonneville International, along with others, has at times put unusual pressure on the FCC when it felt that any of its broadcasting interests might be threatened. One example occurred in March 1983 when the recommendation was made by the Daytime Broadcasters Association (DBA) that the FCC permit all daytime radio stations to operate from two hours before sunrise until two hours after sunset where dominant stations suffer no debilitating interference. Various networks and media companies offered brief objections to this proposal. But the most vehement objection not only to DBA's proposal but also to several proposals proffered by the National Association of Broadcasters (NAB) came from Bonneville International.

Bonneville reminded the FCC that as "a long-time and active member of the NAB" it felt the NAB did an injustice by choosing "to support one segment of its membership against another." Bonneville found fault with the NAB's inclination to help more than 2,000 daytime stations expand their broadcast time while ignoring the interests of long-time, established, clear channel stations of which there are no more than fifty. Bonneville claimed that it was a case of choosing numbers instead of strength. It recommended that the FCC totally disregard NAB's support for DBA's request. A prime reason for this strong retaliatory action was that KSL-AM, one of the Bonneville stations, might experience some broadcast interference from local daytime stations if the other stations' air time were expanded by several hours each day. The president of DBA severely rebuked Bonneville International for its self-serving attitude, referring to Bonneville as one of "the dinosaurs of radio" that treat daytime stations and their listeners as "peasants who deserve nothing better than slavery." Not content with such rhetoric, the president of DBA added that Bonneville's attack on the NAB was "unwarranted."[51]

Salt Lake City's Church-owned KSL has consistently received preferential, even protective treatment from the FCC. In 1968, when two Salt Lake City residents, Ethel C. Hale and W. Paul Wharton, protested Mormon control of media in the Great Salt Basin during

KSL's license renewal process, it was Mormon FCC Chairman Rosel H. Hyde who not only squelched the chances for public hearings on the matter (despite requests from 3 commissioners to hold such hearings) but also cast the deciding vote in favor of renewing KSL's licenses. In 1974 KSL again came up for renewal of its radio and television licenses. This time the U.S. Department of Justice petitioned the FCC to deny renewal on the grounds that "a grant of the renewal applications would be inconsistent with the public interest since the renewals would perpetuate the high degree of concentration in the dissemination of local news and advertising that now exists in Salt Lake City."[52] The Justice Department pointed out that KSL, Inc., was under common ownership with the Deseret News Publishing Company. Not only did the latter publish the *Deseret News*, one of Salt Lake City's two daily newspapers, but it also owned half of the Newspaper Agency Corporation (the joint venture that operated the business and production facilities of both the *Deseret News* and the *Salt Lake Tribune*). Among other problems cited by the Justice Department (using Dun & Bradstreet financial estimates) was that KSL and the Newspaper Agency Corporation together could obtain 81 percent of all local advertising in the Salt Lake area. Renewing KSL's licenses, in short, amounted to condoning a monopoly of media in the region.

Though he had retired from the FCC in 1969, Rosel H. Hyde worked closely on this matter with the Church's Washington, D.C., law firm that represents all its media interests. In the end the FCC refused to deny KSL's relicensing and dismissed the Justice Department's petition. This example of apparent Mormon influence in the FCC is particularly interesting because it involved another unusual aspect. Not only did the *Salt Lake Tribune* (the non-Mormon competitor to the *Deseret News*) oppose the Justice Department's petition and put its own attorneys on the case, but Vernon B. Romney, the Utah attorney general and a Mormon, collected affidavits endorsing KSL from many prominent Utah citizens (including state and national politicians as well as non-Mormon religious leaders) and sent a lengthy memorandum to the FCC.[53] This was a highly unusual action by a state official in a matter involving the federal government and a private organization.

Looking back over his twenty-three years on the FCC, Rosel H. Hyde said candidly in an interview after his retirement, "I must admit, though, my beliefs in what the Church stands for influenced some of my decisions." Recalling the KSL licensing issue, he mused, "I know the feeling that came over me when certain liberal commissioners wanted to deny the renewal of a license for KSL. I was determined to push hard in the other direction for renewal. This is the kind of thing I'm quite sure any other good member would be inclined to feel. It's an instinct, I guess, to protect something you love and are close to."[54]

The strategic presence of Mormons in influential government offices like the FCC is one major way the LDS Church can wield influence in the media industry disproportionate to the Church's size in American society. There are other examples. The new chairman of the board of directors of the Public Broadcasting Service is former Brigham Young University President Dallin Oaks (now a Church apostle). The new head of this public television network's powerful lobbying group, the National Association of Public Television Stations, is also a devout Mormon and a former director of BYU's public television station KBYU-TV. In fact, he was nominated to the post by President Reagan, thanks to the endorsement of Dallin Oaks. Arch L. Madsen, former president of Bonneville International, has served on the board of directors of Radio Free Europe and Radio Liberty. In May 1983 President Reagan appointed him, with subsequent Senate confirmation, to the Board for International Broadcasting.

Perhaps the most outstanding case of Mormon influence in the electronic media involves the Voice of America, the federal agency charged with broadcasting pro-American propaganda to hundreds of millions of people behind the Iron Curtain. In 1981 President Reagan appointed James Conkling, a Mormon and former head of Bonneville Entertainment (an LDS-owned film company), to head VOA. Conkling is a member of the Chevy Chase, Maryland, Church ward, a Mormon parish that also can claim Mormons Mark Austead (former ambassador to Norway), columnist Jack Anderson, and hotel magnate J. Willard Marriott. Conkling described his first months at the agency as "pretty rough — trying to clear out all of the deadwood left from previous administrations." He told us, "I really went to town and cleaned house," reassigning staff "to other places in the government," in order to make room for his own people. "But," he concluded, "we now have two members of the Church here and another coming in pretty soon." Conkling told us that the Church was delighted by his appointment, partly because he intended to step up religious broadcasting on VOA. "I intend to use a lot of material from the radio "Homefront Series" on our VOA broadcasts to Eastern Europe, Africa, South America, and places where I think it could do the most good. I couldn't give them [the Church] a credit line, though I'd like to."[55]

Some of Conkling's aggressive tactics in other areas caused considerable opposition from within VOA itself. Consequently he chose to resign at the beginning of 1983, and the "Homefront Series" was never aired through VOA.

Mormons and Space Satellites

One of Mormonism's greatest strengths is its willingness to adopt means and strategies to fit changing circumstances. The Church's recent but impressive investment in the latest space communications technology is a case in point. In 1981 it ordered 500 satellite receiver dish antennas to establish the world's largest television network using a satellite. As one official of Bonneville Satellite (a subsidiary of Bonneville International) pointed out, there are larger radio, audio, and data networks using satellites for relaying transmissions, but none used for television is more extensive.[56] This recent purchase brings the total number of receiver dishes in the United States owned by the LDS Church to almost 700. And this project is just the beginning. Bonneville International has already appropriated more than $75 million to purchase new equipment by 1990. New dishes are planned for Canada and Mexico. Bruce Hough, Bonneville Satellite vice-president, told us in 1982 that the Church was conducting talks with the Canadian Radio and Television Commission and the U.S. Federal Communications Commission to waive the law that prohibits Canadians from taking transmission from a U.S. satellite. With such a waiver Bonneville Satellite then intends to place hundreds of such dishes in all stakes of both countries. Since that interview, the LDS Church has become the largest private satellite video network owner in the world, with the added capability of tying into any cable system in North America.[57]

Not only are the Church's General Authorities planning future receiver dishes for South America (broadcasting has already begun to Mexico), Europe, Asia, and even the Philippines, but eventually

Mormons will undoubtedly send up their own commercial satellite. The prospect has already been discussed at high-level meetings. The primary obstacle is cost — roughly $70 to $100 million per satellite, still a formidable amount to raise even for a prosperous religious bureaucracy at the start-up phase of media development. But a Mormon satellite is not far off.[58]

What is this elaborate, expensive satellite/receiver system to be used for? Its purposes dovetail with the Church's post-millennial mission to create a literal kingdom of God on earth before Jesus Christ's expected return. For some Church leaders the use of satellites and space-age hardware is perceived as a more efficient means to make the "Restored Gospel" message available to believers and nonbelievers alike. The ebullient words of one spokesperson reflected this missionary enthusiasm: "The manner in which the good word is going abroad is striking indeed. Ancient prophets said that it would be shouted from the house tops. Now, today, it goes far beyond that. It resounds from the tops of the mountains, yes, and even from space."[59]

For other Mormon leaders the earth station network will better connect the 5 million Mormons worldwide with the Salt Lake City headquarters and give them a stronger sense of participation in the national as well as local Church. Peter Pratt of the Information Systems Division of the LDS Church (which leases satellite time from Bonneville Satellite) noted: "The future is open for making transmissions two-way, and in fact, for devising an entire telecommunications network involving satellites, computers, and the Church's broadcasting stations."[60]

A dramatic example of this capability occurred in April 1980 when the Church used its technology to create a special telecast celebrating its sesquicentennial. An address by Church President Spencer W. Kimball was carried live from the restored log cabin of Peter Whitmer, an early Mormon, in Fayette, New York, where Joseph Smith formally organized the LDS organization in 1830, to Mormons throughout the United States. The broadcasting of this address, as well as the sessions of the Church's semiannual general conference, was made possible by use of the Westar I satellite orbiting the earth and a special portable earth station transmitter (concave dish) provided by Bonneville Satellite. The transmission was sent to selected receivers across the country.[61] Many Mormons have a strong nostalgic sense of history, and the broadcast from this symbolic place, in addition to the novelty of being able to see the important annual general conference, made this effort a major event for them. The broadcast also gave Mormons some sense of return on their investment dollars at the grass roots level, since individual stakes had to pay between $3,000 and $4,000 of the $10,000 average cost to install each receiver dish.[62]

The satellite system is also intended to create innovations in such fields as youth training and missionary work. By fall 1982 the *Church News* could report that Mormon "firesides," a traditional discussion/indoctrination format directed at teenagers, were being successfully integrated into the high-tech media with films and live presentations.[63]

In the area of missions the satellite system may well revolutionize the traditional door-to-door witnessing rite of passage undergone by many young Mormon men. A representative of the Information Systems Division of the LDS Church explained that plans were under way to begin using the satellite network in missionary work. He predicted that U.S. and Canadian missionaries, including those in the "home church ministry," would be able to provide a more sophisticated introduction to Mormonism for their "investigators" (that is, prospective converts).[64]

Finally, the growing use of satellite technology fits with the Mormon apocalyptic expectation we described in the previous chapter: that the day is not far off when the United States will be in chaos, ripped apart by civil war or a similar catastrophe, and the Mormons will then be in a unique position to save the nation. To outsiders this belief may smack of egotism or doomsday paranoia; to many members it is a prophetic certainty. As LDS members see it, the satellite communication system being constructed by the Church is part of the Church's preparedness for this anticipated time of catastrophes. Indeed, many of the same Church officials who decide the satellite budget also preach the doomsday message. An informant in the Church's Information Systems Division concurred with the use of such high-speed communications for a possible Church-wide mobilization, declaring that "the General Authorities expect the time to come when they will be able to notify as many as 3 million Church members throughout the U.S., Canada, and Mexico *in less than an hour!*"[65]

MORMONS AND THE MOVIES

The motion picture industry has had an enormous impact, both cultural and financial, on American society. Not surprisingly, the course of its growth at times has become intertwined with the fortunes of the LDS Church. The relationship has ranged from hostile to cordial. Originally Mormons were the subjects, not the writers, of Hollywood screenplays. In the early days movies, like the culture, were far less sympathetic to this sectarian religion than they later became. This shift of sentiment tells us something about how the Gentile public sees (or would like to see) the LDS Church and similarly how the Church would like to be seen.

The earliest movies dealing with Mormons as a people and with their Church carried into celluloid the stereotypes of nine-teenth-century anti-Church tracts. Richard Alan Nelson, a scholar of mass communications, has written:

> Early Hollywood movies focused mainly on Mormon pioneer life with attacks upon the supposed evils of polygamy. Although most early moviemakers could not be called dedicated anti-Mormons, their unfamiliarity with LDS doctrine and history, as well as a lack of contemporary information about Utah led them to sensationalized screen interpretations.[66]

Most of these baldly anti-Mormon pictures were made during the silent film era — movies such as the 1911 Danish *A Victim of the Mormons* (which used the standard white-slave themes of inno-cent young girls seduced into polygamous slavery by licentious mis-sionaries). The year 1912 saw *The Mormon* and a sensationalized version of the *Mountain Meadows Massacre* (with Brigham Young and Joseph Smith, no less, supposedly hatching the details of the ambush). Other films of the genre included *The Danites* (in which Mormons rode about in white sheets like Ku Klux Klansmen); *Marriage or Death*; the British *Trapped by the Mormons*; *Married to a Mormon*; and *Deadwood Dick Spoils Brigham Young*. The famous producer Cecil B. DeMille even tried his hand with the forgettable *A Mormon Maid* in 1917.

The Mormons fought back with more sympathetic self-portrayals. In addition to travelogues, they produced their own his-torical epic, *One Hundred Years of Mormonism*, in 1913. The film received little exposure, but it showed early Mormon awareness of the cinema's potential impact and illustrated the Church's determination to use available technology to establish a better public image. A truce of sorts was achieved between Hollywood and Salt Lake City in 1921 when U.S. Senator Reed Smoot (also an apostle in the Church) negotiated with producer William Fox to stop the release of two anti-Mormon movies based on popular Zane Grey novels, *Riders of the Purple Sage* and *The Rainbow Trail*. Fox wanted to squash a congressional bill that would levy a 30 percent film industry tax on movies and hurt production profits. Smoot agreed to help if the movies were withdrawn from national and international distribution and all references to Mormonism were deleted from the remakes. Fox accordingly had the films removed from movie houses, and from that date anti-Mormonism quickly faded from Hollywood. Richard Alan Nelson notes that

allegations of a Mormon "conspiracy" to spirit away unsuspecting women waned. The long cherished image of an evil theocratic kingdom in Utah faded along with other frontier trappings. Now moviemakers, too, realized that their conception of the state and its people was no longer big box office.[67]

Hollywood in the 1940s became more interested in the heroic, rather than the lurid, possibilities of Mormonism. Whenever possible the Church was most anxious to cooperate in promoting the former. When Mormon writer Vardis Fisher won the 1939–40 Harper Book Prize for his novel *Children of God* and one year later producer Darryl F. Zanuck and Twentieth Century–Fox were filming it as the epic *Brigham Young*, Church leaders, at first hesitant, decided to cooperate with the producers, opening their library to its writers and consulting on its scripts. In the end the collaboration proved enormously worthwhile. *Brigham Young*, starring Dean Jagger (as Young), Tyrone Power (as a Mormon scout), Linda Darnell (as Power's Gentile wife), Mary Astor (as one of Brigham's wives), and Vincent Price (as Joseph Smith) was a colossal success and definitely a public relations coup for the Church. Its portrayal of the Mormons as decent, oppressed pilgrims fleeing bigotry and taming an inhospitable desert in the name of God struck a sympathetic chord in Gentile American consciousness.

Brigham Young helped to reverse the hitherto negative Mormon image advanced by commercial motion pictures, although many Mormons took exception to their prophet-hero Brigham Young being depicted as an often weak and indecisive figure in the film. Reviews of the film all across the country were laudatory and compared *Brigham Young's* social statement about persecution to that made in *Grapes of Wrath*.[68]

A succession of premieres featuring personal appearances by the movie's stars, lavish receptions hosted by the Church, a magnificent parade through downtown Salt Lake City — all this portended a new Hollywood image for the Church, no longer sinister but romantic and noble. With *Brigham Young* the Church almost overnight became identified with the American frontier ethos, a mark of mainline respectability invaluable to a religious organization seeking to shed its sectarian reputation. Indeed, Oscar-winning actor Dean Jagger converted to Mormonism thirty years later and became an active Church spokesperson.

Hollywood has never returned to its early hostile view of Mormonism. At worst it has treated Mormons comically but gently, as in the musical *Paint Your Wagon* (1969), in which Jean Seberg uses the Mormon example of polygamy to justify taking two husbands at once; the George Segal–Goldie Hawn western farce *The Duchess and the Dirtwater Fox* (1976); or the Italian shoot-'em-up *They Call Me Trinity* (1972), in which Mormons act like straitlaced, pacifist Quakers. Mormon portrayals on television also generally made them out to be honest and unwavering individuals, a far cry from the villains of early days.

The LDS Church has come to realize the potential of films not just for profit but, more important, for public relations. *Brigham Young* showed that the old Gentile prejudices had largely abated. Indeed, there was a positive Mormon image to be exploited and a country of non-Mormons willing to applaud it. If Gentiles could exploit the image successfully, so went the logic, why couldn't the Mormons? Thus, a number of attempts were made to produce movies glorifying Mormon themes, either as stories taken from the *Book of Mormon* (though not always identified as such) or as epic biographies of Church leaders such as Joseph Smith and Brigham Young. However, these generally washed out before completion.[69]

The founder and former director of the Brigham Young University film studios (now Media Marketing) recalled that the Church once even gave serious thought to filming the story of the *Book of Mormon* before abandoning the project as too vast for a single script.[70]

In the mid-1970s Philip Yordan, a Hollywood screenwriter-producer whose successes included *King of Kings, El Cid*, and *55 Days at Peking*, developed the last major attempt at creating a film extravaganza about Mormonism. Entitled *Brigham*, the movie was panned as "a disappointment" by the *Salt Lake Tribune* and quickly faded into oblivion.

More commercially successful have been the Church's less publicized (and less controversial) films distributed by Media Marketing at Brigham Young University. Its founder, Wetzel O. Whitaker, worked with Walt Disney Studios before arriving at Provo, Utah. Since 1960 Media Marketing has sold well over 25,000 educational films with titles such as "Run Dick, Run Jane" (on jogging) and "Coronary Counter Attack," both twenty-minute health shorts, "Cipher in the Snow," and "The Mailbox." Who buys them? One Media Marketing representative reported that Media Marketing's biggest customers were other Christian groups, such as Seventh-day Adventists and various Baptist sects as well as Roman Catholics, Lutherans, and Methodists. He saw a definite missionary role for such films: "It gives you a nice feeling of pride to know that the Church is able to influence other religions this way without being too obvious about it. That's the best missionary trick of all, they tell me — preach without being noticed."[71]

The Church does well in films when its messages, but not its name, are represented. Bonneville Productions, a subsidiary of Bonneville International, produces not only the numerous thirty-second and sixty-second "Homefront" spots for television and radio but also a number of high-quality holiday/family made-for-television films. In recent years commercial television networks have broadcast such Mormon productions as "A Christmas Child" (1974); "The Family. . .and Other Living Things" (1976) starring popular actors and actresses Bill Bixby, Gary Burghoff, Ruth Buzzi, the Lennon Sisters, and the Osmond Family; and "Mr. Kruger's Christmas" (1980) starring veteran actor James Stewart.

Another example is the spectacular ABC-TV space-epic series "Battlestar Galactica." Produced and developed independent of the

Church by Mormon Glen Larson (who also produced the "Buck Rogers" television series and movie), this series dwelt heavily on Mormon themes. The *Daily Universe*, the campus newspaper of Brigham Young University, reported:

> Larson's LDS heritage is obvious in his work. Many Mormon concepts crop up in the show: the leaders of the 12 tribes are known as the Council of the Twelve [analogous to the Church's Council of the Twelve Apostles] and people aboard the Galactica marry for time and eternity [a unique Mormon concept]. The Galactica crew are searching for peace and sanctuary on the planet "Kobol" [similar to Kolob in Mormon theology]. And in a recent two-part episode Starbuck and Apollo meet a higher life form which most people would call "angels." One of these "angels," responding to Starbuck's question as to where they come from, paraphrases [former Mormon President] Lorenzo Snow's famed couplet by saying, "As you now are, we once were; and as we are now, you may become." The "angel" further explains the principle of free-agency and tells wayward Starbuck that straight-arrow Apollo has the mission of fellowshipping him and helping find truth.[72]

Indeed, Mormon themes were so prevalent in the "Battlestar Galactica" series that the Salt Lake City edition of *TV Guide* (though not in other areas of the country) advertised:

> With sealing marriages for all time and a Quorum of Twelve, this space epic is filled with Mormon theological overtures.[73]

The television station carrying a documentary news magazine that emphasized these parallels was Mormon-owned KSL-TV.

THE MORMON PUBLIC RELATIONS QUEST

Two scholars reviewing how the Church has been perceived by outsiders during the last decade comment:

> Perhaps more than the members of any other religious sect, Mormons are preoccupied with their public image. It may be argued that such preoccupation is a form of narcissism unworthy of the Restored Gospel, but given the unfavorable stereotypes of Mormonism that have persisted throughout its history, it is under-

standable that faithful Latter-day Saints should eagerly welcome sympathetic treatment of the Church and its programs.[74]

One reporter who visited the Church's Public Communications Department, with its fifty-some workers, found a well-organized, "slick" public relations operation and noted: "It seemed that every time I asked a question they handed me six new brochures and rushed me down the hall to see another movie."[75]

The modern LDS Church has grown comfortable with its hard-won respectability and has witnessed a general decline in rabid prejudice except from some diehard Baptists and other, fundamentalist Christians. Mormonism nourishes a warm yet efficient corporate reputation that, by de-emphasizing the Church's radical post-millennialism, makes it more acceptable to mainstream Christian Americans. Meanwhile it invests a good deal of time and money in selling this image.

One major organ to accomplish this is the Church's Public Communications Department, established in 1972 to promote positive Mormon visibility throughout the Gentile world. President Harold B. Lee directed this office not merely to correct misimpressions and to stave off attacks but also to assume "the initiative in dealing with the public and particularly with the news media."[76] By the end of the decade it was fulfilling its purpose and had its hands in many projects, employing over a thousand people internationally, all dedicated to impressing the public with the positive qualities of Mormonism. Seven overseas public communications offices strengthen the Church's image in countries as diverse as Switzerland, Portugal, the Scandinavian group, Brazil, Argentina, Japan, Tahiti, and Fiji. The Public Communications Department uses sophisticated social science research and marketing techniques, including polling by mail and telephone, computer analysis, and advertising evaluation. The results can sometimes be myth-shattering. For example, Lorry Rytting, head of communications analysis for the Church, found that most of the people who visit Mormon visitor centers in the United States are Mormons and *not* the hoped-for prospective converts, the Gentiles. Other surveys revealed that the Mormon Tabernacle Choir, long believed by the Church to be an important image-promoting force before the public, actually had low audience ratings. Rytting admitted: "We found throughout the country that the choir has a very low listenership. Most of the listeners are female and over 45 years old."[77]

An example of state-of-the-art Mormon media outreach could be seen in 1978 when the Mormons placed a series of eight-page removable pamphlets in that bastion of middle-class values, the *Reader's Digest*. Each pamphlet dealt with spiritual and family problems, carrying titles like "Can You Have a Happier Life?" and "Can You Feel More Secure in Life?" Jerry Cahill, assistant director of the LDS Public Communications Department (which prepared the pamphlets jointly with the Church's Missionary Department), admitted copying their format from the Shell Oil automobile servicing booklets that *Reader's Digest* had carried earlier.[78] The Mormon pamphlets appeared in U.S. and German editions of *Reader's Digest*, which by 1978 had a combined circulation of almost 20 million copies and more than 50 million readers. Altogether this promotion cost the Church about $12 million. But the returns delighted the Church. Cahill claimed that 10,000 persons had written in response to the December 1978 pamphlet alone. (That pamphlet dealt in part with the "family solidarity" of the popular Osmond family, staunch Mormons all.)[79]

In 1982 the Church even printed its own edition of the King James Bible, featuring footnotes referring readers to relevant cross-references in the *Book of Mormon* and other LDS scriptures. Does this mean that travelers sojourning in Marriott Inns will soon find the Church-approved Bible alongside the familiar blue-and-gold paperback edition of the *Book of Mormon*? Possibly, for the Church has great confidence in its low-key, persistent public relations strategy. (The newest editions of the *Book of Mormon*, incidentally, now carry the subtitle "Another Testament of Jesus Christ.")

The Church media people know how to capitalize on events that help the Church's image. It was more than happy to help lionize Dr. Barney Clark, the retired Mormon dentist who became the world's first permanent artificial heart recipient and lived for 112 days after the operation. (Dr. William C. DeVries, the surgeon who placed the heart in Barney Clark, is also a Mormon.) More than one hundred members of Congress sponsored a resolution calling for the presidential Medal of Freedom (the highest civilian award the government can present) to be awarded posthumously to Clark. At his Seattle, Washington, funeral Clark was eulogized by Church elders as well as federal officials such as William D. Ruckelshaus, director of the Environmental Protection Agency and President Reagan's official representative at the funeral. (Clark's Jack-Mormon habits of smoking and drinking were glossed over during the ceremonies.)

In other areas the Church has had to work more behind the scenes. Obtaining media attention in various parts of Europe, where Mormons have often been regarded as cultic, was arduous work until some well-connected Mormon public officials smoothed the way, as Norman R. Bowen, director of the Church's International Public Communications Department, noted in an interview. An important factor in helping the Church receive better media coverage was the appointment of active Church members to top-level government positions. Three of the four former U.S. ambassadors to Scandinavia, for example, were Mormons — ambassadors Mark Austad of Norway, Keith F. Nyborg of Finland, and Franklin S. Forsbergy of Sweden — and each of them originally served a Church mission to his assigned country. Bowen noted:

> Before their appointments, we were lucky if we got a few inches a year in the newspapers in each of these countries. But now we're getting half-pages and occasionally entire pages of coverage. That's what we like to see. If you build the image of the Church, baptisms will increase, too. As a result of the coverage these brethren have been getting, there has been a definite upsurge in conversions throughout these three countries.[80]

The Church media people can also wield considerable clout to discourage criticism of LDS operations. A 1976 published interview with Wendell J. Ashton, managing director of the Church's Public Communications Department, quoted him as claiming:

> A news article about the Church which is fair and generally positive, which may criticize us in one or two places, is more helpful to us than something that's all sweetness and light. Such a news article is actually more believable and those of us with experience in marketing know the importance of believability.[81]

While Ashton was correct that admitting to "minor sins" makes any religious group appear more credible, the truth is that the Church is thin-skinned about what it considers negative publicity, no matter how constructive it might be. As we have shown, unflattering news pertaining to the Church or its decisions rarely reaches the pages of the *Deseret News*. This attitude is reflected elsewhere. When *Ms. Magazine* ran a feature story on Sonia Johnson, the Mormon feminist who refused to recant her outspoken support of the Equal Rights Amendment (and who was summarily excommunicated), copies of that issue were difficult to obtain anywhere in Utah.[82]

One well-publicized example of Mormon displeasure with outsiders' media treatment of the Church and of the retribution the Church can exact is the *60 Minutes* incident. Respected for its probing investigative journalism, *60 Minutes* is the most popular news magazine program in television history. In 1979, *60 Minutes* took on an assignment about the Mormon Church's dealing with one member's farm. The subsequent report generated a small furor. Under pressure from the Church, reporter Harry Reasoner later rescinded his version of the broadcast report, a producer was fired, and the Church essentially emerged vindicated. The details are complex, but the story basically unfolded as follows:

Utah Mormon cherry processor and orchard owner Garn L. Baum ran into financial problems in 1971 and 1972. A severe frost one year coupled with other problems had brought him to the point of foreclosure on his farm. A group of growers, including the LDS Church (through its Elberta Farms, Inc.) and a partnership owned by the Utah Department of Agriculture official whose office granted licenses to growers, approached Baum with an offer to buy his operation. They also offered to let him stay on and run it for a percentage of the profits. They could not offer enough, however, and negotiations broke down. Baum meanwhile managed to raise the capital to stay in business through 1974.

But Baum's situation worsened. He claimed a growers' boycott was organized by those who wanted to take over his farm, and his business dropped drastically. A small group of growers, including the Church's representatives, sued Baum for back payment allegedly due on deliveries of cherries. Baum had increasing problems with the state's Department of Agriculture, particularly with the office of the man who had tried earlier to buy Baum's farm. Finally, in an attempt to salvage what he could before he sank hopelessly into debt, Baum and his family approached John H. Vandenberg, a Church assistant to the Council of Twelve and also president of

Elberta Farms, Inc. and of Deseret Title Holding Corporation. Baum's entire operation had been appraised in 1973 (before recent improvements) at $1.7 million. He offered it for sale to the Church at the bargain price of $800,000 (with his home, valued at $50,000, excluded). The Church offered $500,000. Baum refused, and the Provo, Utah, bank foreclosed on his mortgage. In 1975, the property went up for public auction, and the LDS Church-owned Deseret Title Holding Corporation bought Baum's property. Baum in turn initiated an antitrust suit against the LDS Church, claiming its officers, in conspiracy with the official in the Utah Department of Agriculture, had engaged in "predatory anti-competitive conduct" that drove him out of business.[83]

It was a complex tale but with enough suggested conflicts of interest to attract the *60 Minutes* reporters. Veteran Harry Reasoner did the broadcast with an obvious sympathy for Baum's side of the controversy. The little-guy-up-against-the-greedy-corporation theme fit well with *60 Minutes'* consumer-advocacy reputation. Reasoner portrayed Baum as a Mormon loner up against a Church-dominated political machine and stated that many people in Utah with direct knowledge of the case chose not to be interviewed or quoted about the matter.

The Church fought back, criticizing what it saw as flaws in the report. The Church pointed out that Baum's antitrust suit was thrown out of a U.S. district court because of inadequate evidence; that *60 Minutes* pictured the eventual death of Baum's cherry orchard from lack of water as the Church's deliberate cruelty rather than Baum's decision; and that two guards sent from Brigham Young University to water the orchard told CBS News that they had been physically threatened by Baum if they did not leave his property.

In general the Church accused the CBS report of being one-sided and of ignoring much pertinent information that could have given the broadcast more balance. Accuracy in Media, Inc., a research organization that publishes the *AIM Report,* edited by Reed Irvine, a Mormon, took *60 Minutes* to task for sloppy journalism. The Church repeatedly attacked the CBS program in the *Church News* and initiated a letter-writing campaign. AIM's Reed Irvine observed that it wasn't enough simply to call the complaints to the network's attention through letters:

You have to expose them publicly, embarrass them enough so that they will do something about their mistake. I know that Bonneville International was leaning on them pretty hard to begin with, since they maintain close relations with CBS anyway. Then when we entered the picture, that added more fuel to the fire.[84]

Harry Reasoner appeared not long after the Baum episode on *60 Minutes* and apologized for inaccuracies. In a *TV Guide* interview he was asked, "Can you think of an example of a bad *60 Minutes* piece?" He replied:

I did a story . . . [about] alleged persecution of a farmer by the Mormon Church in Utah . . . For various reasons, for which I am willing to share the guilt, it wasn't there . . . Whether the basic idea was true or not, it was not a solid piece.[85]

It is not often that a prominent investigative journalist offers such mea culpas for a story.

The producer of the *60 Minutes* piece, Richard Clark, was fired, probably as a result of the incident. Clark had done much of the background research in preparation for the story and saw more investigative data than Reasoner's apologies implied. The Church's position that it had been unfairly treated seems questionable at best. Clark told us, for example, that *60 Minutes* had made specific requests for interviews with many Church officials named in court papers, only to be referred to the Church's Public Relations Director. He, in effect, answered all charges and questions with the uniform statement that the Church, or its officials, would never do such things. Such details as the Mormon guards' claim that Garn Baum had threatened them physically were, according to Clark, dubious. Clark had interviewed each guard personally, and they had denied ever being threatened by Baum.[86] According to the Church's later version of events, the guards were not threatened.

The full truth of the charges and counteraccusations in the Garn Baum case will never be fully sorted out. The case demonstrates, however, the Church's determination that it, rather than others, should define its identity for millions of other Americans. Producer Richard Clark had every reason to be bitter in an interview about the Baum incident:

I think you can put me down on record as saying that the Mormon Church can get extremely ugly and nasty if they want to, when something is done to make them look bad or give them a negative image. And it doesn't matter how well researched or how much truth the piece may contain.[87]

The Church's concern for positive public opinion has taken numerous forms. The best example, perhaps, deals with its 1978 decision to admit blacks to the priesthood. For almost a century and a half people with any known trace of Negro blood had been denied access to the Temple, to the priesthood, and thus to full Mormon membership. During the 1960s and the civil rights movement, this prohibition became a thorn in the side of the Church. Two sociologists note that because of the Church's policy on nonwhites,

the late sixties found the Brigham Young University the focal point of militant protests. Sports events provided the context for protests, boycotts, disrupted games, mass demonstrations, and "riots." At one point the conflict among schools within the Western Athletic Conference became so intense that the conference almost disbanded. Administrators, already embroiled in student demonstrations over Vietnam, began to separate themselves from the Mormon school. Stanford University, for instance, severed all relations with Brigham Young University.[88]

There has been a good deal of debate over the reasons that Church President Spencer W. Kimball announced in 1978 the most significant "revelation" made to modern Mormonism. Some observers cynically cite it as a political decision made in response to a cluster of outside pressures on the Church: bad publicity from the media and civil rights organizations, hostility from the liberal white community, and the ongoing Mormon pursuit of respectability. In particular the tremendous potential for Third World Mormon growth could not be realized if the race prohibition stood. This was a point driven home to Church leaders in 1975 after they announced the construction of a new temple in São Paulo, Brazil, the first to be built in South America. The cynical view holds that the "revelation" to admit blacks to the priesthood was conveniently timed: long enough after the "cooling down" of the civil rights movement so that it was not condemned as opportunistic but just ahead of the crest of significant Third World conversions that the Church and other groups, such as the Jehovah's Witnesses, were making.

Defenders of the Church argue that there was little external pressure on President Kimball for such a "revelation." The activist phase of the civil rights movement, for example, had largely subsided by the late 1970s. The defenders' view holds that the "revelation" cannot be explained away by circumstantial evidence or the conjecture of adverse public opinion. No specific "smoking guns" can be produced to link outside influences to the Prophet Kimball's announcement; hence it is assumed to have come literally through revelation from God Almighty.[89]

In fact, evidence exists that the Church made its much-publicized decision to admit blacks to the Mormon priesthood after a deliberate, rational consideration of public opinion, future Church membership growth, and similar factors. In 1971 the First Presidency acquired the services of one of America's largest general management and consulting firms, Crescent, McCormick & Paget (CMP) in New York City. This firm had built a solid reputation in managing such corporate strategies as mergers and acquisitions for well-known clients like Ford and General Motors. On the advice of Mormon corporate advisers, such as J. Willard Marriott and David Kennedy, LDS President Harold B. Lee requested that CMP study how the Church's communications organization could commit resources more efficiently to improve internal communications as well as public relations. No mention was made in the CMP report of the Church's racial policy, but Church leaders seemed interested in applying modern management perspectives to their own goals and problems.

In 1974 and 1975 the First Presidency under new President Spencer W. Kimball authorized three more studies by CMP. One study produced a report for the Church's Health Services Corporation on how to streamline its operations and make the organization more cost-efficient and resulted in the Church's divesting itself entirely of its unprofitable hospital system. Two other studies were done for the LDS Social Services Department and Welfare Department and for the Presiding Bishopric's Office.

In 1975 one final CMP study was carried out for the LDS Church. This effort produced the consulting firm's longest report, dealing with the role and organization of the Presiding Bishopric itself, Church policy positions and administrative procedures, and other internal matters. Most important, among the recommendations made by the consulting firm were "a careful review" of certain potentially embarrassing "doctrinal policies" such as the Negro issue and "a serious reconsideration" of such policies in light of past public relations problems that they had caused. The report strongly urged that Church leaders reassess the race issue and its "relevancy" for the future. The problem posed by building a new temple in São Paulo, with a population largely of mixed blood, was specifically mentioned in this report. Two additional consultants hired for the same purpose voiced similar concerns about the wisdom of continuing a restriction of the Mormon priesthood to whites.[90]

Many organizational changes touching the average LDS member were made as a result of these reports, but from the standpoint of public relations, none was as important as the change resulting from the consultants' unanimous recommendations about LDS racial policy. Three years later, on June 9, 1978, Church authorities announced the "revelation" rescinding the traditional ban on a black priesthood. The "revelation" had been preceded by a great deal of prayer, meditation, and meetings among President Kimball and the members of the Council of the Twelve. Whether one wants to credit its inspiration to any divine agency is ultimately unimportant. (Church leaders themselves admitted that the racial issue had been on their minds for a long time.) What is important is that not long before the Church president and prophet's decision (conscious or subconscious) to announce a new racial policy based on divine "revelation," several professional consulting firms in which the Church had previously demonstrated confidence suggested to Church leaders that they reconsider the status of blacks in the Mormon Church as part of a major overhaul of Church policy. The fact that such firms were retained in the first place is in no way inconsistent with the Church's past concern either for its public image or for its long-range theological goals. No other religious group in American society has conducted such a sustained campaign to gain public respectability, nor has such respectability been so integral a part of any other group's sense of its own destiny.

The change of heart over admitting blacks to the Mormon priesthood had precisely the public relations effect that the consultants expected. In the eastern United States both *Time* and

Newsweek magazines actually stopped their presses to include the story of the LDS president's "revelation" in their weekend editions. President Jimmy Carter commended President Kimball for his "compassionate and courageous" decision.[91] Most Americans now saw one less peculiar characteristic in the Latter-day Saints.

MORMON WEALTH IN COMMUNICATIONS

What are Mormon investments in the communications industry worth as of the mid-1980s? The fact is that even the Church probably does not know the precise value of its own holdings because of fluctuating markets, inflation, and similar factors. Moreover, the Church is extremely reticent about offering even rough estimates. Our own figures on the LDS communications empire are based on comparative values (that is, comparisons of Mormon-owned properties and similar media organizations), the estimates by authorities both within and outside the Church, and what little public information we could find on the subject. Compiling these figures required several years of interviews with media brokers and television and radio station owners, extensive searches in publications of the media industry, and reasonable assessments of Mormon media ownership. In every case we have used conservative figures. Given the rate at which LDS media investments are appreciating, we are undoubtedly providing many underestimates.

Limitations of space do not permit us to give a complete account of all sources and of how we constructed each estimate. We present here only the sum figures and offer interested readers the opportunity to inspect our more detailed notes that led to these estimates.[92]

ESTIMATED VALUE OF ALL COMMUNICATIONS HOLDINGS OF THE CHURCH OF JESUS CHRIST OF LATTER-DAY SAINTS, 1983

Bonneville International Corporation Broadcast Properties

Television Stations KSL-TV (Salt Lake City)	$ 71,000,000
KIRO-TV (Seattle)	107,200,000
Total	$178,200,000

Radio Stations	KSL-AM (Salt Lake City)	$ 23,000,000
	KBIG-FM (Los Angeles)	23,500,000
	KOIT-AM/FM (San Francisco)	12,250,000
	KIRO-AM/KSEA-FM (Seattle)	17,500,00
	KAAM-AM/KAFM-FM (Dallas)	16,250,000
	KMBR-FM/KMBZ-AM	
	(Kansas City, Mo.)	14,000,000
	WCLR-FM (Chicago)	9,400,000
	WRFM-FM (New York City)	19,000,000
	Total	$134,900,000

Total of All Bonneville International Radio and Television Stations $313,100,000

Other Bonneville International Holdings	
Washington, D.C., News Bureau	$ 300,000
Bonneville Broadcast Consultants (Tenafly, N.J.)	2,000,000
Torbet Radio (sold in 1984) (New York City)	11,000,000
Bonneville Entertainment Corporation	
(North Hollywood, Calif.)	1,100,000
Bonneville Productions (Salt Lake City)	27,700,000
Programming Division	10,200,000
Audio Projection Division	6,500,000
Video West Division	11,000,000
Total	$ 42,100,000
Radio Data Systems (Mt. Laurel, N.J.)	$ 13,200,000
Bonneville Satellite Corporation (Salt Lake City)	17,810,000
Total of Other Bonneville International Holdings	$ 73,110,000

Total of All Bonneville International Corporation Broadcast Properties $386,210,000

Other LDS Church Broadcast Properties	
Satellite Division of the Information	
Systems Division of LDS Church	$ 6,180,000
University Television and Radio Stations	
(Provo, Utah, and Rexburg, Idaho)	4,650,000
Total of All LDS Church Broadcast Properties	$ 10,830,000

Total of All LDS Church and Subsidiary Broadcast Companies $397,040,000

Other LDS Church Media Interests

Deseret News (Salt Lake City)	$ 59,500,000
Times-Mirror Corporation Stock	54,000,000
Deseret Book Company (stores and facilities in Utah, Idaho, and California)	12,300,000
Deseret Press (Salt Lake City)	7,800,000
Brigham Young University Press (Provo, UT)	7,100,000
LDS Church Distribution Center (Salt Lake City)	4,500,000
Brigham Young University Film/Media Marketing	5,400,000
Total of All LDS Church Other Media Interests	**$150,600,000**
Total of All Other LDS Church Broadcast Properties and Media Interests	**$161,430,000**
Grand Total, All LDS Church Communications Properties	**$547,640,000**

These figures represent only the direct communications holdings of the LDS Church. Many other holdings are owned by Mormon families known for their devotion to the Church and longtime influence in Church affairs. For example, the Marriott family-owned First Media Corporation owns ten radio stations.

Another example is the Simmons family holdings. Roy W. Simmons is president of Zion's First National Bank (which the Church once totally owned and now retains a major share of) and is also on the board of directors of Beneficial Life Insurance Company, which is owned 100 percent by the Church. Simmons is also a close adviser to the Church on financial matters. The Simmons family presently owns two Salt Lake City radio stations (KSFI-FM and KWMS-AM) and in the early 1980s has been negotiating to buy more.

The list of persons who own communications businesses and who are active in the Mormon Church and sympathetic to its goals is longer. The extent to which the Church is actually influential in such people's management of their media holdings is a relative unknown, although most knowledgeable people to whom we talked agreed that the Church is pleased to see its members accumulate such properties.

In this section we have emphasized only the broadest outlines and most visible communications interests of the Church. The LDS Church currently is the largest religious media owner in the world, its properties *conservatively* valued at more than half a billion dollars. It is a widely diversified and profitable conglomerate. Moreover, its growth continues as we write.

MORMON COMMUNICATIONS AND THE KINGDOM OF GOD

Mormon zeal in acquiring communications technology furthers one important goal: to prepare the way for the millennium of Jesus Christ. As we have shown, to Mormons the electronic and printed media are not simply good investments. They are means, not ends. These media promote a wholesome, benevolent, decent image of Mormonism while simultaneously spreading in a low-key but effective way the Mormon perspective. These media have also been used to discredit or silence what the Church perceives as threats to its mission. Implicit in this widespread ownership are serious considerations about the free dissemination of news and the control of public opinion. It is one thing for Mormons to gain a monopoly over the media that serve their own people (though many would argue against the long-run benefit of that). But as the Church continues to accumulate properties that ostensibly serve the general non-Mormon public, much of which does not agree with Mormon millennial goals and beliefs, the pattern takes on a new significance. In our final chapter we discuss the implications of the emerging Mormon media monopoly for American democracy and religious pluralism.

3

LDS, Incorporated

There is no subject more sensitive to the Church of Jesus Christ of Latter-day Saints than its enormous wealth and business interests. President N. Eldon Tanner, the late first counselor to Mormon President and Prophet Spencer W. Kimball, once bluntly told two Associated Press journalists about Church finances, "I don't think the public needs to have that information."[1] When leaders do comment on the Mormon Church's holdings, they are evasive about the magnitude of its corporate involvement. Thus presidential counselor Gordon B. Hinckley was quoted in the *Wall Street Journal*, "The business involvement which we have is a very, very minor part of our activity." Likewise, he pushed aside any notions that a Mormon economic conglomerate exists by assuring a reporter, "We try to operate the *few*—and I emphasize that—the *few* business interests that we do have in a business-like prudent way, as any prudent business corporation would do, and use them for the public good."[2]

But, in fact, the LDS Church has considerably more than a few business interests. The Church's investments are enormous, constantly shifting to take advantage of profit margins in the stock market, and highly diversified. The Church runs a virtual business empire, with assets close to $8 billion by conservative estimates. These Church operations have been run basically for their economic returns and not necessarily for the public good (whether the "public" is defined as Mormon or non-Mormon).

In Chapter 2 we examined the LDS Church's impressive investments (and the theological rationale for them) in only one sector

— mass communications. In this chapter we present the larger picture of the Church as a key investor, entrepreneur, and rising force in the American economy. We examine its growing membership base, the character of its leadership, its attempts to plan financially for the expected millennium and attendant disasters, and its vast wealth. Looking at the myriad Mormon financial involvements in the state of California alone, one journalist recently reached a conclusion that could apply just as well to the entire LDS economic giant:

It might seem strange, almost slightly blasphemous, to refer to a church as a corporation, but the analogy here is simply inescapable. The Church is undeniably corporate.[3]

Indeed, there is nothing "otherworldly" about Mormonism in the ordinary sense of the term. As religion and as dynamic organization, it is dedicated to "this-worldly" change aimed at establishing a communally owned and operated business empire and a theocratically ruled, unified world society. For members of the Church of Jesus Christ of Latter-day Saints, the material aspects of human existence are raised to the same status as spiritual concerns, in contrast to Roman Catholic and mainline Protestant traditions. Mormon historian Leonard J. Arrington has written:

Among the Mormons, things temporal have always been important along with things eternal, for salvation in this world and the next is seen as one and the same continuing process of endless growth. Building Zion, a literal Kingdom of God on earth, has therefore meant an identity of religious and economic values: in the daily affairs of the Kingdom, Latter-day Saint scriptures call for *unity* ("Be ye one"), *welfare* ("Care for the poor"), and *economic independence* ("Let thy garments be the workmanship of thine own hands").[4]

Thus economic growth is an integral part of Mormon theology. Indeed, of some 112 revelations received by the prophet Joseph Smith, 88 dealt directly with economic matters. In the *Doctrine and Covenants*, 9,614 verses address temporal affairs; of those, 2,618 affirm that economics and religion are not "easily separated."[5] The roots of this outlook can be traced to Joseph Smith and Brigham Young, and they continue to exert influence at the highest levels of the LDS hierarchy. It is this aspect of the Church, perhaps more than any other, that has recently reemerged to generate controversy about Church activities just as it did more than 150 years ago in midwestern America.

During its earliest days the opponents of the LDS Church complained that its burgeoning wealth posed a threat to larger society. Mormon settlers, accepting Joseph Smith's pronouncements that Jackson County, Missouri, was to be the gathering place for Zion before the Second Coming, bought huge plots of land there and established communally operated, Mormon-patronized businesses. Their neighbors did not appreciate either their millennial hopes or their investments. Parley P. Pratt, an early apostle, recalled:

> That portion of the inhabitants of Jackson County which did not belong to the Church became jealous of our growing influence and numbers. Political demagogues were afraid we should rule the county; and religious priests and bigots felt that we were powerful rivals, and about to excel all other societies in the State in numbers, and in power and influence. . . [We were charged with being] guilty of immigrating rapidly from the different States, and of purchasing large quantities of land, and of being more enterprising and industrious than [our] neighbors.[6]

Gentile fears and thus persecution prevailed. The Mormons evacuated Jackson County and moved on to Clay County, Missouri. But there the pattern repeated itself: Mormon temporal and spiritual concerns united. Financial success followed, spreading fears among the Gentiles of theocratic conspiracy and empire building. In 1839 the Mormons were pushed out of Missouri. At Nauvoo, Illinois, they tried once more to found a viable economic and political base that would become Zion. However, Joseph Smith's murder in 1844 and the growing enmity of nearly all non-Mormon officials convinced them finally to strike out for inhospitable lands far enough away that their enemies would be unlikely ever to pursue them. But even in Utah their prosperity threatened outsiders. The unique Mormon blend of religion and economics proved too successful, some felt. As Leonard J. Arrington writes:

> Over a fifteen-year period [in the late 1800s], in what is known as the Cooperative Movement, the Mormons constructed over

200 miles of territorial railroad, a $300,000 woolen mill, a large cotton factory, a wholesale-retail concern with sales of $6,000,000 a year, more than 150 local general stores, and at least 500 local cooperative manufacturing and service enterprises. . . The most controversial aspect of this movement was the policy of expecting Latter-day Saints to give exclusive patronage to these church- and cooperatively-sponsored enterprises.[7]

The Edmunds-Tucker Act, passed by Congress in 1887, was designed to disincorporate, and thus break up, the growing Mormon business conglomerate in Utah. It did, for a time.

LDS, INC.

The modern LDS corporate conglomerate is complex, made up of many layers of subsidiaries (which in turn often control their own subsidiaries) with names that may or may not reveal their Mormon connection, as Figure 3–1 illustrates. Given the Church's unforthcoming policy on releasing financial figures, its total wealth and revenues are usually matters of informed estimates made by investigative reporters who must struggle with a diverse set of sources and no help from the Mormon Church. Frequently observers do not arrive at the same final figures. For example, journalists Bill Beecham and David Briscoe, who did a study of Church finances in the mid-1970s, estimated the Church's gross business income at $500 million per year, with another half billion dollars coming annually from members' tithing (that is, contributing 10 percent of before-tax income) and other gifts. In other words, they claimed the Church was making almost $3 million *per day*. (In another article the two reporters cited a former non-Mormon mayor of Salt Lake City who claimed to have seen in 1962 a confidential Church financial statement giving a figure of $1 million per day — not necessarily a contradiction, considering rapid Church growth in the intervening years.)[8] Another journalist at the *Kansas City Times* calculated at least $2 million each day flowing in from tithing alone.[9]

In addition to the Church's reluctance to disclose its financial worth there is the sheer size of the LDS corporate conglomerate to consider. The organization is so diversified that few people even

FIGURE 3.1

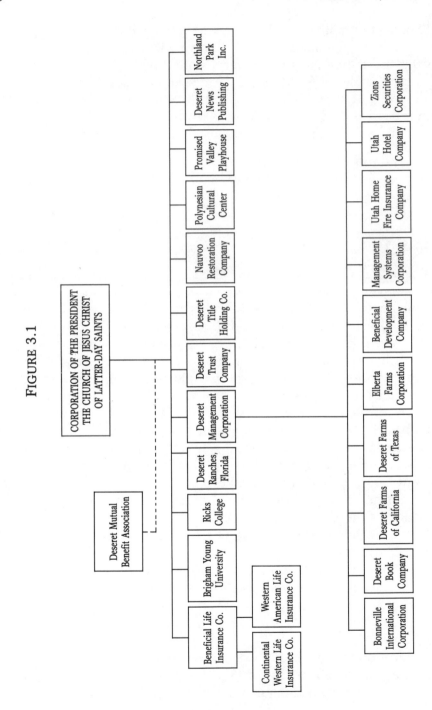

in the uppermost levels have the overview needed to assemble a precise tally of assets and cash flows. When one writer asked Wendell Ashton, executive vice-president and publisher of Salt Lake City's *Deseret News*, what people besides the late N. Eldon Tanner (financial adviser to the Church's first presidency office) had a comprehensive picture of its wealth, Ashton replied, "I guess you can name them on the fingers of one hand."[10]

In the spring of 1959 the Church reported expenses totaling $72.8 million. That was the last detailed financial statement the Church made public. Later in this chapter we provide the most comprehensive figures available on Mormon wealth. However, before considering specific investments in such disparate areas as shopping malls, apartment complexes, agribusinesses, and public utility stocks, it is worth looking at the most significant resource that the Church possesses: its membership base. A minimum of one-third of Mormons currently tithe regularly, while many others exceed even that generosity. Given that the LDS Church is currently the fastest-growing religious body in the United States, membership size is (and should continue to be at least for the near future) an important source of its income.

Mormon Membership

The LDS Church is growing so fast that membership figures are difficult to compute. As of spring 1985, Mormon membership worldwide had climbed to a record high of approximately 5.7 million people, of whom fewer than 3.2 million are in the United States. At that time the Church had 47 temples completed or in some phase of construction, 6,500 Church-owned buildings used as meeting-houses or chapels, 1,520 stakes, and approximately 28,000 full-time missionaries. By the year 2000, projections call for total membership to reach 12 to 14 million, with 84 completed temples, 16,000 chapels, and 2,600 stakes. Mormon membership on the average has doubled every 15 years since World War II, but from 1970 to 1985, it nearly tripled in size. In many places it has grown considerably faster. In the United States, for example, the Texas and Georgia membership doubles every ten years; Pennsylvania's membership doubles every nine years.[11]

But it is outside North America that Mormon membership growth is most impressive. In Latin America alone the Church laims more than 900,000 members, 3,200 local congregations, and 270 stakes.[12] According to Robert Swenson of the Church Missionary Department, there were over 7,200 missionaries with an average combined baptism rate of 8,400 converts per month throughout all Latin America as of May 1985. "It's our most productive area right now," he informed us. "And we expect to see that number of baptisms almost double in another five years or less."

In an extemporaneous address before the Mormon History Association in 1982, Donald R. Snow, professor of mathematics at Brigham Young University, spoke on "Models used in Projecting Mormon Growth."[13] Snow showed that after 1950 the Church experienced a sharp increase in growth (as did most American churches during the "baby boom"). Using both United Nations population figures and Church statistics, he projected estimates for LDS growth outside North America over the remainder of the twentieth century. His estimates are given in Table 3–1.

Table 3–1 Projected LDS Membership Growth for Various Countries

COUNTRY	RATE OF GROWTH	1980	2000
Brazil	Doubles every 4 yrs.	400,000	1.5 million
Chili	Doubles every 2½ yrs.	1 million	~12 million
Colombia	Doubles every 3 yrs.	200,000	2 million
Mexico	Doubles every 8 yrs.	500,000	1 million
Peru	Doubles every 4 yrs.	170,000	800,000
Uruguay	Doubles every 12 yrs.	50,000	85,000
Philippines	Doubles every 4 yrs.	300,000	1.6 million
Italy	Doubles every 4½ yrs.	50,000	270,000
Spain	Doubles every 2½ yrs.	150,000	3 million

This spectacular Third World and southern European growth in Mormon membership is in part the fruit of deliberate labors undertaken by the Church's highest officials as well as rank-and-file missionaries to witness tirelessly. In 1977, for example, LDS President Spencer W. Kimball, along with other officials from the First Presidency, toured Central and South America as well as the Philippines, meeting with Chilean, Bolivian, and Philippino presidents. The Mormon entourage visited cities such as San José (Costa

Rica), Guatemala City (Guatemala), Mexico City, La Paz (Bolivia), Lima (Peru), Santiago (Chile), and São Paulo (Brazil). At that time 250,000 Indian ("Lamanite") LDS members were officially claimed.

In part, the impressive growth record is also the result of the LDS Church's opening its priesthood to non-Caucasians in 1978. Acknowledging this factor, Elder Neal A. Maxwell of the Council of the Twelve predicted that by the Church's bicentennial in 2030 there could be as many as 90 million Mormons worldwide, with hundreds of thousands of full-time missionaries and tens of thousands of stakes.[14]

Yet aggressive expansion into Third World countries is likely to pose new dilemmas for the Church. Inroads made into the affluent North American population are one thing. But most converts in South and Central America are among the world's poorest citizens and could eventually become a drain on Church finances, particularly if they begin to rely on Mormon charities. They could easily draw on resources now being committed by the Church to lucrative investments. The Church would be hard-pressed not to aid them in their desperation. Nineteenth- and twentieth-century Mormon conversions overseas have thus far been profitable for the LDS organization. Since World War II much of the Church's missionary activity has been focused in nations with rapid economic growth: Korea, Japan, Taiwan, Hong Kong, Brazil, and South Africa. But the LDS Church could become entrapped by its own success. Once the impressive statistics on conversions in the remainder of this century have been counted, membership growth in poverty-ridden countries may be as much a curse as a blessing and may challenge the priorities of the Salt Lake hierarchy:

> Church growth among the "poorest of the poor" could demand major financial changes in the operations of the Church along with wholesale behavioral modifications of its members. If this trend continues, Church members will be called upon to make true sacrifices, to become truly Good Samaritans.[15]

Ultimately such growth, if defined as success, may alter the shape of the LDS Church, rechanneling its investments and expenditures and perhaps igniting conflict within the organization. Already American monies are being poured into building programs in many countries where the new members are too poor to contribute even for local chapels and temples. In some areas several stakes (each composed of at least several wards) have to share the same building. The projections cited may be high, but they point in the right direction. In the next several decades the Church will inevitably be faced with decisions about the extent of its commitment to membership growth as well as to financial stability, profitability, and charity toward all its members.

There is one more shadow on the otherwise bright picture of Mormon membership expansion. It is the Church's increasing practice of excommunicating members. Statistics on this unpleasant subject are kept by a Church office called Confidential Records. Of all the information that the Church guards from public scrutiny, the numbers of excommunicants and the reasons they were removed from membership rolls (which for Mormons effectively denies them the chance of salvation) are the most difficult to obtain. The estimates that follow are based on figures provided by informants in that office. Recent changes, enforcing stricter policies of silence, have since been implemented, making it even more unlikely that future researchers will find access to these data.

Total Church membership in 1981 was estimated at more than 4.5 million; by 1982 membership had grown to more than 5 million. About 19,000 members were excommunicated in 1981, and 21,000 in 1982. Measured against the 140,000 converts baptized in 1981 and the 200,000 in 1982, the number of excommunicants seems low, but the causes for excommunication are of interest. Almost half of those excommunicated had committed "adultery and fornication." Homosexuality and lesbianism accounted for only about 200 excommunications in 1981, but that number almost tripled in 1982. "Apostasies" — such as preaching false doctrine, criticizing Church leaders, and withdrawing from the Church — accounted for about 6,500 excommunications in 1981 and almost 7,000 in 1982. The remainder (about 2,500 in 1981 and 3,500 in 1982) are categorized as "other moral offenses," among them heavy petting, incest, cohabitation, and plural marriage.[16]

Excommunications have been on the rise in recent years for several reasons, significant among them the Church hierarchy's growing sensitivity to criticism by its own scholars and intellectuals as well as its intolerance of members' political activities that run counter to the hierarchy's conservative views. (Chapter 5 discusses

Church censorship at greater length.) Church officials have also begun asking more specific questions of its missionaries and family members before giving "temple recommends" (clearance to pass through esoteric temple rituals). These questions focus particularly on adultery (currently accounting for the single largest group of excommunicants) as well as sexual behavior even between husband and wife that does not conform to a narrow range of approved practices. Apostasies, or disloyalty and heresy, also are on the rise.

Excommunications will not threaten the Church's growth in the foreseeable future, although when widely publicized they cause embarrassment for Church leaders by making them look authoritarian and heavy handed (as did the 1979 Church trial of feminist Sonia Johnson, who refused to stop supporting the Equal Rights Amendment and criticizing anti-ERA Church policy). Most active Mormons sincerely love the Church and have no wish to hurt or defy it. Likewise, the large number of inactive Mormons (Jack-Mormons) are currently of little interest to the keepers of Church purity and orthodoxy. In a growth period the organization can afford simply to ignore them.

Yet if the defiance of explicit papal bans on artificial methods of birth control by the majority of Roman Catholics in this country is any indication of how tightly an ecclesiastical organization can or cannot regulate its members' lives, then there is good reason to suspect a fair amount of taboo activity among LDS Church members that might warrant their excommunication if discovered.

Meanwhile, conversions and natural reproduction increase membership at a rate far outstripping defections and excommunications. For example, while most Mormons in the United States do not reside in Utah, that state has seen an enormous population growth, no doubt on account of its largely Mormon population. While the national fertility rate (the number of live births per thousand females aged fifteen to forty-four) was 67.8 in 1981, in Utah it was 117.6. Likewise, the national mortality rate (the number of deaths per thousand people) was 8.7 in 1981, while Utah's mortality rate was 5.4. Whether through conversion or reproduction, the Utah population success story will be multiplied many more times elsewhere, making it very likely that the LDS Church will reach many of its anticipated growth projections.

MORMON LEADERSHIP

Mormon leadership is organized in a pyramidal structure, described in Chapter 1. As one prominent Christian clergyman described it almost a century ago, "No other organization is so perfect as the Mormon Church, except for the German army."[17]

In this section we consider mainly the top Church leadership — those men whose decisions govern the direction of Church investments, growth, and reform. We describe their personal backgrounds, their loyalties and abilities, and their frailties. They are, literally, the directors of "LDS, Inc."

Joseph Smith, Jr., the founder of the LDS Church and the prophet who claimed to receive direct revelations from God, set the pattern for later Mormon leadership. His immediate successor, Brigham Young, continued what became a dual role for all later Mormon Church heads: administrative manager as well as unique charismatic figure — a seer, as the Church officially refers to the function — with special access to God's providence for humanity. While the day-to-day affairs of running one of the fastest-growing religious movements in North America emphasize the former, corporate role, Church members nevertheless cherish the Church president in the latter one.

Such reverence is accorded to the office of Church president as much as or more than it is to the man. There is an undeniable mystique surrounding this living link to God, a mystique reinforced by the Mormon belief that the temporal Church of Jesus Christ of Latter-day Saints represents a mirror image of the spirit realm: that is, the Church of Jesus Christ of Heavenly Saints. For Mormons the Celestial Kingdom (or Heavenly Zion) parallels earthly Zion in both organization and functions. The Celestial Kingdom's Godhead of God the Father, Jesus Christ the Son, and the Holy Ghost are matched on earth by the Church's trinity of the First Presidency (Church president, first counselor, and second counselor). The Council of Heaven in the celestial realm (which broadly refers to the Mormon teaching that Christ and former ancient and more recent prophets meet often to discuss the affairs of this world and of others) has its temporal counterpart in the Council (or Quorum) of the Twelve (Apostles), who meet weekly in the temple at Salt Lake City to set policies on Church affairs. Just as there are various other, lower councils in the Celestial Kingdom, so the earthly LDS Church has its First Council (Quorum) of the Seventy, which oversees the actual administration of diverse Church operations. (The Council of the Seventy, the Council of the Twelve, and the First Presidency constitute the General Authorities of the Church.)

Likewise, below the Celestial Kingdom in the spirit realm are the Terrestrial Kingdom and the "Telestial" Kingdom. Christ and/or His emissaries frequent the Terrestrial Kingdom but not the Telestial Kingdom. On earth the Terrestrial Kingdom finds its analogy in the stakes of Zion (each composed of a stake president and two counselors plus a stake high council of twelve men), while the Telestial Kingdom is represented by the lowest level, the ward. Parallel to the heavenly restrictions, any of the General Authorities may visit the stakes but not the wards (other than their own). Only the stake leaders visit Church wards.

Thus the elements of a theologically justified chain of command and the effective insulation of higher leaders from official dealings with most rank-and-file members (except when the leadership desires it) are well entrenched after 180 years of bureaucratic growth.

There are several outstanding characteristics of the fifty-six men who make up the General Authorities. One significant trait is their combined experience in the corporate world and public affairs. As Table 3–2 shows, in the First Presidency and the Council of the Twelve in 1985 there was no one who has not had a career in business, politics, public relations, or some form of administration, with the exception of surgeon Russell M. Nelson. Among the General Authorities as a whole the largest number (twenty-six, almost half) had been corporate executives, bankers, economists, or financiers. The others had had careers as lawyers, educators, newspaper editors, engineers, professional athletes, career soldiers, or politicians. There is, in short, a vast reserve of administrative talent and financial wisdom at the highest levels of the modern LDS, Inc.

Another important characteristic of the current Church leaders is their genuine sense of duty to the Church. No one has ever seriously suggested that they govern "LDS, Inc.," for personal gain. In an age of exorbitant salaries lavished not only on movie, television, and sports personalities but also on top corporate executives,

the LDS leadership is an anomaly. For example, in the early 1980s
Church President Spencer W. Kimball received a total of approximately $75,000 a year from the Church, not all of which was a
straight salary for his presidential duties. Each of the two counselors in the First Presidency earned approximately $70,000, each
apostle in the Council of the Twelve anywhere from $50,000 to
$65,000 per year. Their specific salaries depended on both their
seniority and responsibilities. The members of the Council of the
Seventy, who often make daily decisions involving tens or hundreds
of millions of dollars, typically received salaries in the decidedly
unimpressive $30,000–$40,000 bracket.[18]

Table 3–2 Selected Profiles of Current LDS Church Leaders

NAME	POSITION	AGE (1985)	CAREER
Spencer W. Kimball	Church President	90	Banker, businessman
Marion G. Romney	Counselor, First Presidency	88	Lawyer, district attorney
Gordon B. Hinckley	Counselor, First Presidency	75	Public communications, public relations
Ezra Taft Benson	President, Quorum of the Twelve	86	Politician, agricultural administrator
Howard W. Hunter	Apostle	78	Corporate lawyer, businessman
Thomas S. Monson	Apostle	58	Newspaper businessman
Boyd K. Packer	Apostle	61	Educational administrator
Marvin J. Ashton	Apostle	70	Businessman
L. Tom Perry	Apostle	63	Businessman, financier
David B. Haight	Apostle	79	Businessman, politician
James E. Faust	Apostle	65	Lawyer, politician, businessman, editor
Neal A. Maxwell	Apostle	59	Educational administrator
Russell M. Nelson	Apostle	61	Surgeon
M. Russell Ballard	Apostle	57	Businessman
Dallin Oaks	Apostle	53	Lawyer, media executive

Compare those salaries with known incomes of other public figures, and the Mormon leaders emerge as grossly underpaid, given the massive corporation they manage. For example, Robert O. Anderson, chairman of the Atlantic Richfield Company, in 1979 earned an estimated $1,650,000 in base salary and other benefits.[19] Walter B. Wriston, chairman of Citicorp, the nation's second-largest bank holding company, received an estimated $779,323 in salary for 1981.[20] Steve Ross, chief executive officer of Warner Communications, earned an estimated $22.5 million in 1981, including benefits and stock interests. Even the late Paul "Bear" Bryant, football coach at the University of Alabama, earned $450,000 in 1981.[21]

Like other important executives, the Mormon leaders enjoy fringe benefits. For example, LDS President Kimball has his housing, cleaning maintenance, and transportation paid by the Church. He may take out loans from the Church (and a number of past presidents have done so when their salaries were smaller) at standard interest rates. These hardly compare with lucrative stock options and many other incentives to build a person's estate so common in the secular corporate world.

Still, it must be noted that the benefits for Church leaders are much better now than even in the recent past. In the early 1970s apostles earned between $18,000 and $23,000 a year. A longtime Church member, Apostle Matthew Cowley, who was earning about $400 a month as Council of the Twelve member during the early 1950s, once remarked to an Oregon stake president that his salary was little more than a glorified welfare program — all honor and not much pay. Some apostles in the past thirty years have subsisted only slightly above the poverty level. In fact, it was common for the more financially solvent apostles occasionally to buy furniture, car parts, or even new cars for their less affluent brethren. Once Apostle Delbert L. Stapley and former counselor to the First Presidency Henry Moyle chipped in to buy a new suit for Joseph Fielding Smith (later to become a Church president), when Smith was an impoverished apostle. All of our informants concurred on one point about the Church leaders: these men have taken on the responsibilities of their different offices out of a sincere sense that they are called by God to do so, not for any money or personal fortunes to be made. As one official in the Church's Finance Department commented:

In all my years that I've been connected with this department, I have never witnessed or experienced any financial malfeasance by any of the brethren in the Council of the Twelve or in the First Presidency. You can take it on my word that they manage the funds of the Church in an honest way and have never used any of these funds improperly for their own self-aggrandizement.[22]

At the same time, the modern Mormon leader, particularly the apostles, are no longer as threadbare as their predecessors. Many Mormon leaders today have been successful businessmen or have stocks and investments that already provide them with comfortable incomes before Church salaries. Other sources of income for members of the General Authorities come from Church-owned businesses on whose boards many of these men sit. Indeed, many apostles have enough personal affluence that they turn their salaries back over to the Church or sign over considerable royalties from books they have written to promote the Mormon faith.[23]

Much of the credit for molding a modern corporate image and style for Mormonism must go to the late Church president Harold B. Lee. When President Joseph Fielding Smith died in 1972, Lee brought a solid businessman's approach to the First Presidency. He built up the international missionary program, streamlined the already burgeoning Mormon Church bureaucracy, and encouraged the use of computers in Church offices. It was Lee who sought out the New York City consulting firm Crescent, McCormick & Paget (discussed in Chapter 2), authorizing a quarter of a million dollars to be spent on obtaining professional advice to consolidate Mormon holdings and reorganize everything from Church offices to publications. Part of this reorganization resulted, at least indirectly, in the eventual landmark decision to admit blacks to the Mormon priesthood. Though he lived only eighteen months after assuming the presidency, Harold B. Lee was the author of the Church's positive, prosperous, "can do" image in the early 1970s and left a permanent mark on its reshaped administration.

There is one final, inescapable characteristic of the top Mormon leaders: the LDS Church is run by a virtual gerontocracy. In 1982 the average age of First Presidency members was 82; of the Council of the Twelve, 71; and even of the Council of the Seventy (which includes a fair number of younger men), it was 57. (This contrasts with the Church in its earliest days. In the early 1830s the average age of the First Presidency leaders was 33; of the apostles, 29; and of the Council of the Seventy, 32. Joseph Smith, Jr., was only 25 years old when he received the call to become the first Church President.) The logic behind the modern practice of selecting only elderly men is to fill the Church's top positions, particularly the presidency, with mature men who are rich in worldly wisdom and years of loyalty to the Church.

Advanced age as a common characteristic of those called to the First Presidency as well as to the Council of the Twelve has important implications for how the Church is operated. In an era of rapid growth calling for flexibility and quick decisions, it may work against the Church. This has never been as clearly demonstrated as during the early 1980s. In 1985 President Spencer W. Kimball (age 90) was confined a great deal of the time to a wheelchair.* Meanwhile, Marion G. Romney (age 88), First Counselor to the Church president, had been hospitalized with pneumonia in 1982. The second counselor to the Church president, Gordon B. Hinckley, in good health at the age of 75, actually ran the Church in 1983 and 1984 while Kimball and Romney were incapacitated. But the situation was complicated by yet another age-related factor. By tradition the oldest apostle has served as the president of the Council of Twelve and has then been acclaimed new Church president when the incumbent dies. In 1985 that up-and-coming candidate was Ezra Taft Benson (age 86), the outspoken right-wing former U.S. secretary of agriculture.[24]

The significance of the physical infirmities which accompany advanced age in all people, particularly afflict the top Mormon leadership and can seriously affect Church administration. In 1982 and 1983 both a counselor in the First Presidency, N. Eldon Tanner, and an apostle, LeGrand Richards, died. In January 1984 Mark E. Peterson, a vigorous apostle and writer, died suddenly. Yet by spring 1984 no new apostles or counselors had been called to fill these positions because President Kimball, to whom such appointments are supposed to be revealed, was not fully functioning as an administrator because of his health problems, and no new president could assume control of the General Authorities. The next president, if

---

*In November 1985, as we were going to press, Spencer W. Kimball died in his sleep at the age of 90.

tradition held, would be Benson. Two new apostles, lawyer Dallin Oaks and surgeon Russell M. Nelson, did fill the empty spaces on the Council of the Twelve, but they were not called in the traditional way by the First Presidency through revelation. Rather, they were virtually appointed by other apostles and LDS leaders. Soon after, on April 19, 1985, Apostle Bruce R. McConkie died of cancer at the age of 69.

The health problems of the Mormon gerontocracy cannot be easily ignored. Nor are they temporary. Modern medicine may become more adept at keeping these living prophets and patriarchs alive, but it cannot guarantee their usefulness as executives. The Church leadership's conservative bent and the weight of Mormon tradition may continue the practice of recruiting for its highest posts among only its most experienced (that is, elderly) adherents, but in the long run good corporate sense may argue against such a practice.

THE MORMON BUREAUCRACY

Success produces growth in any organization. It comes as no surprise, therefore, that the LDS Church enterprise has witnessed an exponential increase in bureaucrats since World War II. These bureaucrats are the faceless people who make the Mormon corporate empire work in all its many offices and enterprises. If we included all the paid employees in the LDS Church offices, all the employees of LDS-owned companies and their subsidiaries, and the vast grass roots army of volunteer workers at all levels, they would easily number in the hundreds of thousands. Church historians Leonard J. Arrington and Davis Bitton estimate that just in the average Mormon ward (the most fundamental local administrative unit, of which there are thousands) there exist about 200 administrative positions, including clerks and laypersons in charge of monitoring financial, membership, and conversion statistics.[25] In 1975 there were an estimated 3,000 paid employees in the twenty-six departments of the Church's twenty-eight story Salt Lake City headquarters.[26] Even at that time the Church was unquestionably one of Salt Lake City's and Utah's biggest employers. By the late 1970s, the number had swelled to several thousand workers worldwide, ranging from full-time in-house employees in Salt Lake

City to college professors at Brigham Young University to stake secretaries and janitors.[27] If the Salt Lake City employee roster has kept pace with overall Church growth, by the mid-1980s, we estimate, it could reach the 7,500 mark. Mormon Fred C. Esplin commented on this mushrooming organizational growth:

> In much the same way the federal government is burdened with bureaucracy, the Mormon church is stacked with tier after tier of quorum, committee and council. The rapid growth of the church has created a need for "civil service" — thousands of managers, attorneys, clerks, historians, teachers, and architects working for the kingdom . . .
>
> One effect of the church civil service is the "palace guard" effect. The middle-level bureaucracy has the power to dilute the effect of the church president. Full-time employees sift through all recommendations that come in to church leaders, as well as all directives that come out. They often speak "on behalf of the brethren" and make decisions that members believe are sanctioned by the church leadership.[28]

This palace guard atmosphere in the modern Mormon bureaucracy is a post–World War II development, the inevitable result of the continuous splitting of labors within the LDS corporation. It was not always so. The First Presidency was once much more accessible to the average member. It was not unusual for visitors simply to drop in unannounced on the Church president and maintain a first-name acquaintance with virtually all stake presidents.[29] For instance, Henry A. Smith, retired *Church News* editor, recalled how during the 1930s he used to walk into the offices of the LDS president or any other General Authority if he wanted to talk with him, without an appointment.[30] With more than forty members of the Council of the Seventy (assisted by hundreds of paid and unpaid regional representatives) managing the day-to-day operations of the Church in separate offices, the average Mormon today has about as much chance of dropping in on the LDS First Presidency as the average citizen has of paying an impromptu visit to, say, a state governor or the chairman of the board of General Motors.

Various attempts have been made to reduce this swelling bureaucracy. Mormons themselves sensed what LDS writer Dennis L. Lythgoe observed about the Church's growing organizational labyrinth: "The tendency of bureaucratic procedures is to exclude those served by the bureaucracy from decision-making."[31] J. Reuben Clark, former counselor in the First Presidency under three Church presidents, had witnessed the rapid expansion of the federal bureaucracy when he worked in Washington, D.C., in the State Department from 1906 to 1929, and he recognized the same process when he saw it in Salt Lake City. As religious leaders in other denominations and churches before him have done, Clark worried about the incompatibility of dynamic religious inspiration and the bureaucratic inertia when he saw bureaucracy winning out. He wondered if "the increased influence of Church bureaucrats and technocrats" might not dilute the actual authority of prophets, seers, and revelators and cause them to surrender much of their autonomy to such functionaries.[32]

Beginning in late 1979 and continuing over the next three years, the Church undertook a major streamlining of its organization. Many people were dismissed, others were transferred from high-paying positions to lesser-paying ones while their former positions were eliminated. Entire departments were merged. Few new employees were hired even as the Church continued to expand its membership worldwide. Instead, many employees had their workloads doubled, tripled, and in some cases quadrupled. For example, managers and executives within the Church administration began assuming more of the clerical work that secretaries had once done.

The major reason for these changes was economic. In the late 1970s the Church, like many individual Americans and other corporations, felt the effects of the nationwide recession. In addition, there had been a falling off in tithings and fast-offering donations (two days each month members are encouraged to skip a meal and contribute the money they save to the Church). Afraid that their organization was becoming fat, Church leaders looked for areas to cut back. On May 26, 1983, an official from the Church's Personnel Department appeared before the Council on Disposition of Tithes (composed of members of the First Presidency, the Council of the Twelve, and the three men sitting in the Presiding Bishopric) and presented a report on, among other things, executive salaries. This was a significant meeting in the history of the LDS Church. It represented the first time that such confidential information had ever been revealed to the entire Council of the Twelve. Ordinarily only the First Presidency, two of the apostles, and the Presiding Bishopric had access to such figures. However, counselor Gordon B. Hinckley felt that the entire Council should be aware of just how much the Church was spending for its payroll each year relative to Church growth.

Prior to this report there had been some lively discussion among Council members concerning possible excess and unwarranted expenditures by employees. Many apostles in particular suspected that the Church bureaucracy employed too many people and could function just as well with fewer. The Personnel Department report satisfied Council members, however, that there already had been substantial trimming of "excess waste expenditures." According to the report, on a dollar-for-dollar basis the Church was now getting double and triple the work from its employees that it once had.

The Church does receive a good deal of work from its employees, considering the often low wages it pays. Certainly many of its leaders — and not only its First Presidency or apostles — could earn much higher salaries as executives in secular businesses. Many highly trained people have left better-paying jobs to work in the Church at a fraction of their previous salaries.

Why is this sacrifice so common among Mormons who work for the Church? As one anonymous Church administrator explained in an interview:

> A member of the Church responds to a calling in the Church, from the Savior Himself. I personally feel that it's impossible individually for a member of the Church, with the commitment which he has toward the Church, to approach any job separately from his feelings about the job as a calling [from Jesus Christ] because he sees his professional assignment as a part in advancing the Kingdom.

Such an attitude makes for people who are willing to work harder and longer, not for personal financial gain but for spiritual reasons. That type of motivation is an important ingredient in the success of a social movement, as sociological research on other religions has shown.[33] Another altruistic motive among Church workers is knowing that they are helping others. There is also the occasional thrill of meeting a General Authority, such as the president of the Church or an apostle, in the elevator or hallway, perhaps having the chance to shake a hand or strike up a brief conversation.

Keeping salaries and stipends low while interpreting Church employment as service "to the Kingdom" is an old Church policy. For this reason the Church has always vehemently opposed labor unions for its workers. The Church has been charged on at least one occasion by minority employees with exploitation. In the mid-1970s some Fijian students at Brigham Young University's Hawaii campus who also worked at the Church-owned Polynesian Cultural Center went on strike, charging that the Church "had exploited them as 'cheap labor' for the center." Some BYU faculty members in Hawaii told news reporters that many students working for the Polynesian Cultural Center graduated from college in debt because they were forced to accept such low wages. One said, "It smacks of the old plantation system."[34] The striking Fijians were threatened with excommunication by Church officials if they did not return to work, a fact that discouraged other sympathetic students from joining the protest.[35]

In one sense the reasons behind the growth of bureaucracy and impersonality in the Mormon Church are no mystery. Its proliferating local wards and aggressive missionary successes, adding thousands of new "Saints" to the Church rolls each year, have required greater coordination from one centralized source. There is no doubt that this trend is irreversible for the indefinite future as the Church expands into diverse markets for souls and requires a more sophisticated system of monitoring its operations.

But while bureaucracies strengthen the power of religious organizations, they also erode their dynamic spirit. Apathy becomes more common than fervent zeal, generating schisms within the organization between those who seek spiritual renewal and those who accept the bureaucratic status quo. If history holds any lessons, it is that success in building a wealthy, powerful religious empire out of a struggling sect exacts a heavy price from many members.

MORMON TEMPLES

Temples play a crucial role in Mormon Christianity. Temples are the places where the Church's most important rituals are conducted: "celestial" marriages of spouses for "all time and eternity," esoteric rites that bind members to their unique Church traditions, and baptisms of the living as well as the dead. Temples are considered sacred high grounds where Almighty God is transcendentally experienced by believers. Anthropologist Mark P. Leone has described the special place of temples in Mormon life:

> For a Mormon, the temple is as close to the other-worldly as he can come on earth. The temple is God's residence rather more than the local chapel where he does most of his worshipping and all of his congregational meeting. A Mormon visits a temple once a month as a kind of norm, but may go every day, or several times a year. He may also go much less frequently than once a year. But he cannot be a good Mormon and avoid the temple.[36]

Except for the brief period before their dedication, when they are open for public viewing, Mormon temples are closed not only to Gentiles but also to Mormons without "temple recommends," certification by local bishops and others that the members are in good standing. Since Mormons already have chapels and meeting halls similar to mainline Christian churches where they can worship, outsiders have sometimes wondered what really goes on during the rituals conducted in Mormon temples. The best and simplest answer can be summed up as what Mormons call "temple work." Besides marriage ceremonies, temple work consists primarily of baptisms for both the living and the dead. Mormons believe that carefully assembling and scrutinizing their family genealogies and vicariously baptizing contemporary stand-ins for deceased ancestors can give the latter the opportunity for salvation. One *Church News* editorial explained this all-important purpose of Mormon temples:

> We all have a great obligation to do ordinance work for our ancestors, as well as for ourselves. It is a requirement that we cannot escape. The Prophet Joseph Smith made it clear that the salvation of our departed ancestors is inseparably connected with our own. "We, without them, cannot be made perfect," he taught most forcibly.
>
> With that in mind, we must search out our genealogies so that our dead may properly be identified as we perform vicarious work for them. From generation to generation we must be united as the Lord has provided. That can be achieved only through the ordinances of the priesthood available in the temples of the Church.[37]

Economically the Mormon temple network represents a sizable investment for the Church. For example, in 1983 a temple opened in Atlanta, Georgia, and another in Dallas, Texas, in 1984, at an estimated minimum construction cost of $3.5 million and $2.25 million, respectively.[38] The Dallas temple was the United States' eighteenth and the world's thirtieth. Other North American temples were close to completion or under construction at Boise, Idaho, and in suburbs of Chicago, Denver, Las Vegas, Portland, and San Diego and Toronto, Canada. By 1985 there were forty-seven temples worldwide that were already completed, being built, or in the planning stages.

A dramatic increase in the number of temples took place during the 1950s after David O. McKay assumed the Church presidency. It was an era of tremendous membership growth, reflected in the construction of thousands of ward and branch chapels, new buildings at the expanded Brigham Young University campus in Provo, Utah, and the Temple Square Visitors' Center and the twenty-five-story Church Administration Building, both in Salt Lake City. New temples were built around the world in places as wide-ranging as Switzerland, New Zealand, England, and Los Angeles. While the Salt Lake City temple retained the distinction of having the largest square footage (253,015 square feet), the Los Angeles temple was built with the largest circumference. By the early 1970s, the Washington, D.C., temple was known as the tallest (80 feet taller than the 288-foot Salt Lake City original). LDS President Spencer W. Kimball, asked by a reporter if he envisioned an eventual limit to the number of temples constructed, replied: "Oh, I suppose there would be a limit — but we hope not for a long while. Some of the prophets ahead of me said we will have hundreds of temples. So we expect to go right on building temples."[39]

Each temple has its own tale about its location, decor, cost, and polanning. The Tokyo temple was almost built on top of a Church-owned five-story office building in the heart of the city. However, according to Emil B. Fetzer, now retired Church architect, "the Brethren didn't like the idea of having something so important as a temple on top of a building with hundreds of Japanese below scurrying all over the place." Church leaders sold the land for more than $25 million and with only the interest from the invested profit were able to buy other sites in Japan and build a number of chapels. The final location for the Tokyo temple was deliberately chosen for its proximity to a number of foreign embassies.[40]

Not everyone is pleased to see the spread of Mormon temples. "Every time a temple is built there will be opposition," Brigham Young once prophesied amazingly accurately.[41] In 1983 in Dallas, for example, we witnessed protest and concern over the construction of a temple and a new 14,000-square-foot stake administration building. Sun Belt Mormonism had grown considerably during the previous five years, from 1,000 to more than 16,000 members in Dallas alone. Much of this growth, of course, was due to migration into the region: like many Americans, Mormons came in search of jobs and better economic conditions. The Dallas temple was intended to serve more than 100,000 Mormons in Texas, Oklahoma, Louisiana, Arkansas, and Missouri.

The Dallas temple's construction sparked a flurry of familiar anti-Mormon fears and activities. Colleen Ralson, an outspoken ex-Mormon–turned Southern Baptist, led a crusade armed with brochures and films such as *The God Makers*, produced by Saints Alive for Jesus, a West Coast anti-Mormon group made up of former Church members. Welcomed at local Baptist congregations (Southern and independent), she fed already growing concerns as the Southern Baptist Convention faced a four percent decline in baptisms in 1983 (the largest since 1979).[42] Mormons, predictably, were blamed for the decline:

"Do you know that 40 percent of the converts to Mormonism are from Baptist backgrounds?" Dr. Edmund Poole, associate pastor of First Baptist Church, asked his congregation during a recent Sunday service. "Two hundred thirty-one every single day are converts to Mormonism from Baptist backgrounds."[43]

Poole's estimate was disputed by the Southern Baptist Home Mission Board as "exaggerated," "inflated," and without any real research behind it.[44]

In the early 1980s Mormon attempts to build temples across the United States and overseas continued to encounter resistance. In Carlingford, Australia, protestors clashed with a local city council that had approved construction of a temple.[45] In the Denver, Colorado, area the Church twice had to abandon prospective sites because of community hostility but vowed to keep on trying.[46] In Glenview, Illinois (a suburb of Chicago), local residents and environmentalists were outraged that the Church proposed to erect a temple more than one hundred feet tall that would attract over 125,000 Mormons from the Midwest and Canada next to a thirteen-acre nature preserve. One member of a local group organized to protect the preserve and halt the Mormons claimed: "It [the temple] will be in direct view of our most isolated and pristine nature trails, shattering their remoteness . . . Why do Mormons have to put it here?" The Mormon answer came from the project coordinator: "Because it's the perfect spot for our temple . . . I don't think there's anybody in Glenview who realizes what the temple will do for the community — the reverence, the awe, the beauty."[47] The Mormons tried to compromise with a slate rather than a glass roof to minimize artificial light at night and with a 100-foot buffer zone between the temple and the preserve. (Church spokespersons took pains also to intimate what commercial developers, less sensitive to local sentiments, might construct on the site if given the chance.)[48] Soon after the protest, ground-breaking ceremonies were held.

Local protests are not always overcome by negotiation. In Dallas, ground-breaking ceremonies had to be held privately with almost no publicity.[49] In Atlanta the Church overcame angry opposition from conservative Protestants by a concentrated public relations campaign. The Church purchased a large advertisement in the *Atlanta Constitution* (among other newspapers) emphasizing Church members' beliefs in Jesus Christ, the traditional scriptures, and strong family bonds. The mission president of the Georgia-Atlanta Mormon mission recalled how he was instructed from Salt Lake City to have all his missionaries contact all the newspapers in the state. They were to carry with them and offer to the editors or reporters Elder Mark E. Petersen's tract "Jesus Christ, Mediator and Redeemer" to refute the claim that Mormons do not believe in Christ and that Mormonism is a cult. Baptists in the Atlanta area had decided to take out a full-page newspaper advertisement warning people to stay away from the temple open house, but Mormon spokespersons were able to persuade editors at the *Atlanta Constitution* that it would not be in the best interests of the public or the Church to have such "harassment" publicized and legitimized. The editors decided not to print the Baptist ad. Georgia's governor and other important dignitaries were invited to the open house, and the governor made several complimentary speeches about the LDS Church, parts of which were carried by the media.[50]

73971

The Church continues to expand its temple network. In May 1983 Church leaders even broke ground for a temple and stake center in Freiberg, a city 150 miles south of Berlin in the German Democratic Republic (East Germany). This was to be the second temple in continental Europe (the first was built in Bern, Switzerland, in 1955). It might seem surprising that a Communist Eastern Bloc country would even tolerate Mormons, much less allow them to obtain such a foothold as a temple. Yet the ground-breaking was attended with much fanfare by several apostles from the Council of the Twelve and many other Church officials. The large number of East German officials attending suggests that the government was enthusiastic about the Mormon presence. Douglas Tobler, a Brigham Young University scholar of German history, explained the East German government's welcome in terms of its concern for its *own* public image:

A temple would...be an ensign to the people that the government is not as repressive as the press indicates. I'm sure the government hopes that this will make members of the Church more satisfied to stay in the GDR [German Democratic Republic]. The Church is no threat to the government, and they know it's no threat.[51]

As the Church's temple network expands, the Church is sometimes pressed to cut corners on expenses. One such move is to reduce the size of temples, stopping with a single story. Interior decor can provide the illusion of size. In one recently constructed temple the baptistry fountain, traditionally supported on the backs of twelve gold oxen, was built on the backs of only six, with a wall-mirror behind it to give the impression of a full complement. As one writer quipped:

For the creative Latter-day Saint, the usefulness of the mirror has only begun to be realized. In the future, effective placement of mirrors in local chapels could quickly double sacrament meeting attendance while cutting in half the number of officers needed to staff the ward.[52]

Funding the construction of temples ultimately is tied to other Mormon investments in maintaining and increasing membership and financial stability: among these are investments in welfare farms, satellite dishes in stake centers, Mormon-owned radio stations, and public utility stocks. As the Church grows, it continues to keep the extent of its considerable wealth tightly guarded information. It is to the Church's wealth that we will now turn our attention.

TITHING AND DONATIONS

Tithing and donations are the largest source of income for the Church.[53] Our research revealed a total earned income both from tithing and from all Church investments to have been close to $2 billion in 1983, about three quarters of which, we estimate, came from tithes and offerings.

The practice of tithing was first suggested in November 1834 during a private conversation between Joseph Smith and an early apostle, Oliver Cowdery. Four years later it was established as a standing law for Church members.[54] Tithing originally was intended to be a 10 percent obligation "levied on what a man is worth," that is, on his surplus property, interest from investments, and so forth, and not on gross personal income. But the early Church's need for monies reshaped the tithing practice. Brigham Young placed great emphasis on tithing and donations, making this obligation a deciding factor even in how members could enter into fellowship with their neighbors.[55] Gentiles were often aghast at the blatant pressures Young sometimes used and cynically referred to him as "The Profit" Young.[56]

Today only about one-third of Mormons pay at least a full tithe (10 percent of annual income before taxes) to the Church.[57] Their giving nevertheless amounts to a large share of Church revenues because many of them give beyond their tithe share. Such dedicated members believe that if they give more, the Lord will be more generous in return. Biographies and anecdotes about numerous prominent Mormons, such as the famous Marriott family and many Church leaders, reveal a steady pattern of such generosity.[58]

The Church also makes sure that certain of its members do not escape their tithing obligation. For employees of Church-run companies, for example, the pressure is less than subtle. In 1931 Church leaders announced that all employees of Church-supported schools must be full tithe payers or they would face immediate dismissal from their jobs. In 1934 LDS President Heber J. Grant said of some Brigham Young University faculty members who were nontithing, "If they haven't enough loyalty to the Church to do their duty and pay their tithing, I want it recorded right here and now that I want other teachers there." BYU President Franklin S. Harris resisted enforcing this edict. The issue caused friction between Harris and Church leaders, who suspected "that Harris placed more emphasis on scholastic attainment than on the building of testimonies or adherence to fundamental Church practices like the payment of tithing."[59] Dean R. Brimhall, a government official and a Mormon, who persistently criticized his Church's welfare program during the Depression, once complained to his friend Henry D. Moyle (who later became a counselor in the First Presidency) that the Church dunned even destitute Mormons receiving help from the federal Works Projects Administration. He commented: "Many of these unlucky people [helped by the WPA] are devoted tithe payers, and I do not see how the Church can accept this tithing and other donations from the meager earnings of workers."[60]

More recently the Church has stepped up its pressure on members to tithe. *All* Church employees, for example, are expected to pay a full tithe or face immediate termination. How would the Church know if a member had not tithed? In the same way it learns of fornication, adultery, and the other sins it is determined to stamp out: through the rigorous questioning of members seeking temple recommends and through the reports of ward bishops and other local officials as well as the payroll records of Mormon companies.

In summer 1982 five employees of a Church-owned industry brought suit against the Church and were represented by the Utah Chapter of the American Civil Liberties Union. (The national ACLU, it should be noted, has designated the entire state of Utah a "crisis area" in terms of civil rights infringement.)[61] In a "Charge of Discrimination Statement" filed by Christine J. Amos, one of the plaintiffs in the suit, Amos described how the Church can systematically exert pressure on many members and encourage them to become "cheerful givers":

DISCRIMINATION STATEMENT: I believe that I have been discriminated against on the basis of my religion (LDS but not full tithe payer) by being terminated without cause.

1. I worked for Beehive Clothing for approximately six years. In 1982, Beehive Clothing adopted a policy requiring all employees who are members of the LDS Church to be eligible for a temple recommend in order to continue employment.

2. In order to determine whether I was worthy I was required on my own time and without compensation to be interviewed by my Bishop. Because my Bishop wrote that I had been having problems with tithing and therefore that I was not worthy in every way, on May 3, 1982, I was interviewed by Jack Booth from the Personnel Department of the Corporation of the President. Mr. Booth told me that unless I paid my tithing I would be fired in three months.

3. In the last week of July, Roy Chapman and Russ Bourneman from the Personnel Department of the Corporation of the President returned to Beehive Clothing and began to re-interview employees who had been found not worthy in the spring to determine if they had become worthy in the intervening months.

4. I had not paid tithing since May interview. Rather than go through the emotional trauma of another interview, I informed Beehive Clothing that I could not comply with the religious requirements that they were attempting to impose on me. I agreed to work for several more weeks until a replacement was found and trained.

5. Beehive Clothing employs non-members of the LDS Church, and they are not required to comply with the standards of the LDS Church, such as tithing.[62]

However, most LDS members remain silent. Naturally the recent increase in compliance with tithing is not credited to such pressures. Gordon B. Hinckley, second counselor to Church President Spencer W. Kimball, was able to report to the faithful at the April 1983 session of General Conference in the Temple Square Tabernacle that "payment of tithes and offerings has increased as evidence of their [members'] willingness to move forward in faith."

Donations from members are another important part of the

Church's income, sometimes a form of tithing-in-kind. Gifts run the gamut from the valuable to the bizarre: a rare Ming Dynasty incense burner (now in the Church museum), $75,000 worth of Consolidated Edison preferred stock, or a loaded handgun one Salt Lake City member donated to his ward's bishop (the gun made its way to the Salt Lake City Police Department). However, 90 percent of the donations are in the form of stocks, bonds, and other marketable securities.[63] Currently such generosity remains an enormous source of Church wealth.

Brigham Young University, the largest privately owned university in the United States and "the educational showpiece of the Mormon nation," according to one reporter,[64] provides a good illustration of Mormon generosity and high finances. BYU has brought in hundreds of millions of dollars in donations. For instance, J. Willard Marriott, for whom the school's activities center is named, "made a substantial donation of Marriott Corporation stock which helped make the construction of this magnificent structure possible."[65] Marriott added another $1 million in 1982–83. In fact, the majority of Marriott stock that the Church presently holds came in the form of several gifts.

Then there is land — a lot of it — given every year to the school. For example, in the early 1970s a couple from southern California gave BYU more than a thousand acres of valuable property overlooking the ocean in San Clemente. Later the Church received the property on behalf of BYU and entered into a limited partnership with John D. Lusk & Sons, a California contracting and development firm, to build a combination residential-commercial-industrial development called Marblehead. Additional lands have been given to BYU in Las Vegas, Fort Worth, Phoenix, Malibu Beach, and elsewhere. Today, as more than two decades ago, real estate makes up three-quarters of the gifts given to BYU.[66]

In September 1981 BYU officials announced a new five-year campaign to raise $100 million, using the theme "Excellence in the Eighties." Two years later, the campaign half over, $36 million had been raised. By the end of 1983 fund-raisers announced they were ahead of their goal with $44 million already collected.[67] Informants at BYU told us that at the rate donations were pouring in, school officials expected to go over the $100 million mark by as much as $13 to $17 million.

That kind of success is not the result of sheer good fortune or wishful thinking. BYU's impressive fund-raising represents one of the most thoroughly coordinated financial campaigns ever conducted by a major American university. In an era when even the most prestigious and well-established institutions of higher learning must scramble to shore up receding endowments and keep alumni contributing as expenses rise, BYU appears to be downright flush. Much of the credit can be given to the LDS Foundation. In 1966 the LDS Foundation began as the BYU Office of University Development (later renamed BYU Development Fund) with a mandate to raise funds for the school. Appointed as its head was David M. Kennedy, a former chairman of the board and chief executive officer of Continental Illinois National Bank and Trust Company in Chicago (one of Illinois' largest banking systems). In 1969 Kennedy resigned his position at BYU to become secretary of the U.S. Treasury under President Nixon. Kennedy was typical of the corporate-wise administrators that BYU placed at the helm of this ongoing fund-raising endeavor: his successors have been corporate executives, former mayors, retailers, and bankers.

During the early 1980s the Development Board was renamed the Development Office and its mandate was expanded. (The office had been so enormously successful as a fund-raiser for the university that Church leaders once considered designating it as the official fund-raising arm for the entire Church.) In 1982 the Development Office went through one final incarnation to become the LDS Foundation. Its first chairman of the board of directors was J. Alan Blodgett, who was also managing director for all Church investments and reported to the Presiding Bishopric's office.

Headquarters of the LDS Foundation are still maintained at BYU, with additional offices in the Church Office Building in Salt Lake City. Approximately fifty full-time paid professionals make up its staff. Skilled in such specialties as annual giving, planned giving, memorial giving, institutional (corporate and foundation) giving, accounting, financial estate planning, and legal affairs, they are unquestionably effective. In a two-year period (1981–1982) their collective efforts raised more than $57 million.[68]

We interviewed various officials and informants in the LDS Foundation's office. One man, with a background in accounting and financial and estate planning, was responsible for developing philanthropic support for various Church programs as well as for BYU. One strategy he used was to keep in frequent contact with most of the attorneys in his area, making them aware of BYU's interest in worthy donors for specific projects. He worked closely with the LDS Church Public Communications Department as well. He and his staff mounted a continuous effort to contact members of the business community and many area bankers, asking them if they knew anyone who fit the "ideal profile" of a potential donor — middle-aged or retired, with a substantial estate and record of giving generously to worthy educational causes. An assistant director for the former Church development office described the extensive training for workers in the department at such fund-raising tasks:

> Our representatives are trained in personal grooming habits, correct deportment, proper word usage, the right kinds of voice tone for different situations, good telephone procedures, and the like. It's almost an entire remake of the whole person once they've been through the whole program. They are instructed to contact attorneys, certified public accountants, bank officials, and any other officials who handle the financial affairs of elderly, well-to-do clients and tell them about the needs of our school in Provo. You'd be surprised just how well this system works for us.[69]

Perhaps the best testimony in support of that claim is that almost two-thirds of the funds raised by the development office came from *non-Mormons.*

A former BYU development employee described how LDS Foundation workers seek out the elderly rich, the Mormon faithful, and the generally philanthropic who harbor a soft spot for Brigham Young University. He recounted that potential donors were sometimes flown in free to visit the campus, dined (but, if proper Mormons, not wined), even given choice seats at BYU football games in Couger Stadium. He boasted that the secret to inspiring generosity in people was a low-key approach, steadily pursuing possible donors but not doing any "arm-twisting." He noted: "We've had many non-Mormon donors tell us that one reason they finally chose our school over others they previously had in mind is because we don't put a lot of pressure on them like the others do."[70]

In 1981 BYU conducted one of its massive Telefund drives. Student volunteers telephoned peers and alumni from sixty special phones at the school. Dale McCann, director of the annual drive, was quoted as saying, "BYU has one of the most successful student fund-raising programs in the United States."[71] More than $93,000 was collected in the 1981 campaign, but most of the money found its way into numerous investment portfolios owned by BYU but managed by the LDS Church Investment Department. Ironically, despite the millions of dollars flowing into BYU coffers from the kinds of large donations we described earlier, much of the money for the 1981 campaign was donated by students — probably the group least able to afford philanthropy. Indeed, the 1981 Telefund drive was especially notable (given the prosperity of the LDS Foundation) for its appeals aimed at students through the campus newspaper. School President Jeffrey Holland's name and picture appeared beside the text of an advertisement that began, "Charity is the virtue that has distinguished the great of all times," followed by a personal request that every student donate at least $10 per year to the Telefund.[72] Another fund-raising appeal covering a quarter-page of the newspaper quoted deceased Mormon Apostle Richard L. Evans: "We drink every day from wells we have not dug; and warm by fires we have not kindled."[73] But the real "grabber" came in the form of a large black-and-white photograph of LDS Church President Spencer W. Kimball who appealed directly to students:

> Much of what is accomplished at BYU is done with the help of people like you. Contributions help support this great university in an important way, and they free Church funds to be used in other areas where they are badly needed. I hope you will pause now to consider the great purpose of Brigham Young University and how you can help in its divinely directed work.[74]

Kimball was right. The Church does depend on the largesse of its members, and its corporate growth requires the flexibility to take large amounts of cash or in-kind donations and maximize their investment possibilities. Even college students living on shoestring budgets are expected to sacrifice for the cause — for in the final analysis that's what Brigham Young University, like all Church properties and operations, is about — a millennial quest to build the literal Kingdom of God on earth before Christ's return.

THE WEALTH OF LDS, INC.

The wealth of the Mormon empire is massive. Likewise, the interview notes, copies of stock reports, published documents, and similar materials used in forming our own estimates of that wealth bulk large. Even a weeding-out procedure left us with a pile of material several telephone directories thick. There is no adequate way to give all the detailed references, gathered over several years, for the final figures we present. However, to make much of this information available to other researchers, we have placed dozens of pages of original tables, charts, and summary statistics (along with information on how they were collected) in archives.[75] The tables and figures in the remainder of this chapter are selected samples that illustrate the sources of our final estimates.

Two LDS Church historians recently wrote: "It has no substantial block of stock in many of the [Mountain West] area's most powerful enterprises — Union Pacific Railroad, First Security Corporation, Western Airlines, and Utah Power & Light Company . . . among others."[76] This is the view of Mormon investments that the Church understandably prefers to promote. Unfortunately it is contradicted by the facts. For instance, the *Annual Report of Utah Power & Light to the Federal Energy Regulatory Commission* for December 31, 1980, showed the LDS Church to be the fourth-largest stockholder in Utah Power & Light, with 342,172 shares. (This report, like much of the supporting evidence we provide, is available to the public.) And as of December 31, 1983, the Church was listed as the third-largest stockholder in Zion's Utah Bancorporation, with approximately 170,000 shares, as well as the fifth-largest stockholder in First Security Corporation, with approximately 250,000 shares. Both corporations are not only among Utah's leading banking enterprises but also two of the western United States' largest bank-holding conglomerates. Together both blocks of stock were worth an estimated $12,305,000 at the end of 1983.

The LDS Church avoids public disclosure of its wealth and does not advertise its heavy investments in banks, public utilities, insurance, electronic communications, and agribusiness. Former *New York Times* reporter Wallace Turner noted the obstacles to obtaining information on Church finances:

> In all particulars, it is difficult to discuss the financial status of the LDS Church. Precise information is lacking. The Church has

a policy of secrecy on financial matters that makes it difficult to check the accuracy of reports picked up from non-Church sources.[77]

One informant in the Church Investment Department bluntly told us that the Church's policy on disclosure of its finances is to try to stay out of the press and public eye as much as possible. Church officials do not even like to comment on any articles written about the financial holdings of the LDS organization.[78]

Yet there are ways to gain enough information to form reasonable estimates despite this secrecy. The remainder of this chapter examines the Church's investments, income, and profits. We have broken the wealth of the Church into five general areas: stocks and bonds investments, land and buildings, mass communication holdings, archival and library holdings, and insurance.

Church Stocks and Bonds Investments

As recently as the early 1960s the LDS Church had few or no stocks and bonds in its investment portfolios. Rather, it bought short-term notes that made money easily available when it needed to be spent.[79] In 1963, however, N. Eldon Tanner, a wealthy Canadian politician and industrialist, became first counselor to the Church president. He dramatically reshaped Church investment practices and built its impressive stock portfolios. Men with corporate savvy and investment instincts began to rise quickly through the Church bureaucracy during Tanner's years in the First Presidency. Tanner regularly consulted with financiers and bankers. Management of Church investments became more aggressive and, despite some losses during recessions (particularly during the mid-1970s), the new strategies produced impressive returns.

In the 1980s the Church bond substitute portion of its portfolio occasionally has taken a beating. One of the main reasons is the Church's heavy investment in public utilities amid the growing controversy over nuclear power plants. A number of companies in which the Church owns stock have confronted mounting public opposition to the construction of nuclear plants and come under sharp scrutiny by the Nuclear Regulatory Commission. One newspaper reported:

Between October 1974 and July 1983, according to the U.S. Nuclear Regulatory Commission, 49 nuclear plants were canceled before construction permits were issued. An additional 25 plants were canceled after permits had been issued . . . for a total of 74 aborted nuclear projects.[80]

Table 3–3 gives an idea of the Church's heavy investment in a part of the energy industry that has rapidly lost much of its promise of near-future profitability for investors.[81]

Table 3–3 LDS Church Investments in Utilities Relying on Nuclear Power

POWER COMPANY	NUMBER OF NUCLEAR PLANTS UNDER CONSTRUCTION OR NEARLY COMPLETED	NAME OF NUCLEAR PROJECT	APPROXIMATE NUMBER OF SHARES LDS CHURCH HOLDS
Arizona Public Service	3	Powell Verde Units I, II, III	220,000
Baltimore Gas & Electric	2	Calvert Cliffs I, II	410,000
Cincinnati Gas & Electric	1	Zimmer Plant (since converted to coal)	315,000
Cleveland Electric	2	Perry Units	200,000
Houston Industries	2	South Texas Units I, II	300,000
Long Island Lighting	1	Shoreham Plant	680,000
Middlesouth Utilities	5	Arkansas Power & Light (2) Mississippi Power & Light (2) (Grand Gulf I, II) Louisiana Power & Light (1) (Waterford III)	360,000
Northeast Utilities	3	Millstone I, II, III	250,000
Public Service of Colorado	1	Fort Saint-Vrain	375,000
Rochester Gas & Electric	1	Ginna Unit	314,000
Texas Utilities	2	Comanche Peak I, II	320,000

Source: Figures were compiled from numerous annual reports from utility companies to the Federal Energy Regulatory Commission.

But the Church is still a long way from the poorhouse with its public utilities investments. Table 3–4 shows the annual dividend rates, paid quarterly, only for those utilities in which the Church holds 100,000 shares or more of common stock. (It actually has many smaller holdings in other utilities not mentioned here.) Stocks in only these companies paid the Church approximately $20,325,000 in 1983. When public utilities bonds and common stocks are combined, the Church holds total investments in this portfolio alone valued at $255 million.[82]

Table 3–4 LDS Church Bond Substitute Portfolio (1983)

Public Utilities Bonds			$ 80,000,000
Public Utilities Common Stocks			$175,000,000
Total Investments in Portfolio			$255,000,000
PUBLIC UTILITIES	APPROXIMATE NUMBER OF SHARES	ANNUAL DIVIDEND (1983)	APPROXIMATE TOTAL PAID (1983)
Central Illinois Public Service	140,000	$1.52	$ 212,800
Commonwealth Edison	360,000	$3.00	$1,080,000
Wisconsin Public Service	130,000	$2.32	$ 301,600
Public Service of Indiana	230,000	$2.88	$ 662,400
Kansas Power & Light	450,000	$2.24	$1,008,000
Baltimore Gas & Electric	410,000	$3.00	$1,230,000
Long Island Lighting	680,000	$2.02	$1,373,600
Middlesouth Utilities	360,000	$1.74	$ 626,400
Texas Utilities	320,000	$2.20	$ 704,000
Southern Co.	260,000	$1.80	$ 468,000
Arizona Public Service	220,000	$2.60	$ 572,000
Idaho Power Co.	210,000	$3.08	$ 646,800
Montana Power	250,000	$2.68	$ 670,000
Public Service of Colorado	375,000	$1.84	$ 690,000
Florida Power Corp.	150,000	$3.60	$ 540,000
Utah Power & Light	345,000	$2.32	$ 800,400
Southern California Edison	110,000	$3.80	$ 418,000
El Paso Electric	100,000	$1.40	$ 140,000
Indianapolis Power & Light	115,000	$2.76	$ 317,400
Southern Indiana Gas & Electric	124,000	$2.28	$ 282,720
Northeast Utilities	250,000	$1.38	$ 345,000
Rochester Gas & Electric	314,000	$1.84	$ 577,760
Virginia Electric (Dominion Resources)	290,000	$2.56	$ 742,400
Cincinnati Gas & Electric	315,000	$2.16	$ 680,400
Cleveland Electric Illuminating Co.	200,000	$2.40	$ 480,000
Gulf States Utilities	165,000	$1.64	$ 270,600
Houston Lighting (Houston Industries)	300,000	$2.32	$ 696,000

The accounting and investment departments of the Church are governed by two powerful committees. In 1983 the Investment Policy Committee included Gordon B. Hinckley as chair (Hinckley was second counselor to President Spencer W. Kimball but because of Kimball's illness, he was the *de facto* head of the Church), Ezra Taft Benson, and Howard W. Hunter (both members of the Council of the Twelve), and all three members of the Presiding Bishopric. The committee establishes general investment policies and guidelines without usually dealing in specifics. Below this committee is the Investment Securities Committee, made up of seven members, which meets every month and determines the allocations for various investment portfolios — bonds, equities, farm management programs, cash accounts, meetinghouses and temples, and so forth.

The Church maintains a number of investment portfolios for specific purposes, such as numerous real estate portfolios covering their farms and ranches, their commercial properties, and their industrial parks. By looking at the investments made by just one Church-owned operation — in this case the Beneficial Life Insurance Company — we obtain a good idea of how the Church invests its money (in this case tithing funds). There is a fair amount of "corporate inbreeding," or interlocking directorships, at the top of the Mormon pyramid. For example, Ezra Taft Benson and Howard W. Hunter, in addition to serving on the Investment Policy Committee, also sit on Beneficial's board of directors. According to one member of the Investment Securities Committee, "The structure of the [Beneficial] portfolio is rather like that of a large pension fund."[83] The portfolio has long been involved in traditional investments such as stocks and bonds, and, until recently, its equities investments have been largely conservative and "Big Board," or blue chip. In 1982, according to the *Annual Statement of the Beneficial Life Insurance Company,* the company owned a total book value of $16,338,787 in government bonds. Almost two-thirds of these bonds had maturities of five years or less, the rest three years or less. Out of the eleven new government bonds purchased in 1982, only one (valued at $297,818) had a maturity date stretching as far as 1991. Most of the rest matured before 1988. This pattern contrasts with the annual statements of previous years, which show more purchase of government bonds with ten-, twenty-, and even thirty-year maturity dates as well as more commercial stocks.

The reason for such a shift is no mystery. Within the last several years Church leaders have developed a much more sober, even apocalyptic, attitude that influences the Investment Department. They convey a sense of impending economic catastrophe on a national scale, an extension of the doomsday millennial expectations we described in Chapter 1. Some leaders, like Ezra Taft Benson, are hard-line millennialists who expect widespread social upheaval and disorder imminently. Hence they want to maintain a healthy portion of assets that can be liquidated on short notice and used to run the Church, its building programs, and its welfare system for at least a year if tithing and other earnings are suddenly cut off. It is an interesting characteristic of LDS Church leadership that despite the no-nonsense business acumen usually brought to many corporate decisions, the Church's theology and prophecies still shape investment policies. The course of many future investments and hundreds of millions of dollars are profoundly affected.

Informants in the Church Investment Department confirmed that the "Brethren" in 1983 were indeed concerned with investment liquidity. Not long before, they had changed many of their Big Board investments over to more liquid investments such as money market funds, Treasury bills with 30/60/90 days or up to six months' maturity, Treasury notes that usually mature in two years or less, short-term certificates of deposit of a year or less, short-term commercial paper between 30 and 90 days' maturity, and anything else that appeared to be sound, short-term, and yielding a respectable return. After many interviews with brokers, investment counselors, and persons informed about Church investments, and with the recognition of how the Church has shifted allotted investments in various ways, we estimate that the Church currently puts about $509 million into such short-term investments. That number can be only approximate, however, since short-term investments by their very nature are continually in flux.

Gone are many of the Church's heavier investments in a number of eastern industrials such as U.S. Steel, Union Carbide, Ford Motor Company, General Motors, and Chrysler. One financial planning officer for E. F. Hutton (and an active Mormon) commented, "I was astonished at just how much of their entire investment portfolio has changed in such a short period of time. The average turnaround in their portfolio investments was unbelievable." He estimated that in recent years well over 80 percent of the LDS Church's stocks and bonds investments have been made or readjusted to fit into the new liquidity strategy.[84]

At the same time, the Church still maintains an impressive presence in Big Board stock ownership. It owns some 300,000 shares of the Marriott Corporation (1983 market value over $25,000,000), almost 400,000 shares of Exxon (valued at about $15,000,000), and over 100,000 shares each of Standard Oil of California and Phillips Petroleum (value of each over $400,000,000). Table 3-5 presents a summary of the wealth of the LDS Church investments and the income they produce.[85]

Table 3–5 Estimate of LDS Church Investments, 1982–1983

LDS CHURCH INVESTMENTS	APPROXIMATE TOTAL
Short-Term (government bills, bank notes, commercial paper, etc.)	$508,600,000
Public Utilities (bonds and stocks)	$254,600,000
Big Board or Blue Chip (bonds and stocks) (AT&T, IBM, GE, Xerox, General Foods, Sears, Gannett, CBS, etc.)	$190,400,000
Approximate Total LDS Church Stocks and Bonds Investments	$953,600,000
Estimated Earned Income on above Investments	
Short-Term (Average yield 9.2% estimated for $508,600,000)	$ 46,791,200
Public Utilities (Bonds: Average yield 12.5% estimated for $80,000,000)	$ 10,000,000
(Stocks: Average yield 10.5% estimated for $175,000,000)	$ 18,375,000
Blue Chip (Average yield 4% estimated for $190,400,000)	$ 7,616,000
Estimated Earned Income on above Church Investments for 1983	$ 82,782,200
Estimated Earned Income on All Other Business Investments	
Includes agribusiness holdings, commercial real estate, industrial park properties, communications holdings, trusts, and other general undeclared investments.	$198,300,000 (1982) $207,000,000 (1983)

Table 3–6 gives our estimates of total LDS income for selected years.[86] The 1983 figure of $2 billion is a staggering amount considering that much of it is poured back each year into more investments.

Table 3–6 **Approximate LDS Church Total Income**
             from All Sources
             (Tithing, Donations, Earned Income)

Year	Estimated Income
1962	More than $ 365,000,000
1976	More than $1,095,000,000
1978	More than $1,000,000,000
1982	$1,700,000,000
1983	$2,000,000,000

Church Lands and Buildings

For Mormons, Zion is not merely a concept. It is a geographic place, just as Jerusalem is to Jews. Many Mormons still regard Jackson County, Missouri, as Zion, the place where the millennium will occur. Others take a more global interpretation. For them Zion consists of those places the Church owns and controls, that is, its properties as well as its investments. We briefly review the major Church lands and buildings that make up Zion in this latter view.

Meetinghouses

In 1983 there were approximately 4,435 meetinghouses, where local congregations of Mormons meet for regular services, in the United States and Canada. More than 80 percent of the LDS population still resides in the western and northwestern United States, principally in Utah, California, Idaho, Arizona, and Washington, and three-quarters of the meetinghouses are in these states.[87] In addition, there are approximately 2,367 meetinghouses outside North America, but given Church growth in South America and elsewhere such buildings are springing up faster than we have been able to count. One Church leader estimated that over 400 new branch, ward, and stake meetinghouses were being built each year throughout the world to accommodate the rapid membership growth.[88]

Altogether these meetinghouses represent a 1983 minimum value of $3,175,884,000.

Other Religious Edifices

The April 1980 issue of the Church's *Ensign* magazine cites eighty-six edifices of special religious significance to Mormons. These include the Church's administrative headquarters in Salt Lake City; separate genealogical libraries; the Church's famous Granite Mountain Vaults, which protect its records and microfilm family records; museums; distribution centers and mission properties; and the Salt Lake City Tabernacle and Assembly Hall. In 1985 there are about 100 such places in the United States and Canada and 167 outside North America, altogether worth an estimated $208,065,000.

Temples

In 1984 there were forty-two temples completed or scheduled for completion by 1985 around the world. They varied greatly in size. The massive Washington, D.C., temple, for example, is built on a site covering 57 acres. The temple site in London covers 32 acres and the Seattle temple site takes up 23½ acres, yet the Tokyo temple is built on less than one-half acre! The Salt Lake City temple has the largest floor area (253,015 square feet), followed by the Los Angeles temple (190,614 square feet), the Washington, D.C., temple (164,000 square feet), the Jordan, Utah, temple (148,235 square feet), and the Mexico City temple (126,235 square feet). The smallest amount of floor space is in the temple in Freiberg, East Germany (7,800 square feet). Ironically the Tokyo temple, built on such a small site, has more square footage (54,600 square feet) than any other temple outside the United States except the Mexico City temple. Most foreign temples average only 10,000 square feet of floor space.

We estimated the values of acreage and temple buildings from various sources. We consulted the *Deseret News 1983 Church Almanac*, various issues of the *Church News*, assorted newspapers, and other publications to learn the approximate costs and sizes of many temples. We contacted a number of professionals (construction firms, stone and wood craftsmen, architects, and building engineers) to obtain estimates of what it would have cost to build some of the older temples (such as Utah temples at Salt Lake City, Manti, and Logan and at Cardston, Alberta). Besides these experts, we contacted both commercial and residential real estate agencies in a number of states and foreign countries to determine fair market values for the lands on which temples sit. In some instances temples of nearly the same floor space and acreage had very different values, as in the cases of the Tokyo temple (54,600 square feet) and the temple in São Paulo, Brazil (51,279 square feet). Although the land for the Tokyo temple is much smaller, its value far exceeds that in Brazil. Additionally the Tokyo temple required more structural steel and reinforced concrete than the São Paulo temple because of Japan's exceedingly strict building codes for earthquakes and typhoon protection. Thus temples differed greatly in construction cost and present value.

The most valuable temple currently is the original one in Salt Lake City ($79,093,000), followed by the Manti, Utah, temple ($42,000,000), the Washington, D.C., temple ($35,000,000), the Logan, Utah, temple ($31,465,000), and the Cardston, Alberta, temple ($29,225,000). More recent, foreign temples typically are found at the opposite range: the Freiberg, East Germany, temple has the lowest dollar value ($1,600,000), followed by the Guatemala City and Guayaquil, Ecuador, temples ($2,400,000 each).

The total estimated value of all LDS temples in 1983 was $559,443,000.

Educational Facilities

Here we include all educational buildings and acreage at universities, colleges, elementary and secondary schools, and religious institutes and seminaries owned by the LDS Church. Part of the information on buildings and acreage was already available in sources such as *The College Blue Book* or in tax listings. We gathered land values and estimates of replacements costs per square foot for campus buildings by interviewing local real estate agents.[89] Table 3–7 presents a summary of what we learned.

Agribusiness Holdings

The Church has always been a huge landholder. In 1849 the Church leadership envisioned the State of Deseret (to be strictly a Mormon commonwealth) to include that portion of California east of the Sierra Nevada and all of southern California, all of Nevada

Table 3–7 Estimated Value of LDS Educational Facilities (1983)

NAME AND LOCATION	NUMBER OF BUILDINGS	ACREAGE	ESTIMATED VALUE
Brigham Young University Provo, Utah	317	529	$339,330,000
BYU–Ricks College Rexburg, Idaho	33	255	$ 97,000,000
BYU–Hawaii College Laie, Oahu, Hawaii	7	460	$ 56,000,000
LDS Business College Salt Lake City, Utah	5	4	$ 27,000,000
Church College of New Zealand Tuhikaramea, New Zealand	3	86	$ 33,000,000
Liahona Church School Pea, Tonga	4	200	$ 6,315,000
Other Church Schools in Mexico, Central and South America, Samoa, and the South Pacific	—	—	$ 11,000,000
Institutes and Seminaries in the U.S., Canada, and foreign countries	436	315	$ 59,000,000
	Total Estimated Value		$628,645,000

and Utah, the southern portions of Oregon and Idaho, southwestern Wyoming, western Colorado, western New Mexico, and all of Arizona north of the Gila River — roughly an area one and a half times the size of Texas.[90] Its farm and ranch system is more modest, yet its 928,600 total acres (in 1983) make the LDS Church the single largest ranching enterprise in the United States. The next largest is the famous King Ranch in Kingsville, Texas, at 825,000 acres. To put it in a slightly different perspective, the Church's 928,600 acres equal approximately 1,528 square miles, larger than the state of Rhode Island and only slightly smaller than the state of Delaware. Table 3-8 gives a more specific breakdown of the Church's total acreage.[91]

Table 3–8 Approximate Acreage in LDS Church Farm-Ranch System (1983)

NAME	LOCATION	ACREAGE
Deseret Ranch of Florida	Central Fla.	316,000
Deseret Livestock Ranch	Northeastern Utah	201,000
LDS Welfare Farms & Dairies	U.S. and overseas	167,000 (est.)
U & I, Inc.*	Kennewick, Wash.	109,000
Deseret Ranch of Canada	Cardston, Alberta	95,000
Elberta Farms	Elberta, Utah	12,000
Various farm investments	Midwestern U.S.	11,000 (est.)
Deseret Farms of Texas	Pecos, Texas	10,000
Deseret Farms of California	Sacramento-Esparto, Calif.	6,000
Templeview Farms	Hamilton, New Zealand	1,600
	Total	928,600

*The LDS Church owns about 70 percent of the outstanding stock and is the major shareholder.

The Church's real estate division conducts a good deal of selling and buying land. Journalist Jeffrey Kaye conservatively estimated a total of one hundred property transactions per week.[92] Holdings under the agribusiness category include, of course, farm and ranch lands but also canneries for produce grown on church property, Bishops' Storehouses and a transportation system for the welfare program, equipment such as tractors and threshers, roads, irrigation systems, barns and similar buildings, silos, nine flour mills, twenty-seven granaries, thrift stores for Church members, and livestock (approximately 80,000 beef cattle, another 80,000 yearlings and feeder calves, 6,300 milking cows, 3,500 sheep, and 300 horses). Table 3–9 presents figures just on the value of granaries and flour mills to give some sense of the Church's far-flung and considerable investments in agribusiness.[93]

The estimated total of all agribusiness buildings, improvements, equipment, and livestock in 1983 was $283,824,000; of all agribusiness land holdings, $1,900,114,000. Together all agribusiness holdings (land and other considerations) were estimated to be worth $2,183,938,000.

Table 3–9 *Estimated Value of LDS Church Granaries and Flour Mills (1983)*

LOCATION	BUSHEL CAPACITY	APPROXIMATE REPLACEMENT COST PER BUSHEL	ESTIMATED VALUE
Atlanta, Ga.*	50,000	$4.30	$ 225,000
Burley, Idaho	1,300,000	$2.15	$ 2,795,000
Colton, Calif.*	160,000	$3.50	$ 560,000
Denver, Colo.*	75,000	$4.30	$ 322,500
Elberta, Utah	500,000	$2.55	$ 1,275,000
Freemont, Calif.	40,000	$4.30	$ 172,000
Granger, Utah	400,000	$2.70	$ 1,080,000
Hermistown, Oreg.*	500,000	$2.55	$ 1,275,000
Indianapolis, Ind.*	50,000	$4.30	$ 215,000
Kaysville, Utah*	600,000	$2.45	$ 1,470,000
Lindon, Utah	20,000	$4.30	$ 86,000
Los Angeles, Calif.	200,000	$3.20	$ 640,000
McGrath, Alberta*	100,000	$4.10	$ 410,000
Mesa, Ariz.*	200,000	$3.20	$ 640,000
Murray, Utah	27,000	$4.30	$ 116,100
Patterson, Calif.	300,000	$3.20	$ 960,000
Pocatello, Idaho	50,000	$4.30	$ 215,000
Richmond, Va.	20,000	$4.30	$ 86,000
Sacramento, Calif.	40,000	$4.30	$ 172,000
Salt Lake City, Utah	300,000	$2.85	$ 855,000
San Diego, Calif.	75,000	$4.30	$ 322,500
San Fernando, Calif.	40,000	$4.30	$ 172,000
Seattle, Wash.	40,000	$4.30	$ 172,000
Spokane, Wash.	50,000	$4.30	$ 215,000
St. George, Utah	40,000	$4.30	$ 172,000
Ucon, Idaho	150,000	$3.50	$ 525,000
Washington, D.C.*	50,000	$4.30	$ 215,000

Total Bushel Capacity	5,377,000	Estimated Total Value (Granaries Only)	$15,353,000
		Estimated Total Value (Flour Mills, etc.)	9,000,000
Estimated Total Value of All Granaries, Flour Mills, etc.			$24,353,000

*Flour Mills

Commercial Real Estate and Industrial Park Properties

The LDS Church owns approximately 30,000 acres of purchased or donated commercial properties that have been or are in the process of being developed or sold for profit. For example, in downtown Salt Lake City these include, among others, the ZCMI Center Mall, the Kennecott Office Building, the Hotel Utah and Temple Square Hotel, the Promised Valley Playhouse, and the Eagle Gate

Apartments. These properties alone are worth $204,000,000.[94] The LDS Church is the largest private property owner in the state of Utah.[95] But its commercial properties can also be found in Los Angeles, Phoenix, Boston, Kansas City (Mo.), Honolulu, Tokyo, São Paulo, Seoul, and Sydney.

Altogether these properties carry a conservative estimated 1983 market value of $757,382,000.

Historical Properties

The original Joseph Smith farm at Manchester, New York; the nearby Hill Cumorah; the Martin Harris farm near Palmyra, New York; the Carthage Jail at Carthage, Illinois, and much of nearby restored Nauvoo; the John Johnson farm at Hiram, Ohio — most non-Mormons would not recognize, much less care about, these properties. But to Mormons they have both historical and religious significance. They are to Mormons what the Holy Land is to other Christians and Jews. They make up something less than 20,000 acres, but in terms of tourism, renovation, and the Church's costs for preservation, they represent an important LDS investment.[96]

Our estimated total value of such LDS historical properties in 1983 is $50,107,800, the sum of the following specific holdings.

Church Archival and Library Holdings   No religion has ever possessed a more vital sense of its own history — its unique place in God's design for human events — than does Mormonism. This is undoubtedly a carryover from Old Testament Judaism with which Mormons so consciously identify. Their sense of history, coupled with their theological mission to scour the archives of the United States and Europe in search of more ancestors to baptize, has resulted in a strong value placed on saving records and documents. Mormons have always been careful about preserving records such as notes, diaries, correspondence, pamphlets, works of art, artifacts, and out-of-print publications. At Brigham Young University in Provo, at the Ricks College Library, in the Church's Historical Department library and genealogical library, and at its Granite Mountain vaults (to cite a few locations) the Church maintains extensive collections of written and, more recently, microfilmed data. These range from a first edition of the *Book of Mormon* (worth $7,500) to a page from the Gutenberg Bible to a copy of *Manuscript* *of Fixed-Star Catalogue* by Johann Hevelius (worth $50,000). There are good collections of rare anti-Mormon pamphlets and a nearly complete collection of first edition works by Charles Dickens, many with letters-laid-in by Dickens or autographed by him.

At Granite Mountain the Mormons store their genealogical files on 100-foot rolls of microfilm (processing some 60,000 rolls each year at $7.50 per roll). Deep within this impenetrable natural fortress high in Little Cottonwood Canyon, the Church hopes eventually to store records containing 6 billion names. Huge ten- and fourteen-ton steel vault doors and blast locks keep out contaminated air and provide access to the six vaults, which are semicircles lined with white corrugated steel stretching for about 200 feet. The caverns are entered through a bunker watched continuously by a closed-circuit television camera. The vaults were designed to withstand any major catastrophe, such as flood, earthquake, or even nuclear war. They have been characterized by one non-Mormon as "one of the most desperate monuments to the dream of human immortality."[97]

The total estimated value in 1983 of the Church's archival and library holdings is $157,717,000.[98]

Church Communications Holdings   In chapter 2 we paid particular attention to the theology and logic behind the LDS Church's considerable investments in all forms of mass communications. There is little need to review those figures here except to reiterate the bottom-line dollar estimate on Church communications holdings in 1983: $547,640,000.

Church Insurance Investments   The Beneficial Life Insurance Company was founded primarily to provide life insurance for members of the Church of Jesus Christ of Latter-day Saints. For years that was its single activity. In the past decade, however, Beneficial has been acquiring several other companies, with plans for expansion. Far from just a single subsidiary of the Church, it is now a major investment.[99]

The LDS Church's insurance portfolio reveals both life-health and property-casualty companies. The Deseret Mutual Benefit Association is directly owned by the Corporation of the President of the Church of Jesus Christ of Latter-day Saints (estimated value

$20,000,000). The Beneficial Life Group includes the Beneficial Life Insurance Company, the Continental Western Life Insurance Company, the Pacific Heritage Assurance Life Insurance Company, and the Western American Life Insurance Company. We estimated their combined value at $94,000,000.[100] The Utah Home Fire Insurance Company, first organized in 1886, has an estimated value of $4,000,000.

Altogether, as of 1983 the Church's insurance investments have an estimated market value of $118,500,000.

SUMMARY OF LDS CHURCH WEALTH

Throughout the previous pages we have frequently cited eight- and even nine-digit dollar estimates for Mormon Church holdings. These are careful assessments based on interviews and consultations with financial experts and other professionals as well as on research in specific industry publications. In most cases we actually were presented with two possible figures — a high probable and a low probable estimate — and settled on an average between them for our own estimates. Therefore we may well have underestimated a good deal of the LDS Church's wealth. We suspect this also because as we finished this estimation process new developments and business transactions of the Church became public, allowing us to check our estimates with true figures. A good example is Torbet Radio (a Church-owned advertising agency), which, according to *Broadcast* magazine, the Bonneville International Corporation sold in late 1983 to Selkirk Communications Ltd. of Toronto for about $11 million. This was $7,250,000 *more* than our own original best estimate of $3,750,000 based on January 1982 interviews with Torbet personnel and others, cited in Chapter 2.

Thus the "final" figures we arrived at here are not really final. Despite our efforts to validate estimates and continually update them as we prepared this book, there is a more than even chance that the wealth of the LDS Church is greater than we have indicated. Before making a final comment on the implications of this enormous wealth, we summarize our findings on the Church's assets in Table 3–10.

Table 3- 10 Total Assets of the LDS Church (1983)

Lands and buildings (meetinghouses, other religious edifices, temples, educational facilities, agribusiness holdings, commercial real estate and industrial park properties, historical properties)	$7,071,576,000
Church archival and library holdings	157,717,000
Church insurance companies	118,500,000
Church communications properties	547,640,000
Total	$7,895,433,000

A FINAL LOOK

The inevitable question many people will want to ask is "But how does LDS Church wealth compare to that of the much older Roman Catholic Church and other religious groups?" In the case of the Roman Catholic Church, property, stock portfolios, and other holdings are owned by individual dioceses, not by Rome, so such a comparison of total wealth is not feasible. Nor can comparisons of Mormon wealth easily be made with other American religious groups, however we might wish it. Some groups, like the Christian Scientists, jealously guard information on such basic facts as their overall membership size. No studies have been done on their wealth. Other groups, such as mainline denominations like the United Methodists, the Southern Baptists, or the various Lutheran groups, have not yet been comparably studied. Such organizations blend into mainstream respectability so well that most scholars have not asked probing questions about their capital investments, diversified assets, and so forth.

In fact, very little is known in social science about the economic operation of religious institutions. The entire subject has been largely cloaked in secrecy by the religious groups themselves and avoided by polite journalists and researchers. The few groups that have yielded facts about their financial operations have in general done so unwillingly in court litigations and government investigations or through defectors who exposed what they knew, the Unification Church of Sun Myung Moon being a prime example. Many scholars consider the LDS Church's success such an anomaly in the history of frequent failures in most American sectarian religions, so valid comparison with other groups, even if more information were available, might not be possible.[101]

In a few areas, such as mass communications, we know the LDS Church dwarfs any other group of religious owners and investors. The much-publicized "televangelists" of the "electronic church," such as the Reverends Jerry Falwell, Oral Roberts, and Jim Bakker, are small-time by comparison.[102] Likewise, the millions of dollars of self-appointed messiahs like Sun Myung Moon, much ballyhooed by the sensationalist press, are not even in the same league.[103]

Moreover, control of the Mormons' vast wealth is concentrated in the hands of a small group of directors. We know from the structure of the Church hierarchy that no more than a dozen men really make significant decisions about investment policies and priorities. As we saw from recent changes made in the Church's stock investment plans, the religious outlooks and preoccupations of just a relatively few key persons can affect hundreds of millions of dollars and, indirectly, the lives and careers of millions of Church members tied by employment and investment to those monies.

In our final chapter we consider broader implications of any religion's holding such power. Here we conclude by noting that the very virtues that helped the Mormons overcome persecution, tame a virtually barren wilderness, and move beyond mere survival into true prosperity have created a corporate monolith that may irrevocably be crushing out many of those virtues. Prosperity in religious sects in the past has produced public acceptance, which Mormons have desperately wanted and largely achieved, but also compromise. The cost of succeeding in a Gentile economy is that Gentile standards of success have to be acknowledged. This economic success is a new yoke on the necks of many Mormons, wrote LDS scholar Marden Clark, and it must be lifted if the Church is to survive spiritually. He warned Mormon readers:

> Our emphasis on welfare, food storage, staying out of debt, sound finances, and so forth has made many of us hyper-conscious of the role of money in our lives. We have placed a good deal of emphasis on success, both monetary and otherwise. It is no accident that some of the best known of the new breed of financial advisors are Mormons. All those hundreds of talks on success are

both symptom and cause. So is our intense preoccupation with and honoring of the wealthy, the famous, the champion. We almost canonize our Willard Marriotts, our Johnny Millers, our Danny Ainges, our Osmonds. . . I can't help wondering if some of the things we glory in most don't get twisted to support the easy-money hunger.[104]

Yet this financial success is precisely what must happen, according to the Church's ambitions for a literal Kingdom of God on earth ruled by the Saints. Modern nations have generally become strangers to theocracy, but in an era of rapid transportation, instant communication, and high finance the old rules may no longer apply. No one can predict the amount of national and international stability to come, for example, and how such factors will interact with Church goals is an unknown. To better interpret the Church's attempts to chart its own destiny, however, we need to examine its political as well as its economic power.

4

Political and Military Power of the Latter-day Saints

P resident Ronald Reagan wrote to Jacob Edwin Garn, son of U.S. Senator Jake Garn, shortly before the young man left to do Mormon missionary work in England: "I have such great respect for your Church...Although I am not a Mormon, I very much respect your Mormon values."[1]

What are these values? We have already mentioned many of them: courage, resourcefulness, independence, volunteerism, honesty. Others, as we will see, include patriotism and conservatism. Reagan's full letter to the younger Garn was a classic statement of the popular late-twentieth-century image of Mormons. This image was confirmed in an October 1983 national Gallup poll, which showed that positive reactions of respondents to Mormonism far outnumbered negative ones. As George Gallup, Jr., summed up his results, "The Church of Jesus Christ of Latter-day Saints, while representing only about one percent of the adult population in the United States, is clearly having a profound impact on the United States as a whole."[2]

Gallup was right. Although Mormons were once persecuted by the federal government, many Mormons today have risen into the highest ranks of civilian and military power. While we do not suggest they have done so because of any conspiracy or grand design, nevertheless on occasion, as we demonstrate in this chapter, the LDS leadership has appealed to these members' loyalties as a lever for exerting Church influence on domestic and international policies of the U.S. government. The Mormon Church is indeed having a "profound impact" on American society. This impact has been produced not so much by any moral example the Church sets as by the assimilation of certain Mormons into key national institutions. Before examining Mormon connections to political and military power, however, it is useful to consider briefly the historical ambivalence of Mormonism toward the political realm of its original enemies, the Gentiles.

MORMONISM AND CAESAR

Mormonism in the twentieth century holds what could be called an ambivalent attitude toward the U.S. government and politics. The repression and rejection that Mormons suffered from federal officials even some years after LDS President Wilford Woodruff had issued the 1890 Manifesto repealing polygamy are not forgotten. It must be added that earlier Mormon leaders were not reticent in their response, frequently reviling U.S. presidents with fervor. For example, in 1857 LDS President Heber C. Kimball prophesied about U.S. President James Buchanan:

Will the President that sits in the chair of state be tipped from his seat? Yes, he will die an untimely death, and God Almighty will curse him; and He will also curse his successor, if he takes the same anti-Mormon stand.[3]

Though Church leaders today are kinder toward national executives, many still foresee a coming erosion and weakening of the U.S. government until "the Constitution hangs by a thread," to be rescued by the LDS Church with its divine mandate. The U.S. government is, in their view, only a temporary convenience until the Church has established its millennial kingdom. First Amendment freedoms are divinely provided as fertile soil to allow the seed of Joseph Smith's revelations to take root and thrive. But ultimately the social order and government that sponsored such a nurturing climate will be replaced. This was the vision of the early Church leaders, and it is still commonly presented to Mormons today. It can be seen in the following excerpt from a 1982 (*not* 1882) *Church News* editorial:

Most people in this nation do not understand the origin and destiny of the United States as the Latter-day Saints do. . . How wonderful it would be if all Americans viewed the marvelous country in which we live in the same light as the Latter-day Saints. . . .

The Lord created the United States for a specific purpose. He provided freedom of speech, press, assembly and worship. . . .

Here He had determined to restore the gospel. From here it would be taken abroad. From here, during the Millennium, Christ will govern the world.[4]

Yet, as we will show in this chapter, most Mormons are proud of their patriotism and are strongly anti-Communist and pro–U.S. military. They are particularly recruited for ROTC programs and for positions in the Central Intelligence Agency and other parts of the intelligence community because of these sentiments. Mormonism is the most successful, totally home-grown American religion, and its members have never forgotten their nationalist roots. Even in 1846, during the time of persecution, 500 Mormon volunteers went to fight in the Mexican-American War. Fifteen years later, a volunteer regiment of Mormons fought in the Civil War.[5]

Mormons cannot help being involved in the political arena; it is their heritage. Partly because they know the Church's fate is irrevocably tied to that of the United States and partly because they have learned that without influence in the political estate they cannot hope to move beyond this society, Mormons involve themselves in temporal politics to an extent unusual for a millennial movement. J. D. Williams, a Mormon and a professor of political science at the University of Utah, sees Mormon political activities as a means to ensure Church progress:

The Church of Jesus Christ of Latter-day Saints or its individual leaders have never been able to ignore Caesar's world for very long. Caesar has not always been kind to Mormons, and Mormons have consequently sought to have Caesar with them rather than against them.[6]

Williams has outlined the reasons behind Mormon involvement in politics. Such involvement, he believes, is inevitable but at the same time provokes uncertainty and dilemmas for many Church members who want also to be good citizens.

Where do loyalty and duty lie, for example, when your Stake President asks you as president of the Mormon Elders' Quorum to have your quorum distribute campaign pamphlets for a one-senator-per-county reapportionment measure — a measure you strongly disapprove?...What should your reaction be when an Apostle of your Church uses the pulpit at General Conference to charge the President of the United States, whom you worked to elect, with unconstitutional programs which are leading the nation to socialism?[7]

Williams identified four characteristics of Mormonism that can help us understand the Church's (and its members') political activities. First is the Church's emphasis on *continuing modern-day revelation* through inspired LDS leaders. One recent *Church News* editorial put it plainly:

No man holds divine authority equal to or above the president of the Church. In his position he is pre-eminent!
Let us understand fully the clear identity of the president of the Church. He is the mouthpiece of God on earth for us today.[8]

As Williams notes, such a doctrine has political significance because of the belief of many Mormons that Church leaders' divine inspiration might be transferred to secular (including political) affairs.

A second important characteristic is the Church's strong line of authority. The church is a hierarchical pyramid, and even the lowest ward committee clerk can trace his or her authority upward through the ward bishop, stake officials, and ultimately to the current LDS president and prophet. Conversely, revelations, whether on sacred or secular matters, can quickly (and with minimal challenge) be passed down to rank-and-file members.

A third related characteristic is the Church's organization at the grass roots ward level. Active Mormons are united in a network that can mobilize them for Church purposes quickly and efficiently, as we demonstrate in the next section. However, the millions of American Mormons are not homogeneous in their political sympathies. Given the first two characteristics, it is obvious that there is potential within the Mormon organization for a fair amount of friction.

Fourth, the *Book of Mormon* and early Church history contain precedents both for and against political involvement. For instance, Mormon tradition and leaders regard the U.S. Constitution as a divinely revealed document; hence, the First Amendment's separation of church and state is also considered inviolate while the government still stands. Yet early Mormon leaders, like many figures in the *Book of Mormon,* wore several hats. Joseph Smith was the first Church president *and* mayor of Nauvoo, Illinois, *and* general of the Nauvoo Legion militia. In 1844 he even announced himself as a candidate for the presidency of the United States. His successor, Brigham Young, was simultaneously president of the Church and territorial governor from 1850 to 1858.

Despite the tensions that political involvement can cause, Mormons have many reasons for not remaining aloof from such affairs. Political involvement is in the best interests of the Church's millennial mission. It is also a natural consequence of Mormons' unquestioned success in other spheres of American society.

MORMON POLITICAL CLOUT

In 1898 Elder Brigham H. Roberts campaigned for Congress and won a seat in the House of Representatives. He was allowed to run only with the cautious permission of the First Presidency. In 1895 Church leaders had issued a Political Manifesto, "which attested that the Church had not been involved in politics and required henceforth that all high officeholders in the Church should obtain prior clearance from their ecclesiastical superiors before ever running for political office."[9] (One candidate, an apostle in the Council of the Twelve named Moses Thatcher, had not sought such permission. As punishment for his insubordination he was dropped from the Council and denounced as an apostate.) Roberts had been given the Church's blessing and won the election, yet the House of Representatives refused to seat him because he was an admitted polygamist.

Roberts's example shows just how far the LDS Church has come in a little over eighty years. Not only are Church leaders now enthusiastic about members seeking public office in state and national governments, but these governments in turn no longer discriminate against them. Far from it. Mormons are among the most astute political creatures in America, and their acceptance in national government is the best evidence of this.

Reed Smoot, not Brigham H. Roberts, established Mormon legitimacy in national politics. Smoot was elected to the Senate (as a Republican) not long after being ordained an LDS apostle in 1902. Like Roberts, he found his seat challenged, this time because anti-Mormons believed the Church still secretly practiced polygamy. And this time, improving on its efforts in the Roberts case, the Church fought back masterfully. During the three years of investigations, hearings, and controversy that elapsed before Smoot was finally installed as a Senator, Church leaders paraded before committees and the press in Washington, D.C., to testify to the Church's benign, antipolygamous nature. In the Smoot struggle the Church had a perfect opportunity to develop and hone its public relations skills. LDS representatives performed well. When the smoke had finally cleared, the Senate investigating committee still recommended to deny Smoot his seat, but the Senate as a whole had been so impressed with what they had heard and seen that they installed him over all objections.

Smoot went on to a distinguished thirty-year career in the Senate. In a progressive era when government began to enact many social reforms advocated by liberals, Smoot was regarded as a conservative. Serving on numerous Senate committees, he always kept a sharp eye on expenditures. In 1922 President Warren G. Harding appointed him to the World War Foreign Debt Commission. Later Smoot became chairman of the powerful Senate Finance Committee as well as a recognized expert on tariffs. Here he used his influence to pass the Smoot-Hawley Tariff Act, which, by raising stiff tariffs on foreign imports and by angering numerous foreign exporters, may have triggered a global trade war that caused the crash of 1929 on Wall Street.[10]

Smoot gradually gained the image of being his own man, but he continued discreetly to look out for the Church's interests. In Chapter 2 we cited the 1921 case when Smoot and movie producer William Fox traded Smoot's opposition to pending legislation on a motion picture tax for Fox's removal from movie houses of a film unflattering to Mormons. Other times he directly promoted their economic interests. During the 1920s the Church invested heavily in the domestic sugar industry. Despite considerable opposition in the Senate, Smoot succeeded in raising protective tariffs on imported sugar. In August 1922 Church President Heber J. Grant wrote to thank Smoot for obtaining a higher duty to be levied on Cuban sugar.[11] Grant had had another reason to be grateful the previous year. In 1921 the Church had been trying to work its way out of debt and was having trouble obtaining loans from New York banks until Smoot arranged for it to receive a $10 million loan from the War Finance Corporation.[12] Given federal aid, the Church suddenly became a creditor with a much better rating and found other lending institutions more than willing to help it.

Before and shortly after World War II several other outstanding Mormon men made their mark in Washington, D.C., establishing the confidence of Gentile administrators. J. Reuben Clark, Jr., who later joined the First Presidency of the Church, served under seven American presidents in a variety of capacities: as assistant solicitor and later solicitor for the Department of State; in the judge advocate general's office; as a counsel to the State Department and on various other commissions; as under secretary of state; as ambassador to Mexico; and in many other roles. Marriner S. Eccles, a successful Utah businessman, became secretary of the Treasury in 1934 and that same year was nominated to be chairman of the Federal Reserve Board, a post he held until 1951. Unlike his contemporary Smoot, Eccles advocated deficit spending to stimulate the economy and was a champion of Roosevelt's New Deal.

Another Mormon New Dealer was Senator Elbert D. Thomas, a former University of Utah professor, who served in office from 1932 to 1951. Unlike many influential Mormons, Thomas was pro-labor and pro-union nationally and internationally. He served on many important Senate committees (such as Foreign Relations, Civil Liberties, Labor and Public Welfare, Military Affairs, and Education and Labor). A politician of a different ideological stripe, right-wing Ezra Taft Benson (who in 1985 was president of the Council of the Twelve, next in line to succeed Spencer W. Kimball as LDS president) served as secretary of agriculture for eight years, beginning in 1953 under President Dwight D. Eisenhower. During those years Benson proposed much important agricultural legislation that later shaped federal policies toward government subsidies of farmers.

Things have definitely changed since the days of the Political

Manifesto. A number of current or recent apostles and members of the First Presidency have backgrounds that include politics, among them the following:

N. Eldon Tanner	Former minister of lands and mines and legislator in Alberta, Canada
Marion G. Romney	Former Utah legislator
Ezra Taft Benson	Secretary of agriculture under Dwight D. Eisenhower
David B. Haight	Former mayor of Palo Alto, California, and governor of the San Francisco Bay Area Council of Mayors
Neal A. Maxwell	Former legislative assistant to U.S. Senator Wallace F. Bennett of Utah
James E. Faust	Former Utah legislator
Marvin J. Ashton	Former Utah state senator

The *Deseret News 1983 Church Almanac* listed living Mormons who had served at high levels in the U.S. government. As of October 1982 they totaled seven Cabinet members, four sub-cabinet members, four ambassadors, twelve senators, and thirty-three representatives.[13] There has also been a host of Mormons working in the government who attract little publicity but nevertheless wield influence, for example:

Richard Richards, until 1983 head of the Republican National Committee; stayed on as consultant to it. He was a conservative but not doctrinaire enough for the New Right enthusiasts who predominated during the first few years of the Reagan administration.

David C. Fischer, a 1976 Brigham Young University Law School graduate, worked for Reagan in previous campaigns and became special assistant to the president when Reagan took office.

Terrel H. Bell, former U.S. secretary of education.

Paul H. Dunn, of the Church's First Council of the Seventy, appointed by Terrel H. Bell to the National Higher Education Board.

Gregory J. Newell II, director of *all* of Reagan's appointments and scheduling in 1981–82. Previously he worked for two years in the White House under President Gerald Ford.

Rex E. Lee, former dean of the BYU Law School; named solicitor general by Reagan. (The solicitor represents the federal government in cases before the Supreme Court.) He won the case in which the Supreme Court ruled that Congress' use of the legislative veto over presidents is unconstitutional.

Charles C. Cox, Securities and Exchange commissioner, nominated by Utah Senator Jake Garn, chair of the Senate Banking Committee.

Angela M. Buchanan, treasurer of the United States.

Richard Wirthlin, former BYU professor, Reagan's pollster and adviser.

Steve Studdert and Rocky Kuonen, both in charge of all advance preparations for trips the president makes away from the Oval Office.

The list could be much longer. In many cases these Mormons were recruited or appointed to important government positions through an informal network of other influential LDS Church members. While professional and other types of networks are a standard way for politicians to recruit qualified persons for appointed positions, the significance of the Mormon network is that it has direct links to the LDS Church leaders in Salt Lake City. Curt Burnett, press secretary for Utah's (Republican) Senator Jake Garn, described such networking in action as he reported that Garn had been "very instrumental" in having about two dozen LDS members (most from Utah) appointed to top-level positions in Washington. These people, Burnett further explained, did not include the hundreds of other Mormons recruited for important positions in the federal government since President Reagan took office in 1981. Burnett credited much of this recruitment to Reagan's personal enthusiasm about the LDS Church and to Senator Paul Laxalt (R-Utah) who helped the President select talented Mormons for specific jobs. Garn's press secretary pointed out another result of Reagan's respect for Mormonism: the President's much-publicized

New Federalism program, which turned over more responsibility for social services and other expenses to individual states, in part borrowed from his advisers' understanding of the LDS welfare program. Burnett also stated that LDS Church leaders were pleased with these developments. Prior to the Reagan administration there were only seven LDS stakes in the Washington, D.C.–Virginia area. By early 1982 there were nine stakes, and wards were being formed on an ongoing basis. In fact, the nation's capital recently achieved the distinction of having the largest concentration of Church members east of the Mississippi. Burnett said with pride: "From an LDS point of view, this gives us a tremendous amount of leverage in the ways things are done in Washington."[14]

We do not mean to suggest that all Mormons in Washington vote on or promote every policy with some knee-jerk concern for how the Salt Lake City elders will react. There is evidence to the contrary. One study done in the late 1960s found that Mormon legislators in the House of Representatives and the Senate noticeably disagreed on such issues as the 1965 Voting Rights Bill, most voting in ways consistent with their party affiliations and political views. When the LDS Church sent each of them a letter stating the Church's position on the bill, they reacted differently. Some resented it, others ignored it. The reactions were largely partisan (Democrats were more negative than positive, and vice versa for Republicans). This is not surprising, given that at the time five of the ten Mormon representatives represented districts that were not made up predominantly of LDS members.[15]

Yet many Mormons in public service are conscious of their role as informal emissaries of the Church and use their official influence to further Church interests. A prime example are the Mormon former ambassadors to Norway (Mark Austad), Sweden (Franklin S. Forsberg), and Finland (Keith F. Nyborg). Keith Nyborg (a former ward bishop, branch president, and officer in a stake presidency) told a *Church News* reporter in 1982 of the overlap between his religious outlook and his diplomatic duties:

We are here because the Lord wants us here; it is not really of our own doing and not entirely political. . . If people ask about the Church, we can explain. But we don't want the news media to pick up on our Church membership and make it a public cause.

The reporter added: "The Finnish LDS public communications office noted that during the year the Nyborgs have been here [in Finland], the Church has been given 1,260 inches of publicity in the press; the year before, it was only 70 inches."[16]

By looking at Utah's best-known national LDS legislators, Senators Orrin Hatch and Jake Garn, we can see this sort of attention paid to Church concerns closer to home. Hatch is well known for his polished, smooth demeanor and his reliance on careful preparation rather than oratory or bluster. In the 97th and 98th Congresses of the early to mid-1980s he wielded considerable influence on Capitol Hill. He is chairman of the Labor and Human Resources Committee (which oversees the Departments of Labor, Education, and Health and Human Services). He serves on the Judiciary Committee (where he is chairman of the Subcommittee on the Constitution). In addition, he serves on the Senate's Budget and Small Business Committees. By appointment of the vice-president of the United States, Orrin Hatch is U.S. delegate to the International Labor Organization in Geneva, Switzerland, and a commissioner on the Commission for Security and Cooperation in Europe. Hatch was rated as one of the top five young senators by the *National Journal* in his first two years in the Senate. In 1981 columnist Jack Anderson named him one of the Senate's ten most effective members.

One Salt Lake City editorial called Hatch an "outrider for the later-arriving wave of conservatives from the Far West who now dominate the Senate."[17] Thoroughly conservative in philosophy, Hatch opposes busing for integration, affirmative action, parts of the Voting Rights Act (he favors an amendment that would ban racial discrimination only if intentional bias can be proved), and the openness provisions of the Freedom of Information Act. He voted against a special bill creating a national holiday honoring slain civil rights leader Martin Luther King, Jr., and helped kill a bill creating a national clearinghouse to monitor family violence in North America. He held hearings on a constitutional amendment that he designed to overturn the Supreme Court decision permitting abortion. To no one's surprise, he vigorously opposed the Equal Rights Amendment. In line with Mormon beliefs, he has also fought for stiffer warnings on cigarette packages about possible cancer dangers as well as an amendment to the Constitution permitting voluntary prayer in public schools.

Environmentalists have criticized him for being "soft" on anti-pollution laws. Labor unions have seen him as anti-union. Before a University of Utah audience, consumer advocate Ralph Nader accused Orrin Hatch and his Utah colleague Jake Garn of representing a government that is "indentured to powerful corporate interest." Said Nader: "[Hatch and Garn] consistently support programs that are not in the interest of their constituency, including tax loopholes for the oil industry and other 'corporate welfare' programs, and increasing their own salaries and tax breaks while opposing anti-trust enforcement."[18]

Hatch's positions on these issues are no different from those of many other conservatives. Hatch, however, could play a vital role in the appointing of Mormons to important jobs in the federal government and, as an elected public official, can promote Mormon values. Hatch declares that, "In the whole four years that I have been in the Senate, I have yet to have any General Authority of the LDS Church give me any instructions concerning how I should vote back in Washington, and I would be shocked if one did...I don't think any church should dictate how a state or federal government should act."[19] Hatch does, however, maintain ties with the LDS leadership. One of his staff assistants mentioned to us that Hatch makes at least one visit each year to the First Presidency, reporting on his activities in Washington, and also attends the semi-annual General Conference in Salt Lake City. On occasion Hatch has done simple favors for Church leaders and consulted with them on legislation. During the late 1970s, for example, the LDS Church was cultivating contacts in the People's Republic of China, in the hope of eventually sending missionaries there. At the request of the LDS "Special Affairs Committee," Hatch arranged such contacts between Gordon B. Hinckley and the Chinese. In 1982 the committee again approached Hatch, asking him to arrange an introduction between Church representatives and other foreign dignitaries, including the Soviet ambassador.

On the domestic scene Hatch's political activities have sometimes reflected close sympathy with Church policies. His staff assistant recalled that during the Carter administration, a bill entitled the Family Protection Act (which would provide federal funds to aid the victims — women and children — of family violence and would help establish women's shelters) was introduced into Congress. Hatch got in touch with the First Presidency's Gordon Hinckley about the bill. Church leaders made it clear that they felt the bill offered the prospect of too much government involvement in family affairs. Hatch was prepared to filibuster but managed to stall the bill in committee until Congress adjourned in the fall 1980. When Congress reconvened, the Republicans had swept into power after the Reagan landslide election victory. The bill was never resurrected. Hatch's staff assistant predicted the same fate for the Equal Rights Amendment (a red-flag issue for Mormon leaders) if supporters tried to reintroduce a bill promoting it. As chairman of the Subcommittee on the Constitution of the Senate Judiciary Committee, he speculated, Hatch would attempt to delay and defeat any such bill.[20]

The Special Affairs Committee mentioned above is the public policy research arm of the Church. The committee monitors and researches any legislation that affects the Church or its mission, such as the Equal Rights Amendment, mission work in Communist countries, and tax exemptions. Begun officially in the mid-1970s, the committee was chaired in 1982 by Gordon B. Hinckley, who also played an instrumental role in creating it. It is a major conduit for the exchange of information and viewpoints between Church leaders and legislators in Washington.

A profile of Senator Jake Garn closely resembles that of Orrin Hatch. Garn sits on or chairs a number of very influential committees. He is chairman of the Senate Banking, Housing and Urban Affairs Committee, which has jurisdiction over the nation's entire financial sector as well as over all federal housing programs and all programs related to cities, such as federal grants for urban renewal. He is on the Senate Appropriations Committee, considered by many to be the most powerful in the Senate because it must approve all federal spending. He is also chairman of the Appropriations Committee Sub-Committee for HUD-Independent Agencies. These positions have earned Garn the nickname "Housing Czar of America" since the chairman of the Banking Committee authorizes spending for housing programs while the chairman of the Appropriations Sub-Committee actually allocates the money for housing. Thus Garn significantly influences much of the legislation concerning cities and homes from beginning to end.

It seems clear that conflicts of loyalties must come up for public

officials, elected or appointed, who also belong to a millennial movement pledged to someday turn this nation into a theocracy. Like
John F. Kennedy, who took pains during his presidential campaign
to assure voters that his primary loyalty as U.S. President would
be to the Constitution rather than to the Vatican, sensitive Mormon
politicians have anticipated the question of conflict of loyalties and
have denied that it has any basis. But from our interviews and the
cases cited in support, we doubt that such a conflict can be so easily
dismissed. Mormon political scientist J. D. Williams observes that

> the practice of Church officials making suggestions to public ad-
> ministrators and lawmakers [since the Church's early days in
> Missouri and Illinois] has never died...In the legislative area,
> relations between Church officials and law makers are still very
> direct. Some are out-in-the-open for the public to see; others are
> behind the scenes. Communiqués to members of Congress are
> periodically sent by the First Presidency. Two famous ones were
> the 1946 admonition to the Utah Congressional delegation to
> oppose a peacetime draft and the 1965 letter to all Mormons in
> Congress to resist the repeal of "right-to-work" laws.[21]

The Church is bolder in Utah and more circumspect in
Washington, D.C., but the operating principle is the same: the designation *Mormon* politician/bureaucrat/official is supposed to mean,
at least in the eyes of some Church officials, special consideration
of LDS Church interests.

This does not mean that Mormon politicians cannot think for
themselves. J. D. Williams notes that five of the Mormon representatives and senators "sternly" replied to the First Presidency's
letter on repeal of the right-to-work laws with a statement asserting
that while they respected and revered the First Presidency of the
Church, they could not "yield to others" their responsibilities to
their constituencies. One member of the First Presidency is reported
to have then good-naturedly commented: "They have the right to
tell us to jump in the lake, and they did just that."[22]

While we are a long way in the United States from a theocracy,
there is nevertheless a *de facto* effort under way that is something
of the sort, not just in Utah but in Washington, D.C. We do not have
the space to review every present Mormon legislator in Washington. But we have described the Mormon network of politicians in

the nation's capital, representing the United States abroad as well, that in the course of meeting daily responsibilities uses official government channels to advance the LDS Church's causes. Their activity does not by any means constitute a conspiracy, for much of it occurs aboveboard though it is not rigorously publicized by the media. Rather, it is something more akin to a social movement.

To an extent the LDS Church has "arrived." No longer the target of official sanctions and repression, it now has a growing voice in shaping domestic policies of the U.S. government.

Grass Roots Mormon Politics

In 1978 Oscar McConkie, an attorney for the Salt Lake City law firm that handles most of the LDS Church's legal work, exhorted a Brigham Young University audience:

> We ought to legislate morality. My experience is that we legislate very little else, but it's a question of whose morality do we legislate — the Lord's or somebody else's?
>
> If we could only convince ourselves that we are the agents of the Lord, we would surely make God's purposes our own. That is what we ought to be doing in the political process.[23]

That is the attitude of many Church leaders: that the democratic process should serve as a vehicle for advancing the millennium according to Mormonism. Some go further. In February 1974 Apostle Ezra Taft Benson was asked during an interview if a good Mormon could also be a liberal Democrat. Benson pessimistically replied: "I think it would be very hard if he was living the gospel and understood it." To this extreme position Ralph Harding, a two-term Idaho Democratic congressman and a Mormon, retorted:

> In fact it is much easier to be a faithful Latter-day Saint and a liberal Democrat than it is to be a faithful church member and a member of the John Birch Society . . . Compassion and tolerance are attributes that are found in faithful church members and liberal Democrats, but seldom in John Birchers and other extreme rightwingers.[24]

How much effect do LDS leadership attitudes have at Mormonism's grass roots level? A lot, state Democratic leaders feel. The image of Republicanism is perceived by many faithful Saints as more closely aligned with Mormon values than that of Democratism. Dale Lambert, an active Mormon and former Democratic party state chairman, has seen many well-known Mormons who declared themselves Democrats when they ran for office and subsequently lost. He said in an interview:

> Our efforts to run a middle course and be true to Democratic constituencies while still appealing to the majority haven't worked. We hear some brave talk, but the party is very discouraged.[25]

There is a joke in Salt Lake City expressing a feeling that Mormon Democrats say they know well. It goes:

> I thought I saw Brother Williams in the Temple last week. Why that's impossible. He's a Democrat, you know.[26]

To Utah Democrats, however, it's no joke. Though many Mormons may not go as far as Ezra Taft Benson in equating membership in the Democratic party with apostasy, Republican philosophy seems to have an edge at election time. Ed Firmage, a University of Utah law professor, liberal Mormon Democrat, and former congressional candidate, thinks the LDS Church should take responsibility both for perpetuating the idea that good Mormons have to be Republicans and for dismantling the stereotype in the future. Said Firmage:

> My main concern isn't as a Democrat, but as a Mormon. We need to look at the universality of the gospel message. The basic Church principles are not liberal or conservative or Republican or Democratic.[27]

Otherwise, Mormon Democrats warn that Republican and Democratic parties would essentially turn into Mormon and Gentile parties, threatening a return to the political polarization of the 1870s in Utah when the Liberal party (founded to represent Utah Gentiles who felt left out of power) engaged in some nasty mud-slinging campaigns against the LDS People's party.

The Republican state chairman, Charles W. Akerlow, disagreed with these published predictions. In his own statement to the press he claimed Utah Democrats were "crying wolf." "Far too much is being made out of this issue," he said, blaming Democrats' woes on their own "tactical errors" and their liberal image. In his analysis,

> their problem is they keep adopting positions that Utahns don't
> like . . . they should just quit whining and blaming the church and
> get good candidates running on the right issues — and they'd win.[28]

Mormon sociologist Armand Mauss set out to study this question systematically in the late 1960s with two surveys of 1,300 Mormons in Salt Lake City and a coastal city in California. Suspicious of claims that Mormon rank-and-file members as well as leaders were overwhelmingly conservative, Mauss observed: "An impression of conservative Republican proclivities as dominant . . . certainly cannot be derived from the voting history of Utah during the present century, nor from the party affiliations of Mormon congressmen, who have been largely Democrats for some years."[29] Mauss found that the majority of the Mormons he studied better fit the description "moderate" than "conservative." Less than a fifth could be considered right wing. His respondents were split almost fifty-fifty into Democratic and Republican camps. Mauss admitted that this is a much larger Republican percentage than can be found in the general population but certainly nothing like a landslide mandate for conservative Republicanism. In addition, the Mormon respondents were rather tolerant of minorities and much less anti-Semitic than other sectarian Christians have been on past surveys. Although Mauss did not say how many of his respondents were actually registered voters, it is safe to assume that many were.

Yet Mormons are part of a larger hierarchical network. Even if their partisan sympathies are moderate and split between the two major political parties, they are still subject periodically to pressures for political action that appeal to the Mormon brand of morality rather than a political ideology. A good illustration of this pressure is the Church's involvement in the drive to kill the Equal Rights Amendment.

The Case of the Equal Rights Amendment

The proposed Equal Rights Amendment to the U.S. Constitution stated:

> Equality of rights under the law shall not be denied or abridged
> by the United States or by any state on account of sex.

A number of conservative groups aimed to stop state legislatures' ratification of this amendment. Some represented the "new religious right," such as Reverend Jerry Falwell's Moral Majority, Inc., and Phyllis Schlafly's Eagle Forum. Others, like the LDS Church and the Roman Catholic Church, were part of what social scientists term the "old religious right." Much of the opposition to the ERA, aside from the fact that it was clearly an outgrowth of feminism and secular liberalism, arose from fears that the traditional roles of men and women would be radically reshaped. Conservatives argued that, armed with the ERA, the federal government would have the authority to seek out sexism within religions and other private arenas. For example, in June 1983 a subcommittee of the Senate Judiciary Committee, chaired by Utah Senator Orrin Hatch, held hearings on the ERA. Hatch questioned pro-ERA witness Massachusetts Senator Paul Tsongas about the amendment's implications for his own western bailiwick:

> There are many churches in this country which deny various rights to women in the exercise of their religious doctrine. The Roman Catholic Church, for instance, denies priesthood to women. The Mormon Church limits certain positions to men. The orthodox Jewish synagogue segregates men and women. In your opinion, would the ERA allow such churches to continue to have tax exemptions and other public benefits?[30]

This line of reasoning admittedly rises above many of the sillier arguments heard at the time, such as the one deploring the ERA because it would force men and women to use the same public restrooms. Hatch's position on the Senate Judiciary Committee also brought publicity to one particular pro-ERA spokesperson, Virginia's Sonia Johnson, who founded Mormons for ERA and was excommunicated by the LDS Church in 1979. (The Church claimed apostasy, not politics; Johnson disagreed, claiming that all she had done was to expose the Church's anti-ERA pressures to which she had refused to accede.) Because several other potential witnesses for the pro-ERA position were unable to attend the hearings on extending the ratification date for the ERA, Sonia Johnson agreed to appear on behalf of Mormons for ERA. A disapproving Orrin Hatch "put on his priesthood voice" (as Mormons would put it) and rebuked her as a Mormon woman, not just as a citizen, before national television cameras, making her an instant celebrity.[31]

More important, the ERA controversy demonstrated the Church's willingness to engage in a lobbying campaign to stop legislation it did not like. Its ability to mobilize grass roots members to oppose the ERA actually was previewed in June 1977 at a two-day meeting of the Utah Women's Conference authorized by the National Commission on the Observance of International Women's Year. This conference was among fifty similar ones held in every state (and funded by Congress) as a consequence of the International Women's Year conference held in 1976 in Mexico City. The main task of each state convention was twofold: (1) to elect fourteen delegates to the national International Women's Year Conference at Houston in November 1977 and (2) to vote on a number of women-oriented policy resolutions drawn up by the National Commission, including proposals covering federally funded day-care centers for working mothers, abortion, and the ERA.

Word went out through the LDS Women's Relief Society, which has chapters in every ward, for each ward Relief Society president to recruit ten women to attend the Utah conference. Mormon writer Dixie Snow Huefner recalled when her Relief Society president asked her to help gather local LDS women as participants. The official assured her that the Church was not trying to instruct Mormon women how to vote but merely wanted to encourage them to attend and reflect "church standards whenever appropriate." A leader in Huefner's stake Relief Society, however, remarked that the conference would be too "liberal" if Mormon women were not present.[32]

Huefner learned of similar approaches made to other Mormon women, some of them directly told by ward leaders how to vote on issues such as the ERA. A letter from the national president of the Relief Society, originally calling for Mormon women to attend the conference, did not go so far but did encourage women to read the *Deseret News* for information about the conference's agenda and rules (the *Deseret News* meanwhile ran antifeminist/anti-ERA editorials). Women were asked to bring female friends, neighbors, and relatives who shared "mutual concerns."

Conference organizers originally had expected 3,000 participants. Instead, *more than 13,000* showed up. In essence, through the Women's Relief Society the Church packed the conference with Mormon women, many of whom were uninformed about the many issues addressed and hostile to what they saw as a feminist control of the conference (even though half the women on the coordinating committee were Mormons, including homemakers as well as professionals). Says observer Huefner:

> To judge by remarks heard from the floor of the convention, the fact that organizers and nominees were generally interested in the women's movement seemed both perverse and conspiratorial to most conference participants — who were not similarly interested and had therefore passed up chances to become involved until the Church had rallied them.[33]

The conference included a number of workshops on specific issues such as the ERA that were to result in resolutions to be voted on by all attending. Since most LDS women lacked information about many issues, special preconference caucuses were suddenly organized by Church leaders with heavily slanted anti-ERA/antifeminist speakers.

> Caucus leaders had represented the politically conservative forces opposed to abortion, the ERA, and the women's movement in general. They had used the Church's organizational mechanisms and their own Church affiliation to encourage attendance at the caucuses. Many persons in attendance accepted such representations unquestioningly, neither challenging the sources of the information nor checking its accuracy.[34]

Caucus attendees had many familiar anti-ERA "horror stories" paraded before them, linking the national resolutions (most of which were economic, such as equal pay for equal work and opening credit opportunities to women) to lesbianism, aborted fetuses, and sexual immorality. Huefner recalls that some caucuses were even told not to read the resolutions because some of them might "sound good" and therefore could deceive the women.[35]

In the end the Church succeeded in obstructing the purpose of the conference. According to the guidelines set down by the National Commission on the Observance of International Women's Year, the slate of fourteen delegates was to achieve geographic, occupational, religious, age, ethnic, and socioeconomic balance. The Mormon majority at the Utah conference ignored these guidelines, electing fourteen delegates and five alternates to the Houston conference, of whom all but one were Mormon, all were Caucasian, all were distinctly middle-class, all but one was forty years of age or older, all but one Republican, and all had been named on the anti-ERA and

anti-abortion "model slates" passed out at the doors of the conference. Moreover, every one of the resolutions drawn up by the National
Commission, including the ERA, was soundly defeated along with
a good many other more general propositions (such as removing legal
handicaps on rape victims). Dixie Snow Heufner summed up what
the Church had achieved by orchestrating this rejection of concerns
so important to so many women:

> A major factor in the negative vote was obviously the acknowl-
> edged philosophical opposition of the majority of the participants
> to both feminism and to the women's movement. They had no wish
> to examine individual issues on their merit but rather were present
> to make a political statement in opposition to the very legitimacy
> of the need for the conference.[36]

But the Equal Rights Amendment, by itself, was the Mormons'
bête noire. On this issue the Church acted with greater concentration
and more care than it had with the International Women's Year conference. The ERA's fate in Nevada shows how the LDS Church can
mobilize its forces and thus is an important case to consider, however
briefly. It was in Nevada, in November 1979, that the ERA was presented to voters in a public referendum during a general election for
a U.S. House of Representatives seat, seven statewide officers from
governor to state treasurer, and fifty state legislature seats. James T.
Richardson, a prominent sociologist of religion at the University of
Nevada at Reno, followed Mormon involvement in that election. When
the ERA referendum failed by a two-to-one margin, effectively killing
its chances for ratification in Nevada, he concluded that considerable
credit had to be given to the Mormons.[37]

In a 1976 election campaign in Nevada there had been apparent
Mormon Church involvement in establishing a citizens' political action
group, which in turn led to an investigation by the Democratic party's
Fair Campaign Practices Committee. QUEST (Citizens' Quest for
Quality Government) began as a small non-Mormon conservative
group that soon obtained endorsements by high-ranking Mormons
in state and regional offices. In Richardson's words:

> The Church organizational structure was used to tell people about
> the group and to gain members for the organization [QUEST]. Each
> ward was assigned a quota of people to send to organizational

meetings . . . and church-appointed leaders served as leaders of the group. This group . . . interviewed candidates using what was called by many an extremely slanted questionnaire, and then issued endorsements of candidates, during both the 1976 and 1978 elections. Charges were made during both campaigns that the endorsements of this group were distributed within the Mormon Church, as well as in some Catholic churches, and that the famous Mormon Relief Society "telephone tree" was used to spread the word about acceptable candidates.[38]

Another group, Citizens for Responsible Government, was accused of issuing misleading and biased information about candidates to Mormon churches. CRG was less important (and has been less studied) than QUEST. Nevertheless Richardson concluded that both groups had heavy Mormon involvement.

In fact, all Mormon churches — so far as Richardson was able to tell — became involved to some extent. Mormons' ward and stake leaders preached on the ERA referendum, urging members to vote against it. Some LDS leaders used such opportunities to recommend favorite anti-ERA candidates. Meetinghouses became places where anti-ERA literature was distributed and anti-ERA speakers found audiences. Richardson learned that some anti-ERA pamphlets, tracts, and newsletters were distributed through the home teacher and visiting teacher networks of the Church. Other such material was inserted in the *Beehive* newspaper (a "nonofficial publication" of the LDS community but distributed through churches). Ward and stake leaders were encouraged to distribute anti-ERA literature and to use telephone trees (particularly through the Women's Relief Society) to promote anti-ERA candidates and generate votes against the amendment. Testimony given at the hearings of the Democratic Fair Campaign Practice Committee by some Church members unhappy at this blatant Church incursion into politics named the highest Mormon leaders in Nevada as directly involved in starting up and controlling both QUEST and CRG.

Richardson describes a last-minute LDS effort to bury the ERA that occurred in Las Vegas:

> Word was received from somewhere that a recent poll showed ERA slightly ahead, and this was used to mobilize the Mormon Church in the Las Vegas area (where over 50 percent of Nevada's

population resides) for one last major effort. A meeting was called on Saturday night of Mormon leaders from throughout the area, and around 2,000 attended. In an emotion-packed meeting, they were strongly encouraged to do everything possible to make sure that ERA was defeated. These people went back to their individual wards (churches), and mobilized them to call others, to distribute literature, to get people to the polls, and to do "poll-watching," using church lists in some cases. Claims and charges have been made since then that up to 9,000 Mormons were involved in calling and literature distribution over the next two days, and that virtually every Mormon in Las Vegas was called and urged to vote, and that literature was "dropped" on virtually every doorstep in Las Vegas the day before the election. . . This writer has been told by Mormons and non-Mormons alike that upwards of 95 percent of all eligible Mormons voted in the election, which, if true, represents an astounding voter turnout which would have put even Mayor Daley and his Chicago Machine to shame.[39]

Finally, the Church called on its members for their "gifts" as well as their energies in the holy war against ERA. The clearest example of outspending ERA support can be found in Florida. In the late 1970s certain states, such as Florida, where the ratification of ERA hung in the balance, suddenly became the focus of unprecedented LDS Church attention. The ERA by that time had been ratified by thirty-five states, but thirty-eight were needed by June 1982. The Florida House of Representatives had ratified the amendment but the Senate had failed repeatedly to follow suit. In the December 1979 ratification vote the amendment had failed by a slim margin of two senators: 21–19. Florida had emerged as a critical state.

In 1978 the Florida secretary of state ordered an investigation to determine if Florida election laws had been violated by a 1978 fund-raising campaign orchestrated by LDS leaders. This campaign put thousands of dollars into the campaign chests of four Republican state Senate candidates and funded a massive anti-ERA advertising campaign that included printing and distributing 425,000 anti-ERA leaflets. The *Miami Herald* published a series of investigative reports on the scandal, revealing a national Mormon effort to kill the ERA in Florida with hefty contributions made to senatorial candidates whose elections might make the difference in passage or defeat of the amendment. *Miami Herald* reporter Linda Cicero wrote:

> Mormon church leaders solicited contributions from members of their congregations in Florida, California, Georgia and Alabama. Hundreds of small checks — that church sources say totaled at least $60,000 — were sent to the four candidates and to a Tallahassee-based political action group working against ERA.[40]

Florida election laws state that any group soliciting or spending more than $100 for political purposes must not only register as a political action committee (PAC) but also disclose how much money is raised, the contributors, and how the money is spent. But the checks given to Families Are Concerned Today (FACT) were never run through its accountants. Much of the money donated to the four Republican candidates did not even come from Mormons in Florida, much less from Mormons in the candidates' districts. Moreover, Florida election laws set maximum limits of $3,000 on any *group's* contribution to a political committee and $1,000 on any *individual's* contribution, yet as much as $26,000 was received by FACT just between October 21 and November 6 through the Mormon campaign and individual Mormons had contributed as much as $3,000 apiece."[41]

Mormon leaders had set a goal of raising $10,000 for each candidate but estimated that at least $60,000 was contributed in the seventeen days before the election. Journalist Linda Cicero reported one Mormon official's boast of effectiveness:

> In just two days, California Mormons alone contributed close to $13,000. A Florida Church leader, explaining how efficiently the [grass roots communication, or telephone tree] system works, said: "The structure exists where I can make 16 calls, and by the end of the day, 2,700 people will know something.[42]

Cicero learned from the four candidates' official campaign records that LDS Church leaders divided Florida along LDS boundaries (ignoring traditional political lines) to decide which congregations would be responsible for helping specific candidates. Accounting for the enormous success of the LDS fund-raising campaign, Jay N. Lybbert, one of three regional representatives of the Mormon Church in Florida and a junior college political science instructor, explained in a classic understatement: "I just talked to a few of my friends." Yet Cicero found that FACT's telephone bills for October through December of that year, for calls made by Lybbert alone, cost $414.80 and involved many levels of leadership.

Ironically, the only large non-Mormon contribution to FACT — $3,000 — came from Phyllis Schlafly's Illinois-based STOP-ERA organization.

The ERA issue provides a clear example of both the LDS Church leadership's determination to act on social and political issues it feels are closely tied to its millenial mission as well as its willingness to mobilize members' energies and resources in such pursuit. The Utah International Women's Year conference and the Florida election case exemplify the Church's capabilities to inspire rank-and-file members and to provide either efforts or money for causes on short notice. It is members' loyalty to their Church, and the Church's tightly knit organization, that makes this possible. One woman in Altamonte Springs, Florida, explained to a reporter why she had donated one dollar to one Mormon-approved state Senate candidate whose district was eighty miles away in Tampa:

> I don't even know who he was. I don't even know what he was running for. [I donated] because our church wanted us to support this man.[43]

MORMONS AND THE MORAL MAJORITY

The Mormons represent the "old religious right" in North America, but they have been building bridges to the "new religious right." Woven into this emerging alliance are connections to the John Birch Society and other right-wing groups. The linchpin in this effort is Freemen Institute and its Mormon president, W. Cleon Skousen.

Skousen holds a juris doctor degree from George Washington University and was admitted to practice law in the District of Columbia. A former Salt Lake City chief of police, he also spent sixteen years with the Federal Bureau of Investigation. Later he became editorial director of a national police magazine (*Law and Order*) while teaching thirteen years as an associate professor of religion at Brigham Young University. Skousen has written a number of books, including six college texts and a popular book, *The Naked Communist* (which the late LDS Church President David O. McKay, speaking at General Conference in October 1959, encouraged all Church members to read).[44]

On July 4, 1971, Skousen opened the Freeman Institute in a former two-room judo training hall next to the Brigham Young University campus at Provo, Utah. On September 18 the Institute officially moved to its new offices in a former warehouse building in Provo (Ezra Taft Benson was the principal speaker, with other Church officials and apostles present). By 1979 Skousen retired from the BYU faculty and moved the Institute's headquarters to Salt Lake City. On April 4, 1980, the Institute moved into its present modern two-story location in Salt Lake City, with a largely Mormon staff.⁴⁵

The Freemen Institute, a nonprofit educational foundation, specializes in constitutional studies designed, in its own words, "to inspire Americans to return to the Founders' original success formula." This "success formula" is interpreted to be the "restoration of the Constitution" in the tradition of the founding fathers, that is, laissez faire capitalism. Governed by a board of fourteen directors (with Skousen as its chair), the Freemen Institute publishes the *Freemen Digest* and many books and pamphlets. It also possesses its own library of books, monographs, and similar materials. It is probably best known for its constitutional seminars held across the country, its periodic constitutional rallies, and its media work. It offers the "Miracle of America" constitutional seminars in a home-study package containing twelve cassette tapes (narrated by Skousen) and two illustrated study guides for $59.95. It sells a twelve-cassette-tape series entitled "The Family Crisis," also for $59.95. The Institute claims to have graduated over 140,000 persons from its seminars and to have distributed more than 156,000 cassette tapes of speeches by prominent public figures as well as almost 60 million pages of printed material. It has also produced video cassettes for television.⁴⁶

The Institute's literature claims it is supported through the contributions of many persons, called "pledged Freemen," across the nation. For $10 or more a month ($100 or more per month makes one a member of the Century Club) members receive a subscription to the *Freemen Digest*, a cassette-tape-of-the-month (the Institute's term), and a monthly newsletter written by Skousen, entitled "Behind the Scenes."

Skousen chose the name Freemen for his institute because (say his brochures) America's forefathers considered themselves "free men" before they called themselves Americans. This choice points up an interesting subtlety, the idea that the ideals of the Institute predate the American Republic. The name also contains a Mormon double entendre from one passage in the *Book of Mormon* (Alma 51:6) that reads:

> And those who were desirous that Pahoran should remain chief judge over the land took upon them the name of *freemen*; and thus was the division among them, for the *freemen* had sworn or covenanted to maintain their rights and the privileges of their religion by a free government. (Italics ours)

The Institute's emphasis on "restoration" of the Constitution, one infers, parallels Mormonism's claim to restore the gospel of Jesus Christ. A Freemen Institute official concurred in an interview:

> When we go to foreign countries, we teach a model constitution which has been drawn up by the Freemen Institute here. It is patterned similarly after the U.S. Constitution. We've taken certain concepts of the Restored [LDS] Gospel and incorporated them into our working model of what an ideal constitution should be.[47]

The Freemen Institute claims: "The position of the Freemen Institute is in the balanced center of the public spectrum, right where the Founding Fathers stood."[48] In reality, however, the Freemen Institute is a right-wing think tank. According to the Institute's brochures, it opposes among other things the Occupational Safety and Health Administration, the Environmental Protection Agency, the Federal Communications Commission's fairness doctrine in editorial broadcasting, the federal government's change of the gold standard in currency, all subsidies to farmers, all federal aid to education, all federal social welfare, foreign aid, social security, elimination of public school prayer and Bible reading, and (that familiar right-wing nemesis) the United Nations.

Given this list of policies and projects that the Freemen Institute feels are subversive to America's democratic interests, it is not surprising that the Institute has entered into a coalition with another well known right-wing group.

Freemen Institute Links to the John Birch Society

U.S. Representative Larry P. McDonald, the Georgia Democrat who died tragically on 1 September 1983, in the Korean Air Lines passenger jet shot down by a Soviet fighter, was also national chairman of the John Birch Society. On April 4, 1980, he attended the dedication of the Freemen Institute's new Salt Lake City headquarters (along with Utah Senator Orrin Hatch, Congressman George Hansen from Idaho, Mr. and Mrs. J. Willard Marriott, and others).[49] McDonald had also attended previous Freemen Institute functions.

McDonald had founded Western Goals, an anti-Communist research organization based in Alexandria, Virginia, that compiles computerized dossiers on anyone who "would seek to bring revolutionary change to America." Western Goals' broad definition of such people led them to collect information and, some accused, misinformation on such persons as Atlanta Mayor Andrew Young, Coretta Scott King, former Black Panther Eldridge Cleaver (who, ironically, went through transitions that included becoming a born-again Christian, a Moonie, a speaker at the Freemen Institute, and finally, a Mormon), actress Jane Fonda, Chicago Mayor Harold Washington, presidential candidate and former Senator George McGovern, and former California Governor Jerry Brown.[50] Linda Valentino, director of public information for the American Civil Liberties Union (her dossier was in Western Goals' files), speculated that many law enforcement agencies used Western Goals as a "clearinghouse" for "dirty" information they could not legally keep themselves.[51]

Western Goals' board of directors reads like a who's who of modern right-wing luminaries, including the late Taylor Caldwell, U.S. Representative Phil Crane (R-Illinois), former "red-chaser" and New York lawyer Roy Cohn (of McCarthy hearings fame), four-star General Lewis W. Walt, USMC, and retired Joint Chiefs of Staff Chairman Adm. Thomas H. Morrer. Western Goals had a modest staff of a little more than a half dozen persons in 1983, a mailing list of more than 4,000, and an income of about $2 million provided by contributions. Its editor of publications, John Rees, was also the Washington bureau chief of the weekly *Review of the News*, a newsletter originated by the John Birch Society. Rees's wife was formerly employed on Congressman McDonald's staff.

There are definite ties between the Freemen Institute and Western Goals as well as indirectly to the John Birch Society (beyond Congressman Larry McDonald's evident sympathies for Cleon Skousen). In an interview, an administrative assistant for Western

Goals told us that McDonald and Skousen were friends who kept in close communication. The Freemen Institute had purchased books and other literature from Western Goals as well as provided it with financial contributions. The same could be said for the John Birch Society, the assistant added, which also had a number of ties to McDonald's organization.[52]

LDS Apostle Ezra Taft Benson, who once claimed that "the so-called civil rights movement as it exists today is used as a Communist program for revolution in America"[53] and whose John Birch sympathies are a byword among Mormons, stated at a rally in Scottsdale, Arizona, that "the Lord blesses the work of the Freemen Institute."[54] One of Benson's sons is vice-president of contributions and fundraising at Freemen. Skousen himself paid tribute to the John Birch Society in a Freemen Institute publication:

> Years ago the John Birch Society did some in-depth research and found the liberal Establishment with its hands in the government's multi-billion dollar cookie jar. Then it discovered a lot of other things for which the Establishment has never forgiven them. When the Birch Society tried to tell people what was happening their message was largely drowned out with smears and jeers until even today very few people actually know what the John Birch Society is all about. About all people have heard is that it is "extremist" and "far right."
>
> Actually, the things the John Birch Society has been warning the people about for so many years are not so obvious that it isn't even news any more . . . The John Birch Society has made its own history and needs no defense by me.[55]

Freemen Institute Links to Moral Majority, Inc.

Since their origins, Mormons have been accused by Baptists of being members of a cult. Countless tracts and pamphlets have been written condemning Joseph Smith's visions and the LDS Church's "un-Christian" basis. Baptists, suffice it to say, have been a thorn in the side of the LDS Church for the past 150 years.

Yet on many social issues the Mormon and Baptist (both Southern and Independent) conservative positions are virtually indistinguishable. Therefore, despite their traditional theological distrust and downright enmity toward each other, it is logical — perhaps inevitable — that both camps would eventually align to thwart the evils of so-called secular humanism, feminism, and godless communism (among others). Currently, there are indications that such an alliance is in progress. The "old religious right" (the Mormons) and the "new religious right" (politically alert Christian evangelicals and fundamentalist leaders such as Reverend Jerry Falwell) have been exploring mutual interests and values while seeking out the possible advantages and limits of cooperation.

One clear piece of evidence is the visits by Falwell and his assistants to Freemen Institute officials in Salt Lake City. The vice-president of the Freemen Institute commented:

> Reverend Jerry Falwell and Dr. Skousen are close, personal friends. Brother Skousen invited him to speak at one of our big get-togethers on July 4, 1980. Reverend Falwell uses a lot of our material . . . We send our monthly materials to Reverend Falwell. He especially likes our basic course entitled "Miracle of America," which is a history of our Constitution from the time of the Anglo-Saxons to the present in thirteen hours of cassette tapes. He also likes anything Dr. Skousen may write.[56]

Falwell indeed seemed impressed with the Freemen Institute when he visited it in 1980, particularly with its emphasis on the American family in crisis and its calls for a laissez faire capitalist patriotism coupled with a strong national defense. In a United Press International interview entitled "Falwell Falls for Freeman [sic]," Falwell reportedly praised the Freemen Institute as the "leading conservative group in the country" and called it "the conservative answer to the Brookings Institute." The article went on:

> "Every conservative group in the country relies on the Freemen Institute for the best quality research on Constitutional questions," Falwell said in a news conference prior to an "I Love America" rally at the Utah state capital. "I have the highest respect for the work of the Institute, and feel we agree on everything."[57]

Falwell has made use of "The Miracle of America" seminars for his own workers in the past. He also has addressed audiences in Salt Lake City and endorsed the Freemen Institute's work, saying "we have to do what Dr. Skousen says . . . teach the principles of the Founding Fathers."[58] Falwell's picture, taken with Skousen at a press conference they held on Constitution Day 1980, is proudly displayed in the Freemen Institute's brochure.

Less publicized contacts between the Freemen Institute and the Moral Majority organization as well as other groups in the "new religious right" and political right wing have been ongoing since the start of the decade. Cal Thomas, secretary of Moral Majority, Inc., told us by telephone from Lynchburg, Virginia:

> In 1981 I went out to Salt Lake City and had dinner with Dr. Skousen. We spent a great deal of time together discussing all the things we had in common. We reviewed a lot of their material, and he gave us a lot to take back with us. I found Dr. Skousen's brief on the social security system especially interesting. Reverend Falwell liked it too. More material was sent to us later on. There may come a situation in the future where both of us [Skousen's people and Falwell's organization] may have to be co-combatives together and pool our resources to defend those principles we believe in so much. It is very probable that this could happen under the right kind of situation.[59]

The Freemen Institute may bring the LDS Church into an alliance with the Moral Majority, in spite of traditional unpleasantness between Mormons and Baptists, because they have so much in common about what they dislike in American society and the world at large. They may continue to run parallel courses, the evangelicals and fundamentalists unwilling to admit the Mormons into the "true" Christian fold and thus not willing to treat them as allies. Or they may fall away from any possible cooperative effort altogether.

The current prospects for some sort of cooperation look hopeful. The Freemen Institute's Skousen has been wooing other conservatives, such as Roman Catholic antifeminist Phyllis Schlafly (the caption beneath the picture of her with Skousen in the Freemen Institute's brochure says she has given many of her Eagle Forum leaders scholarships to attend Skousen's constitutional seminars). Howard Phillips, National Director of the Conservative Caucus, Inc., is cited in the brochure as praising Skousen's work during a speaking engagement. Skousen has also appeared publicly with noted antihumanist evangelical writer Tim LaHaye.[60]

Skousen continues also to keep his channels open to more mainline, Mormon power holders, such as U.S. Senator Orrin Hatch and former U.S. Representative George Hansen, featured speakers at past Freemen Institute Constitution rallies. In September 1984 the Freemen Institute changed its name to the National Center for Constitutional Studies, to emphasize its commitment to right-wing politics in the name of America's blueprint for democratic government and also to avoid long explanations of the name Freemen.

MORMON THINK TANKS

On March 23, 1983, President Reagan appeared on television to deliver what has become known as his "Star Wars" speech. In this address Reagan announced that he wanted research to begin on a ballistic missile defense system that would protect the United States and its allies from a massive enemy attack. He called on the nation's scientists to perfect a ballistic missile defense shield that could use lasers, particle or microwave beams, or some other advanced technology to blunt or deflect an enemy missile attack, even if the effort took the rest of the century.

William E. Burrows, director of New York University's Science and Environmental Reporting Program, said the Star Wars speech "galvanized the aerospace industry, which is heavily dependent on defense contracts."[61] If that is true, then the Mormons will undoubtedly ride the crest of this high-tech weapons boom through one of their little-publicized but important properties: the Eyring Research Center. What the Freemen Institute has been to right-wing political ideology Eyring is to sophisticated missile guidance systems and electronics. The Eyring Research Center at Provo, Utah, was founded in July 1973. Originally set up as a nonprofit organization, it became very profitable and, as its by-laws dictated, then was turned over to the LDS Corporation of the First Presidency.[62]

The Eyring Research Center employs 170 people at its Provo, Utah, facilities and about 115 more at Hill Air Force Base in Ogden, Utah. (Hill Air Force Base is one of the most important military installations in the western United States. It is home to the Ogden Air Logistics Center, one of five such centers in the country, which is responsible for worldwide logistics management and maintenance support for the Minutemen and Titan II missiles as well as Bomarc drone missiles, Maverick air-to-ground missiles, and the Emergency Rocket Communication System.)[63] Eyring also employs about a dozen Brigham Young University faculty as consultants and both graduate and undergraduate students from BYU as assistants.

Over 70 percent of the research done at Eyring is on government contract (approximately $15 million worth), and most of that is for the U.S. Air Force. Much of this work is classified (such as monitoring the Minute Man missile system, missile simulation and trajectory testing, and miscellaneous work with the MX missile). With the help of the BYU engineering department, Eyring has pioneered in the field of missile guidance systems, particularly for the Peacemaker Missile System.

At a time of increased military and political interest and investment in the special types of hardware and software that the Eyring Research Center has to offer, the Church has become involved in a very important way with this nation's security. It has other Star Wars connections as well. Consider this final excerpt from the *Harper's* article by William E. Burrows:

> The Star Wars speech in effect created a Defensive Technologies Study Team, headed by former NASA administrator James C. Fletcher, which sent the president a detailed recommendation for ABM research in October. The report suggests spending $21.1 billion on research and development through fiscal 1989...The Fletcher group's report...has been endorsed by Secretary of Defense Caspar Weinberger.[64]

Dr. James C. Fletcher has had a distinguished career since World War II working with guided missiles. Former president and chairman of the board of the Space General Corporation, former administrator of NASA (Richard Nixon's appointment), and during the mid-1960s president of the University of Utah, Fletcher is currently a professor holding an endowed chair at the University of Pittsburgh. He is also a devout member of the LDS Church.

Another think tank of sorts connected to the LDS Church is less spectacular than the Eyring Research Center but quite active — Automated Language Processing Systems, Inc., no longer directly owned by the Church but still closely associated with it. ALPS had its beginnings in the early 1970s at Brigham Young University with a group of linguists, including one who became vice-president of ALPS' Research and Development. The LDS Church, through BYU President Ernest L. Wilkinson, provided a grant of over $1 million to develop a computer system capable of rapid translations. The original goal was to speed up translations of the *Book of Mormon* for export to foreign missions. But the system had so much promise that both the Church and the U.S. government invested several more million dollars in the project.

The translation market is growing worldwide. Currently estimated at $5 billion, the amount of business is expected to increase to $8 billion by the mid- to late 1980s. Private firms such as National Cash Register and Hewlett-Packard have contacted ALPS about installing translation systems in places as far apart as Zurich, Switzerland, and Guadalajara, Mexico. In a rapidly shrinking world, the business need for a fast way to translate documents in and out of more than one language is enormous.

But what does ALPS have to do with either the LDS Church or the military? Simply this: ALPS' investors and officers (such as its chairman of the board of directors and the directors themselves) are predominantly Mormons, some also acting as advisers to Church leaders. At the same time, ALPS has expanded its scope beyond translating the *Book of Mormon* and the business world. ALPS now contracts with the military (principally the Army) to translate intelligence and espionage materials. Said one ALPS official:

Most of what we'll be doing is translating an enormous amount of technological data, documents, and stuff like that. The East Germans are heavily influenced by Russian technology and a lot of their terminology now is a modified form of Russian. Say, for instance, if the Russians have a word for "floppy disk," then the East Germans will modify that to their own use. And this kind of modification drives the Army batty. They are unable to figure out what the stuff says or means.

This same official predicted that in the near future approximately 20–30 percent of ALPS' business would come from either the military or the Central Intelligence Agency.[65]

THE CIA/FBI CONNECTION

Despite the popularity of spy movies in the late 1960s and 1970s, those years were not kind to the American intelligence community. Student demonstrations, antiwar sentiment, and the public's disillusionment with America's involvement in international affairs made recruiters for the Central Intelligence Agency an endangered species on many college campuses. The federal government, too, clearly had its doubts about the agency. President Lyndon Johnson once described the Central Intelligence Agency with acerbity as "Murder, Inc."[66] During the 1970s, the CIA's budget was cut by 50 percent and its personnel reduced by 40 percent.[67]

All that has changed. Charles E. Jackson, chief of recruitment for the CIA, reports: "Business is booming. We're seeing more resumes than we ever have."[68] A recession and tough employment climate, a resurgence of political conservatism among young adults, and the Reagan administration's budget priorities restored much of the CIA's attraction as well as its budget. And as the CIA's fortunes have blossomed, so has the LDS Church's involvement with the CIA.

One example was Robert R. Mullen and Company, which handled international public relations for the Mormon Church and served as "an overseas cover for CIA activities" from 1959 to 1972.[69] (Mormon Mullen once wrote an apologetic entitled *The Latter-day Saints: The Mormon's Yesterday and Today*.) Indeed, according to the Rockefeller Report on the CIA issued in 1975:

> Robert Mullen had . . . for many years cooperated with the CIA making some of his overseas offices available at different times as a cover for Agency employees operating abroad. This existence of Mullen's relationship with the CIA was, of course, kept secret to protect the secrecy of the cover arrangements.[70]

Mormon Robert Bennett, son of U.S. Senator Wallace F. Bennett (R-Utah), bought the Mullen company in 1971 and employed ex-CIA Watergate burglar E. Howard Hunt at the time of the notorious Watergate Hotel break-in. Robert Bennett had been active in the Republican party and once worked at the U.S. Department of Transportation. These political connections led Bennett and the Mullen company to become involved with Hunt and the Watergate burglars. In fact, Hunt and the others discussed their plans for the break-in in meetings at the Mullen company offices.[71]

Another connection between the LDS Church and the CIA is through the agency's extensive recruitment of young Mormon men shortly after they finish their missions and college education. This recruitment takes the CIA regularly to the Brigham Young University main campus in Provo, Utah. Journalist Kenneth C. Danforth wrote in a *Harper's* article that he had heard many references to the high proportion of Mormon CIA employees. He asked Church leader Wendell J. Ashton, "Why is it that such huge numbers of Mormons are attracted to the CIA?" Ashton's reply: "The question is, 'Are our young men attracted to the CIA or is the CIA attracted to them?' "[72]

Denver CIA recruiter Jack Hansen said during one recruitment visit to the Provo campus:

> Utah is one of our good sources. A lot of people here have language or foreign culture experience. That's what we look for.[73]

Another CIA recruiter, Charles Jackson, claimed that additional factors about Mormons make them good candidates for CIA work, namely their reputation for a "sense of conformity and respect for authority," their sobriety (as abstainers from drugs and alcohol), and their patriotism.[74]

Stan A. Taylor, director of BYU's Center for International and Area Study, downplayed CIA recruitment at his institution during an interview. Noting that the Church expressly prohibits the CIA from using its missionaries overseas as covert agents, he claimed that few of the young people at BYU are ever accepted for employment by the CIA. He also doubted that the CIA has ever shown any "active interest" in hiring returning LDS missionaries.[75]

In fact BYU would appear to be a major recruiting center for the CIA. Dr. Gary Williams, chairman of the BYU Asian Studies Department, offered his own assessment of the rosy employment future some BYU graduates can look forward to if they consider the CIA at graduation:

> We've never had any trouble placing anyone who has applied to the CIA. Every year, they take almost anybody who applies. Former Mormon missionaries have the three qualities the CIA wants: foreign language ability, training in a foreign culture, and former residence in a foreign country.[76]

In fact, Dr. Williams reports that some missionaries leaving for foreign missions have occasionally been approached to do additional work for the CIA while in the field. It is no coincidence that some returning missionaries report having had people accuse them of being CIA operatives in places such as Spain, France, and Peru. Patrick J. McGarvey, a former CIA employee, wrote in *C.I.A.: The Myth and the Madness* about deep cover operations, in which men accept an undercover foreign assignment for seven to nine years, performing discreet tasks for the Agency. He noted: "CIA has a surprising number of Mormon Church members in its employ, and the fact that many of these men had spent two years in a Mormon mission in Latin America or the Far East is not overlooked by CIA. A friend found himself back in the Mormon mission in Hong Kong after his training."[77]

But the most definitive confirmation of the Mormon-CIA connection comes from knowledgeable CIA employees who are also Mormons. Mormon Bishop Jeffrey Willis, personnel director for the CIA (he was the principal LDS Church official responsible for the excommunication of pro-ERA activist Sonia Johnson, a member of his ward), elaborated on the desirability of former Mormon missionaries for CIA positions. He affirmed that the Central Intelligence Agency would hire "a good Mormon," especially a returned missionary, "right on the spot." In fact, he said, CIA recruiters prefer returned missionaries over any other kind of applicant. Returned missionaries have a language capacity highly prized by the Agency. Furthermore, their understanding of the country in which they've served, their knowledge and expertise concerning its government, the customs of the people, and so forth are valuable commodities. Willis pointed out that returned missionaries are also much sought after by CIA recruiters because of their integrity, devotion to their country and to their Church, and because of their "hard work ethic." Willis described how the CIA keeps a "bio-profile" on everyone who works for the Agency; having "Returned Missionary of the Church of Jesus Christ of Latter-day Saints" on this record is a "definite plus" for applicants and career men. Willis was not free to discuss the number of returned missionaries currently working within the CIA or what their job assignments were. He did say that "a relatively good number of them are currently engaged in analytic work" in the United States and in various parts of the world, but he declined to be more specific. He ended the interview with a frank statement about the value of LDS missionaries to the CIA: "Without the large number of returned missionaries currently working for this Agency, I seriously doubt whether we would be as effective as we now are. We place more value on their kind than most people in government may realize."[78]

Jack Hansen, a Mormon recruiting officer for the CIA in Denver, Colorado, reiterated personnel director Willis's emphasis on the CIA's efforts to obtain Mormon missionaries with foreign experience. He also pointed out the reciprocal benefits of the Mormon missionary program for both the intelligence community and the LDS Church: the CIA obtains reliable, trained personnel and the Church offers its university's graduates a chance to serve their country. Hansen said that he recruited "on the average" about 300 applicants per year from all of the western schools he visited. Of those who finally are accepted, the majority are returned missionaries from Brigham Young University, and he remarked that a few ex–mission presidents as well eventually reach top levels in the CIA. Hansen estimated that about 20 percent of the Mormons employed by the CIA are directly in the spying business, while the other 80 percent are staff personnel consisting of management, clerical people, and "office paper shufflers." He acknowledged a "significant percentage of returned missionaries currently involved in espionage work somewhere overseas."[79]

Many of these young men work only a few years in the CIA, for most intelligence efforts resemble more the plodding meticulousness of academic scholarship than the exotic cloak-and-dagger adventures of James Bond. One ex-missionary who became disillusioned with CIA work and left after only one year was Neal Maxwell, now an apostle of the Council of the Twelve. On the other hand, many Mormons stay and rise within the agency's ranks, as did Michael J. Barrett, assistant general counsel to the director of the CIA.

Sometimes the Mormon-CIA connection threatens to embarrass the Church, as it did in the spring of 1984. On April 4, FBI agents arrested Mormon Richard Craig Smith on charges that he sold Russian agents information concerning six American double-agent operations directed at the Soviet Union's KGB intelligence agency. According to numerous newspaper accounts at the time, Smith claimed he was set up to infiltrate the KGB but then abandoned by the CIA. (The CIA was tight-lipped about details of Smith's alleged mission.) As of this writing, Smith has not yet gone to trial. In any event, Smith's career with the CIA followed a trajectory not much different from that of many Mormons recruited by that agency. A native Utahn, Smith was raised in a devout Mormon family. His first job after high school was with the CIA, but after six months he resigned to serve a missionary stint in France. Later, after attending Brigham Young University for two years (he later finished his undergraduate degree), he served in Army intelligence during the Vietnam War and saw tours of duty in various Asian and Middle Eastern countries. After the Army he drifted into a series of jobs that led him once again to become involved with intelligence community–connected persons, including his former San Francisco bishop, who was an FBI agent.

The Federal Bureau of Investigation also has a connection to the Mormon Church. For years the FBI kept a file on the late Church President David O. McKay, but the record was "clean." McKay had supposedly maintained a cordial, long-distance relationship with FBI director J. Edgar Hoover and in 1962 even offered Hoover the unusual opportunity to address a Church General Conference. In 1966, using ex-FBI agent Cleon Skousen (later of Freemen Institute fame) as a go-between, McKay had even tried to bring Hoover out to Brigham Young University to receive an honorary doctorate, but Hoover pleaded a busy schedule and never went.[80]

The FBI, like the CIA, recruits heavily from the Mormon ranks. The extent of Mormon employment in the FBI recently became public when the Bureau arrested one of its own agents, Richard W. Miller, a twenty-year veteran, charging him with espionage. In October 1984, Miller was accused of selling classified documents to a female Soviet KGB agent and her estranged husband in Los Angeles. (Miller's case was being tried in the summer of 1985 as this volume was going to press.)

Miller was a Mormon and had graduated from Brigham Young University in 1963 with a bachelor's degree in Spanish.[81] This fact in itself might seem unremarkable if it had not triggered some interesting disclaimers and new revelations about FBI-LDS relations.

For example, Richard W. Bretzing, special agent in charge of the FBI's Los Angeles office, was both Miller's superior and a

Mormon bishop. Sometime before his arrest Miller had been excommunicated; afterwards, Bretzing had appealed to Miller's past Mormon faith and urged him to "repent" of his mistakes.[82] Miller's defense attorney asked a U.S. district judge to dismiss the charges on the grounds that Bretzing was using Miller as a scapegoat to prove that Bretzing does not favor Mormon agents.[83] This was a logical move on Bretzing's part, the attorney argued, since Bretzing had been recently accused of favoritism toward his LDS peers. One agent, for example, had complained to reporters that "the Mormon Mafia was running the office and giving choice assignments to their own people."[84] Bretzing resisted this accusation and issued the following statement:

> There are dozens, perhaps hundreds of special agents of the FBI currently on the rolls and serving throughout the world who are members of the Church of Jesus Christ of Latter-day Saints. I believe it is unfair to impugn them or their religion based on the activities of another individual with a common religious background. The suggestion that preferential treatment has been given or is being given to anyone based on his or her personal religious preference is totally inconsistent with exercising our rights and privileges guaranteed by the United States Constitution.[85]

The Miller incident revealed more than just office politics with a possible religious slant in the FBI's Los Angeles office. Rather, these events point to a considerable Mormon presence in the FBI, though at this time it is difficult to estimate precisely how many agents are Mormons. Like the CIA, the FBI has placed a premium on returned LDS missionaries for some offices. One FBI recruiter affirmed this in a recent interview: "Utah, because of all the returned [LDS] missionaries, leads the nation in the number of new recruits under the [FBI's] language program."[86]

Yet a further interesting twist to the LDS Church–intelligence community relationship is that the LDS Church Security System has been known to recruit Mormons away from the CIA and FBI.[87] LDS Church Security has a number of responsibilities, among them protecting Church property from unwanted intruders and vandalism, protecting Church officials such as the president and his two counselors (much as the U.S. Secret Service protects the president), and investigating breaches of information security in

Church administration. Church Security is virtually a separate Mormon police force, just as BYU campus police is in Provo, operating not just on Temple Square in Salt Lake City but also on Church-owned property including many business blocks surrounding Temple Square. Like many private security systems hired by industries, Church Security agents cannot technically arrest (though they detain) or fingerprint (though they work closely with the Salt Lake City police department and Salt Lake sheriff's department to get virtually any fingerprints they desire nationwide), but they do make it a practice to photograph "troublemakers" for future dossiers.

There are more than 300 Church Security police presently employed by the Church. Nearly two-thirds of them work in Salt Lake City (the rest are connected with temples scattered around North America). In many ways their neat, uniform, conservative appearance (aside from age) renders them indistinguishable from the young Mormon missionaries who walk door to door in American suburbs.

Most important for our purposes are the upper administrative members of the Security System. The head of Church Security is a retired FBI agent. Other Security officers include former CIA agents and men involved in military intelligence (one in the Air Force for over twenty years) and law enforcement (former deputy sheriffs from places as far away as Los Angeles County, BYU campus police officers, various state highway patrol officers, and assorted local city detectives). While the Church–intelligence community relationship in no way resembles a two-way street for the career-minded, traffic does not flow exclusively *from* Salt Lake City *to* Washington, D.C. Sometimes it runs the other way.[88]

MORMONS AND THE U.S. MILITARY

Frances Lang wrote in a 1971 *Ramparts* article: "The Mormon Church has become a fantastically potent force in the United States. It has a hand in the control of critically important institutions in this country."[89] Nowhere is this conclusion better demonstrated than in the U.S. military establishment, which has offered a rewarding career track for Mormons since World War II.

The Mormon Church is the only major American religion to have had at least three organized militias. The first of these was a military company called Zion's Camp, organized in May 1834 at Kirtland, Ohio, for the march to Jackson County, Missouri, to regain confiscated properties of resident Latter-day Saints. Zion's Camp was made up of about 150 males, many only teenagers. But to its leaders it was "an Army of the Lord."[90]

When the Latter-day Saints migrated to Missouri in the mid-1830s, they organized militia companies in several counties, to the consternation of nearby Gentiles. To Gentiles it appeared that Mormons were fast overwhelming the rest of the population with sheer numbers. For example, by the summer of 1838 the population of Caldwell County, Missouri, was about 5,000, of which 4,900 were Mormons.[91] The Missourians joined against the Mormons in armed mobs, and the Saints reacted by mustering their militia, called the Host of Israel. As we discussed in Chapter 1, Mormon leaders did not believe in passively turning the other cheek in response to harassment by Gentiles. The Host of Israel engaged in a number of conflicts, and a number of Mormons died in the hostilities.

On the banks of the Mississippi River at Nauvoo, Illinois, Joseph Smith organized yet a third Mormon militia: the Nauvoo Legion. In 1840 all Mormon males between the ages of sixteen and fifty were enrolled in the Legion. Modeled after the Roman army, it was divided into two cohorts and then into regiments, battalions, and companies.[92] Smith was elected as its lieutenant general, a role he clearly relished as he donned an ornate uniform and saber whenever he reviewed his troops or entertained dignitaries. Smith was later given a commission from the Illinois governor (as were the Legion's officers), and the militia was authorized by several acts of the Illinois legislature. At the time of Joseph Smith's martyrdom in June 1844 there were approximately 5,000 Mormons enlisted in the Nauvoo Legion. It was the largest private standing army in the continental United States, second only to the United States Army itself. An American Army artillery officer, after witnessing a parade of the Nauvoo Legion (which he admitted "made a very noble and imposing appearance"), went on to record:

The evolutions of the troops would do honor to any body of armed militia, and closely approximates our own forces. There are no troops in the state like them in point of enthusiasm and warlike aspects, yea warlike character.[93]

In the Great Salt Lake Basin, as we noted in Chapter 1, the Mormons had good reason to reinstate militias in local frontier communities. The frequent overlap between Church offices and militia rank undoubtedly was a key factor in the Church's ability to frustrate federal troops by guerrilla tactics when they invaded the region during the Utah War of 1857, with bishops and stake presidents shifting roles easily to become lieutenants and captains.

Since that time, however, Mormons have distinguished themselves in all wars and major military conflicts in which the United States has engaged. Looking in 1983 at the backgrounds of just members of the Council of the Twelve and the First Presidency, we found a former Army artillery officer, a former Air Force intelligence officer, a former Marine, a World War II bomber pilot, and several other naval and army officers. The conservatism and patriotism of Church members that has made them so attractive to civilian government officials has also suited them for military service, particularly as a career. Brigham Young University also serves as one important location for military recruitment. Indeed, BYU has the largest ROTC program of any major American university and a special Military Week that regularly draws top Pentagon brass as commencement and commissioning ceremony speakers. In December 1982, for example, Brigadier General Charles D. Bussey, second-ranking spokesman for the U.S. Army, spoke at commissioning ceremonies for fifteen Army and Air Force ROTC graduates. In April 1983, Major General Robert Sullivan, responsible for all ROTC units nationally, spoke at ROTC commencement exercises at BYU. After touring the Missionary Training Center and sitting in on several missionary classes, he remarked to one BYU faculty host:

> There's only one thing wrong with that. They aren't all officers in the United States Army! What a strength they would give us.[94]

On another occasion that same faculty member heard a brigadier general tell a conference of military science professors: "If I had to do away with all of the schools in my region but one, I'd keep the program at Brigham Young University because the officers they commission have been returned Mormon missionaries." The faculty member thought that most ROTC graduates at BYU were returned missionaries.

Mormons have not always had such an easy time integrating the military, however. The government permitted only a half dozen Mormon chaplains as recently as the early days of the Vietnam War in the 1960s. Church President Harold B. Lee sent Elder Boyd K. Packer directly to President Lyndon Johnson to appeal for a relaxation of restrictions in the number of LDS chaplains, telling Packer to "remind President Johnson it isn't 1830, and there aren't just six of us now." Packer met with Johnson in the White House, arguing that six LDS chaplains were simply inadequate to minister to the large numbers of Mormons in military service. Johnson reportedly told his defense secretary later: "Give the Mormons what they want." And the number of LDS chaplains began to increase.[95] Mormon chaplains are now as accepted as those of any other denomination. In 1980 a conference for all chaplains in the armed services was held at Brigham Young University, where the Church public relations office made sure that the visitors were shown (among other things) the Church's Missionary Training Center.

A full account of all Mormons in top-level military positions would require much more space than we have here. The *Church News* frequently mentions enough names and impressive credentials of Church members in the military to suggest that the real number is large. One *Church News* article in January 1982 reported that Brien D. Ward, a brigadier general promoted to major general on recommendation of President Reagan (and confirmation of the U.S. Senate), had become director of laboratories for the Air Force Systems Command headquartered at Andrews Air Force Base in Maryland. A West Point graduate, Ward was responsible for "providing policy, planning and technical direction to 14 research and development laboratories, five liaison offices and the European Office of Aerospace Research and Development."[96] It is easy to name others in such positions. Brigadier General Robert Oaks (a relative of Apostle Dallin Oaks, the Utah lawyer once appointed by Ronald Reagan to work at the Public Broadcasting System's lobbying arm) is the Commander of the 86th Tactical Fighter Wing at Ramstein Air Force Base in West Germany. One Pentagon informant pointed to Oaks as a serious candidate for the chief of staff of the United States Air Force in the near future. Or there is Lieutenant General Richard E. Merkling, deputy commander of Air Force Logistics and Engineering at Wright-Patterson Air Force Base in Dayton, Ohio. (Merkling has also been on his region's stake High Council.) Or the U.S. Coast Guard's Rear Admiral Alexander Yost, who makes periodic speaking trips to BYU. Or Lieutenant General W. F. Ulmer, Jr., former West Point commandant and, until recently, commander at Fort Hood in Killeen, Texas, the largest Army land base in the United States.

One Air Force officer with whom we talked claimed that the Mormons' reputation as a reliable patriotic group had been a benefit to his own career in several ways. He had deliberately implemented the same kind of rigid administration he had known in the Church in his own work, with successful results. Gentiles in the military and the government, he believes, show a "remarkable acceptance" of LDS peers and seek them for their loyalty, integrity, and "perfect obedience." In fact, the officer estimates that his previous military assignments were made particularly because he is a Mormon, even though he knew of other officers better qualified or more experienced.[97]

This officer is also a valuable asset to the LDS Church in the same way that U.S. Senators Jake Garn and Orrin Hatch (among other Mormon officials in Washington) are through the Mormon network in the nation's capital. He told one of us that he has always made it a point to discuss any vital decisions that might be made with some of the brethren in Salt Lake City. Proud of his close relationship with most of the Council of the Twelve, he declares that Gordon B. Hinckley of the First Presidency is "a good and dear friend."[98]

But this high-ranking individual's contacts with LDS Church leadership involve more than mere moral uplift. For example, he was instrumental in helping the General Authorities secure permission from the East German government to build the Freiberg temple there (discussed in Chapter 5). Church leaders have not overlooked his worth. On several occasions when he thought seriously about retiring from the Air Force, high-level leaders, specifically the late LDS President Harold B. Lee, Gordon B. Hinckley, and several apostles, asked him to stay on in the interests of the Church.[99]

Thus far we have argued only that the military services like to recruit red-blooded patriotic Mormons, that such Mormons often excel in military careers, and that given the opportunity such career soldiers will help out their faith. But the implications are much broader than that, surely more than just lending assistance to building a temple (and a small one at that) in East Germany. Decisions on the international level, affecting all Americans, Mormon and Gentile, present and future, are affected by such conflicting loyalties. A sobering example is the MX missile controversy in the early 1980s.

The irony about the controversy was that many Utahns (including its legislators) have traditionally encouraged heavy defense spending, particularly in their state. During World War II the Army and other branches of the federal government poured more than one billion dollars into bases, depots, arsenals, and other installations throughout Utah.[100] Ever since, Utah has been a prime recipient of defense dollars, not just for air and land weapons but also for war research. The state's wide open, unpopulated spaces, coupled with the LDS Church's generally supportive posture on the U.S. military and its lack of tolerance for pacificists and conscientious objectors within its own ranks, made the state a logical choice for placement of the MX missile system.

The missile system was a plan calling for the U.S. Air Force to place a minimum of 200 missiles somewhere beneath the surface of the Great Basin desert of Utah and Nevada. It was to be a complicated network of 4,600 shelters and 9,000 miles of underground roads. Over these roads flatbed vehicles would continually shuttle missiles (each tipped with ten nuclear warheads) back and forth in an attempt to keep the Soviet Union unsure about what subterranean silos would be used to fire missiles during a nuclear war. *Time* magazine described the proposed $56 billion system a "brobdingnagian shell game designed to foil a Soviet attack on the missiles."[101] Critics attacked the plan as not only ineffective but harmful to the ecology even if the nightmare of nuclear war failed to bring environmental disaster. Secretary of Defense Caspar Weinberger claimed the system was "vital" to the nation's defense.

It seemed at first like another boost for the Utah economy. Government contracts would pump massive amounts of money into the state. Jobs would be plentiful for years, regardless of recessions elsewhere in the nation. But then "overnight the weight of public opinion shifted to 70 percent [of Utahns] being opposed to MX deployment in Utah."[102] The reason was simple: on May 5, 1981, the LDS First Presidency issued a statement condemning any basing of the MX missile in Utah and Nevada.

The statement gave a number of curious reasons for putting the missiles elsewhere. For example, the First Presidency complained that "with such concentration [of missiles], one segment of the population would bear a highly disproportionate share of the burden . . . in case of attack." The statement noted that "history indicates that men have seldom created armaments that eventually were not put to use." It went on: "It is ironic, and a denial of the very essence of that [Mormon] gospel, that in this same general area [where peace-seeking persecuted settlers came to live] there should be constructed a mammoth weapons system potentially capable of destroying much of civilization." It decried the possible environmental hazards of the missile system's construction and even the possible "grave sociological problems" of the expected influx of workers brought in to build it — this last fear paradoxically coming from a region that had previously welcomed all the defense contracts Washington had to distribute. The usually pro-military First Presidency even resorted to piety and pacifist ideals, claiming that the Mormons had settled Utah to "establish a base from which to carry the gospel of peace."[103]

The LDS Church leaders did everything in their statement but confront the real reason for their opposition to the MX missile basing strategy. We suspect that they did not want to air their conviction that Mormons consider the Salt Lake Basin to be the new Zion, the capital of the forthcoming Kingdom of God on earth and the cradle of Jesus Christ's imminent millennium. The outspoken patriotism and confident conservatism underlying Mormon support of the American military establishment, its foreign policy, and its industrial entanglements suddenly waffled as the Mormon Church had to confront for the first time the real possibility that its North American Zion could be ground zero in a Soviet missile attack. Mormons apparently were prepared for the millennium, but only on their own terms. As good post-millennialists, Mormons believed that Jesus Christ can return to earth only when His kingdom is economically and politically prepared for Him to rule. A nuclear war in Utah would therefore be a theological as well as a national disaster.

Reactions to the Mormon statement were not usually put in such fundamental theological terms as in our analysis, but most were unremittingly critical. Liberal columnist Carl T. Rowan branded the Mormons as hypocrites. He wrote scathingly:

I am not a booster of the MX. But [President] Kimball's statement troubles me, because it illustrates that even our religious leaders invoke ''morality'' in ways that say, ''Let someone else make the sacrifices, run the risks, while I remain prosperous and secure.''

Does a Mormon in Utah have a greater exemption from the problems and perils of national defense than a Methodist in Michigan or a Catholic in Maine?. . .''state's rights'' takes on a hollow ring when you note that Utah's Sens. Jake Garn and Orrin Hatch, and its Reps. James V. Hansen and Don Marriott, are all hawks, all macho supporters of the MX missile and every other weapons system that someone has told them will defeat communism.

There is something sickeningly phony about people who make pious speeches about the dangers of godless communism, and who cry for the transfer of funds from social programs to weapons systems, but who in the crunch say, ''Don't endanger us by putting those missiles in our state.''[104]

Likewise, conservative columnist William F. Buckley, Jr., asked: ''What on earth got into the elders when they made their pronouncement against the MX missile? The reasoning was not only specious, but provocatively so.'' In May 1981 editorials, the *New York Times* referred to the Church's transparently ''parochial interest'' in the MX matter and called its stance ''disturbingly sanctimonious.''[105]

Even antiwar doves were not entirely pleased with the Church's sudden about-face toward peace, for they argued that the Church had finally taken an antimissile stand (of sorts) for the wrong reasons. That is, it failed to place the MX issue in a more general arms race context and to use that issue to call for arms reduction.

What would have provided real grist for the media and public discussion was some background on one factor critical to why the Utah-Nevada basing plan was scrapped. Earlier in 1981 Church leaders had contacted a high-ranking member in the Department of Defense while he was still a Church Regional Representative.

A loyal Mormon, he traveled with Gordon B. Hinckley to North Carolina one weekend to organize a new stake. During the trip they discussed the MX issue which had weighed heavily on the minds of Spencer W. Kimball and other Church leaders. As a person who by virtue of his position in the defense establishment could be influential in the decision on any MX basing strategy, this individual was later invited to Salt Lake City where he met with members of the Council of the Twelve Apostles. The First Presidency told him that it supported the MX program but not its intended base of deployment. First Presidency members had already drafted the statement on the "error" of placing MX missiles in Utah and Nevada which they intended to release to the press. They allowed the official to make recommendations on slight changes of wording. But, he recalled in an interview with us, it was very difficult to move them on the placing of the missiles and for him to accept their final decision. He appreciated that the usually pro-military Church leaders were in a difficult position. "The whole issue," he concluded, "boiled down to where they didn't want the MX system placed. And that was not in Utah. They didn't seem to care just which state we put it in as long as we kept it out of theirs."[106]

The massive protests of Utah's citizenry and political pressure by high-placed Mormon officials in Washington apparently won. After the Mormon outcry President Reagan backed off the Utah-Nevada MX deployment site and appointed a special committee to study alternative ways to base the MX missile. Heading it was Reagan's special choice, Brent Scowcroft, a man with impeccable credentials: West Point graduate, retired lieutenant general in the Air Force, and deputy to Henry Kissinger on the National Security Council during the Nixon and Ford administrations. Scowcroft himself is also an active Mormon. He and his committee eventually selected Wyoming as an appropriate potential site for the MX.

POLITICS AND PARA-PATRIOTISM

The LDS Church, through its various members employed in important legislative, executive, military, defense-related, and intelligence positions, now is capable of wielding extraordinary influence in the affairs of the American government. As we have seen,

Mormons are capable of acting in concert on issues that LDS leaders consider important to the Church. The complex and inclusive LDS Church structure, with clear lines of authority flowing downward and outward from Salt Lake City headquarters to local wards across the country, means that grass roots members — not just politicians or generals — can be mobilized on amazingly short notice. In our pluralist society where most Americans are not embedded in such tightly run organizations claiming their ultimate allegiance, the Mormon Church has an enormous advantage over other competing interests, secular or religious.

For many years the Church was the distinct underdog in the public policy arena. This obviously is no longer the case. Nor is the Church merely a regional force to be reckoned with, as most nonwesterners have thought. It has members in this nation's most important government positions. The Church apparently makes the assumption that these persons are especially accountable to its own leadership theological agenda, calling on senators and generals when necessary. After all, the United States, its Constitution and traditions of church-state separation, and the virtues of religious pluralism are transient things in the LDS post-millennial long view, useful perhaps for getting a secure foothold and building resources, but ultimately dispensable.

Does this then mean that the faithful Mormons are not or cannot be "good" Americans, loyal to the Constitution? Or that many highly placed Mormon officials in public office or the military, more than a few of whom are war heroes and veterans who made the same sacrifices and took the same risks as their Gentile comrades, are not patriots? Such questions assume there are only two categories possible: patriots and pseudo-patriots. Actually the situation of many Mormon officials is one of *para-patriotism*. They do indeed love this country and patriotically serve it to the best of their abilities. But this loyalty ranks in a hierarchy of others. In the end, for some Mormons para-patriotism serves a greater loyalty as dictated by the Mormon theological scheme.

Consider, for example, this faith testimony of the Air Force officer mentioned earlier:

I think that the Prophet Joseph Smith was right about the Church saving the Constitution. I believe every word of it. But

I just don't know how the Lord will bring this about. Will He use good priesthood brethren [such as the general] in high places in the military and government to give direction and counsel to our present leaders? Or will He give the prophet a revelation for us to move ahead and take command in some sense? It's just hard to say when you don't know what the Lord's got up His sleeve. But I'm convinced that we are going to play a role like we've never before played in the shaping up of things in the world.

I think that doors have already been opened and we've been the men the Lord has selected to walk through those doors... You put together the political, military, and ecclesiastical into a group of men and you've got super-human leaders.[107]

Para-patriotism has only recently become a dilemma for some Church members. It is a logical result of declining religious discrimination that allows Mormons into all levels of national affairs and the old-fashioned Protestant ethic that Joseph Smith built into early Mormonism. But it is more than just the LDS Church's dilemma. As we have shown, it helps shape a variety of public policies, foreign and domestic, that affect everyone.

5

The Darker Side of Mormonism

E very organization, no matter how noble its mission, has a dark side that it prefers not be revealed. For some organizations the dark side is far removed from the mainstream of activities. In others the dark side may be integral to the entire edifice. The larger the organization the greater the chances of an extensive dark side because sheer size requires a bureaucracy to manage it. Bureaucracy is in fact the key. The anonymity and rational pragmatism of any great bureaucracy virtually ensures a dark side. As two social psychologists observe, because "bureaucracies arrange that everyone need only intend to follow the rules, the result is that bureaucracies have a genius for organizing evil."[1]

An enterprise the size of the LDS Church not surprisingly possesses a dark side beyond just the questionable dimensions we have already discussed. In this chapter we focus on other controversial aspects of the corporate Mormon entity. The LDS Church has engaged in a good deal of authoritarian control of its own members, stifling dissent and criticism in a manner inconsistent with democratic ideals. It has been Janus-like in its international dealings — with Jews, Arabs, and Communist nations, to name a few.

These generalizations are not casually made. Before any final assessment of the Church organization can be made, we need to examine the evidence behind them. A good place to start is the best-known and highly touted LDS project: its welfare program. As we will show, all is not as its reputation would have it.

179

THE MYTH OF MORMON WELFARE

President Reagan, champion of the philosophy that communities, businesses, and private philanthropy ought to handle most of the charitable relief now provided by the federal government through welfare programs, praised the LDS Church's welfare system when he visited Utah in 1982 stumping for the reelection of Republican and Mormon U.S. Senator Orrin Hatch. Enamored with the image of self-sufficient Mormons who depend on hard work and Church cooperation rather than stoop to accept government relief during hard times, Reagan hailed the Mormon welfare program as

> one of the great examples in America today of what people can do for themselves if they hadn't been dragooned into the government's doing it for them . . . If more people had had this idea when the Great Depression hit, there wouldn't be any government welfare today or any need for it.[2]

Reagan's love affair with private philanthropy as an alternative to government welfare needs little elaboration. It is undoubtedly one reason that in 1981 he appointed three active and highly placed LDS Church members to a White House task force to encourage volunteer activity and private charity for the poor in America: Elder Thomas S. Monson of the Council of the Twelve; Jeri J. Winger, vice-president of the General Federation of Women's Clubs in the LDS Church; and George W. Romney, former Michigan governor and presidential candidate and head of the National Center for Citizen Involvement.[3]

However, Reagan was poorly informed about the Mormon Church's track record on keeping its members off welfare rolls and unrealistic about thinking other Americans could feasibly imitate the Mormon model. Despite a great deal of popular folklore, public relations news releases, and wishful thinking, the belief that the LDS Church uses and did use its resources to keep the majority of its poorer members off federal aid, now or during the Great Depression, is largely unfounded. The Mormon Church never had the colossal in-house welfare program attributed to it in the 1930s. That the public has come to believe otherwise is a tribute to the Church's public relations talents. Nor does the Church now operate such a program. If anything, the LDS Church is moving further (and faster) away from a realistic welfare program to take care of its own members than at any other time in its history.

The Origin of the Myth

The myth of Mormon welfare began during the Great Depression. It was initially a public relations effort, sometimes bitterly denounced by public officials who knew better, but it succeeded. A typical example of how the popular press extolled the virtues of the Mormon Church appeared in a 1937 article in *Reader's Digest*:

> A year and a half ago [1935] 84,460 Mormons, about one-sixth of the entire Church membership, were on direct relief. Today none of them are. The Church is taking on its own...Within a year every one of the 84,460 Mormons was removed from the government relief rolls all over the country.[4]

The public image of the LDS welfare program was created in the mid-1930s. In 1935 President Franklin D. Roosevelt announced a shift in federal priorities from simple relief programs (that is, charity) to projects that would put unemployed persons to work on socially productive tasks. In this spirit he established the Works Projects Administration (WPA), which became involved in large-scale projects ranging from reforestry to road construction to building dams. Roosevelt envisioned that relief programs were to be left to states and local governments as the federal government increasingly sponsored work-oriented projects to aid individuals temporarily and communities more permanently.

Meanwhile Mormons, like many Americans, were hit hard by the Depression. In 1935 the Church undertook a survey of the standard of living of its members and found that *one out of five* received some form of federal assistance (either as direct relief or from work in federal projects). Widespread reliance on the federal government (the Gentiles) was unpalatable to a church that only two generations before had been the object of fierce persecution and derision by the same power. In 1931, for instance, the *Deseret News* published an editorial that acknowledged the problems many members faced in finding adequate food, clothing, and shelter, but it called for Church funds to be spent on work projects, not on mere handouts. At that time some stakes and wards were providing destitute members with work such as renovating chapels and chopping wood.[5] The editorial called for more to be done.

In April 1936 the LDS leaders announced the Church Security Program. On paper at least, this was a Mormon version of the WPA. There had been a growing sentiment among Mormon officials that the organization ought to consider some Church-wide program to assist its many impoverished members. More important, these leaders knew that cutbacks in federal relief would severely hurt large numbers of Mormons receiving such help. As historians Arrington and Hinton note, "The sequence of events at the time of its establishment makes it clear that the Church Security Program was essentially a reaction to the prospective curtailment of federal relief."[6] Church officials soon after met with President Roosevelt, seeking his public endorsement of their plan. Roosevelt enthusiastically responded, expressing hope that the Mormons "might inspire other groups to do something of a similar nature."[7]

This was to be the widely touted Church Welfare Plan (as the Church Security Program was renamed in 1938). However, it was the plan's widely promoted spiritual agenda that stuck in the public mind. Values of industry, thrift, self-reliance and stubborn independence, and the old-fashioned Protestant ethic were being practiced in an era when many down-and-out souls turned to government bureaucracy for help. Here was an example for all Americans. It was a replay of the epic pioneer saga with which most Americans still identified.

But it was also mostly smokescreen. No one was more tireless in exposing this fact than Dean R. Brimhall, administrative assistant in the Department of Labor Management, of the Works Projects Administration during the mid-to-late 1930s. As a competent bureaucrat Brimhall resented the pro-Mormon publicity that rode on the coattails of publicly administered monies. Many of Brimhall's letters and notes have been preserved at the University of Utah library in the Dean R. Brimhall Papers. They reveal, through the eyes of a first-hand participant, a welfare situation far different from the one paraded before the world.

In the summer of 1936 Brimhall visited Salt Lake City not long after the LDS Church announced the formation of its Security Program; Brimhall met with LDS Apostle Harold B. Lee (later to become Church president from 1972 to 1973). On August 7 Brimhall wrote Lee to reconfirm what had been discussed at their meeting. The contents of the letter provide a picture of the Church Security Program rarely presented to outsiders:

> I . . . understand you to say that for the present the Church had no intention of taking people from any employment financed by any relief agency such as the federal government or even county and city governments.
>
> It was also my understanding that there was no intention on the part of the Church to take the responsibility now assumed by the relief agencies of the State or local communities, whether the people concerned were members of the Church or not.
>
> It was also my understanding that the Church program has not removed anyone from the Federal Works Program or from the direct relief rolls of the State and local communities.

Brimhall added:

> You may recall that I emphasized the fact that the Federal Government did not have and has not had a single person on the dole in Utah for many months.[8]

That was in 1936. The myth that the LDS Church had removed most or all of its members from public assistance persisted, however, while available statistics told a different story. As early as 1935 Bishop Sylvester Q. Cannon of the Presiding Bishopric in Salt Lake City wrote to the Social Service Division director of the Salt Lake County Emergency Relief Administration asking for information on Latter-day Saints receiving aid. In providing statistics the director commented that the numbers were smaller than at first estimated because during the month before, many individuals had found work with WPA. Nevertheless, of 6,786 cases on nonworking relief 4,100 (or *61 percent*) were LDS members.[9] In late 1937 Brimhall noted to a friend that only six states had a "higher load" on the Emergency Works Program than Utah. He concluded:

> I am sorry that I cannot be more flattering to the [LDS] Organization which we watch with so much interest but the fact remains that most of the propaganda that has come out about the efforts of the Utah Church is fictitious.[10]

One year later the Mormons had still failed to reduce significantly the proportion of members dependent on some form of federal aid:

> So far as Utah as a whole is concerned, it has a very heavy federal Works Program load. . . The number of people receiving Old Age Pensions and the Aid to Dependent Children are both among the highest in the United States. I am enclosing a copy of the latest statistical report from the Social Security Board which will give you the facts about Old Age Pensions and Aid to Dependent Children. *You will see that in proportion to its population, Utah is getting assistance for more people on the whole than most any state in the country.* Furthermore, the pensions paid to old age recipients are a good deal above the average in the United States.[11] (Italics ours)

Brimhall (but not the general public) was aware of an official LDS Church policy statement on welfare issued in April 1938. It explicitly stated:

> The Church has not yet made any effort, or pretended to make any effort to take members from governmental work projects. It has merely urged those on such projects to do a full day's work for a day's pay.[12]

Brimhall's own research clearly showed that the picture of Mormons removing thousands (let alone tens of thousands) of their fellow Church members from public welfare rolls to rely instead on Church funds was a statistical impossibility. In an unpublished manuscript entitled "The Myth of Mormon Work Relief," written in January 1938, Brimhall described how the Mormons had managed this public relations coup. After realizing that state and federal relief funds were to be drastically cut and aware that their own in-Church charities had shrunk during the Depression, LDS officials became worried.

> They had carried on, for years, the conventional gifts of food and clothing to a few of their indigent members. They apparently suddenly realized that murmurings of devout members who had paid tithing. . . were asking themselves whether it would not be more sensible to buy an insurance annuity than to pay such a huge percentage of their earnings and then find their church unable to reciprocate by helping them during "evil times."[13]

LDS officials soon learned, Brimhall reported, that in Salt Lake County alone the relief load was 60 percent Mormon. In April 1936 these same officials announced at the General Conference that

the Church had a plan to take care of all its members. They suddenly became violent critics of direct relief and criticized "government" doles, quite ignoring the fact that the Federal government had beaten them to this idea by nearly a year.[14]

Nineteen thirty-six was an election year, with Democrat Franklin D. Roosevelt pitted against Republican Alf Landon. J. Reuben Clark, a prominent Mormon Republican and adviser to Landon as well as first counselor in the presidency of the Church, made much of the Mormon plan in speeches. In October, shortly before the presidential election, Clark announced to the world that

the Church plan had succeeded. All Mormons were off relief. National publicity immediately followed. Numerous articles have been published saying that the Mormons had taken more than 80,000 off the relief rolls. The astonished reactionary press seized on this with avidity. At last someone had shown that "it could be done" without government aid.[15]

The Mormons could never produce the evidence to back up their claims. Brimhall's own statistics showed that the Mormons possibly had about 80,000 men and women receiving some form of unspecified federal assistance at one time, but that number never received straight relief, and that number was never removed from the rolls of public relief or work projects. Rather, Brimhall found:

Less than four thousand persons in all the world who needed assistance worked some time or other on Mormon Church projects. Some may have worked a day or two, some may have worked a month. No man-months or man-years are given . . . From 80,000 or more we come to the published fact that less than 4,000 worked some unknown length of time at some given time during 1936 on some Mormon Church Security program project. Many of these 3,865 were no doubt workers on federal projects who, as devoted Mormons, worked occasionally for the Church.

During this time the federal government continues to spend millions taking care of Mormons not only in Utah but in other states. [Indeed, Brimhall discovered the simple, telling ratio that the greater the proportion of Mormons in a western county the greater the federal relief load.] The Federal Surplus Commodity Corporation, a mere sideshow of the public assistance, has distributed to Mormons many times the amount produced by the Mormons on their "work projects." The WPA School Lunch Program alone, has distributed in Utah many times as much food to needy children as has been produced by the entire Mormon Church Program throughout the world.[16]

By the late 1930s Brimhall, among others, was irked at publicity that praised the LDS Church for its alleged exemplary ability to "take care of its own." Much of the frustration came from a press that found the image of Mormon self-reliance too attractive to re-examine critically. (As we indicated in Chapter 2, it was also an era when many Americans, including Hollywood, rediscovered the Mormon experience in a romantic fashion.) In November 1937 Brimhall had written to reporter John Franklin Carter: "The Mormons are very much concerned about the publicity they have had since they are afraid that the exposure of the true conditions will bring them disrepute."[17] Nevertheless, newspaper editorials and articles across the country, in places such as the New York *Herald Tribune*, called on the federal government to learn from the LDS example and stop pouring relief funds "down the drain." In January 1939 Brimhall wrote to a colleague: "The federal work rolls continue to be very high in Utah so that the non-Mormons are very much put out by the publicity of the Mormon Church because it looks as if practically all the non-Mormons must be on some form of Government Work or relief." Brimhall noted in the same letter that the Old Age Pension benefits in Utah were the second highest in the country but, after investigation by the national Social Security Board, justified. Likewise, approximately 5,000 children were provided for under the Social Security Act. Brimhall pointedly concluded, "You can see, therefore, that the claims of the Mormon Church are absurd from every angle."[18]

Even more galling to federal officials was the willingness of Church security spokespersons to take the credit for WPA projects while simultaneously criticizing the government for its "spending spree" of welfare funds. A massive irrigation project in the Uintah

Basin that included a WPA-built dam was one such episode: in 1938 the *Deseret News* published pictures of the dam describing this as the type of project sponsored by the Church security plan.[19] But the Church Security Program never took on such a spectacular enterprise. It simply never had the manpower.

Gordon Taylor Hyde, a local Salt Lake City bishop, summed up the real dependence of many Mormons on government aid during the Depression. In a letter to a candidate for the U.S. Senate who had spoken contemptuously about persons employed in public works projects, Hyde said:

> It is my opinion, and that of many other Bishops, that without the aid of the present government relief projects it would be impossible to care for the unemployed members of our church. I feel a deep sense of gratitude for the government assistance which has been rendered to the unemployed.[20]

In spite of dubious evidence, the LDS Church's public relations campaign worked. Most Mormons in dire straits continued to receive employment or other aid from the federal government while the Church took the credit. The Church was eventually to establish, for a time, a more substantial welfare enterprise. But these efforts did little to ease the misery of many Mormons during the Depression.

The Rise and Fall of the Mormon Welfare Promise

World War II improved the prospects for a genuine Church welfare system. Tens of thousands of European Saints in war-torn nations such as Holland, Belgium, France, Germany, and England had been reduced to living at a subsistence level. The millennial fears of Mormon leadership — that future global conflict and economic depressions would lead to calamities worse than those of the 1930s — seemed to be coming true during the early 1940s. Large numbers of Church members were about as badly off as any biblical prophecy might have left them.

To its credit the LDS Church did mobilize relief efforts for its European members on an enormous scale. In January 1946 the Church began sending supplies — eventually more than eighty-five railroad freight cars' worth of food, clothing, and bedding in that year alone — across the Atlantic. Elder Ezra Taft Benson was sent as the Church's official emissary to inspect the suffering of Saints in the various countries. Soon after, in a charitable gesture of reconciliation, the Dutch Saints sent the first convoy of sixty tons of foodstuffs to their German counterparts.[21] In this country the Women's Relief Society of the Church enlarged its child welfare department to provide aid for the orphans of European Church families killed. A special Church-wide fast day was established to generate special relief funds to be sent to Europe.

Ironically, this postwar international relief effort generated momentum in the Church's American welfare activities. In 1947 the Welfare Program was declared a permanent operation of the Church, and it began to serve meaningful numbers of Mormons in this country as well as in Europe. The growth of the program during the next decade and a half was phenomenal. Commodities in the Regional Bishops' Storehouses (where relief goods were kept) increased in value from $385,836 in 1946 to $2,420,770 in 1960. The Welfare Program's total assets increased from $4 million to $44 million during that same time, and the number of families assisted by these funds grew from 8,000 to 27,000.[22] By 1971 the Welfare Program was providing annually $17,722,800 in direct assistance from fast offerings, special grants from other Church funds, and commodities donated by members.[23]

Growth in the Church's Welfare Program during the 1970s gave promise of substantiating the public image of a Church both determined and able to take care of its own. For example, on October 1, 1971, Congressman William Springer of Illinois entered remarks into the *Congressional Record* that contrasted a glowing picture of the Mormon welfare system with the federal counterpart (which he described as "bordering on chaos"):

> I know no other religious group which is working on this problem of taking care of the members of its own church without application to the Federal Government for assistance. The real surprising thing is that Mormon welfare rolls have shown a steady decline in the past three years, whereas the U.S. Government welfare rolls have expanded in a tremendously increasing rate over the same period.[24]

Springer admitted that his information was thirdhand. Indeed, his claim does not make statistical sense. It is unlikely, given the massive growth of LDS Church expenditures in this area, that Mormon welfare rolls actually shrank. The indefatigable Dean R. Brimhall — by 1966 retired from government service and living in Utah, but still pricking Mormon balloons when they concerned the welfare issue — wrote the *Salt Lake Tribune* a feisty letter long after the Mormon welfare image had become firmly ensconced in the popular mind. He noted that whenever he asked the Utah State welfare statisticians about the effect of the Church's Welfare Program on the overall state welfare load, he always received the reply that they had no real figures. He went on to comment about the "spate" of letters the *Tribune* has received over the controversy of whether to tax or not to tax LDS welfare properties. He selected two Utah counties, Uintah and Juab, in which many antitax Mormon letter writers lived. He pointed out:

> State and federal expenditures for welfare for Uintah county for February, 1966 (latest current figures) totaled $44,286, and for the same month $18,684 for Juab. (These figures do not include Social Security payments). Now if these expenditures are for one month it is clear that the annual expenditures by the state and federal government in these counties will be well over a half million dollars. If one could get similar reliable figures from the LDS Welfare officials the conflicts of opinion would be pretty well erased.
>
> To assume that these large sums for only two rural counties went only to non-LDS Church members, as is often implied, would be absurd. So, who gets what out of the LDS welfare enterprises? What is the total production and cash collected and who gets what of each? Is the claim that LDS people "Take care of their own" a myth? I fear it is.[25]

Nonetheless, the Church pushed ahead, increasing its welfare resources and plans to provide greater support for its less fortunate members. As mentioned in Chapter 2, during 1974–75 the Church authorized the New York City consulting firm of Crescent, McCormick & Paget to do an intensive evaluation of its Welfare Department and the Presiding Bishopric's office, the committee of three men charged with supervising all accounting and expenditure policies of the Church. One important recommendation of CMP was a major expansion of the welfare services of the Church. The firm proposed a "master plan," or blueprint, for this task that suggested four alternative levels of assistance to poor and needy Saints. Each level entailed meeting the needs of different percentages of the overall membership. Level III, for example, called for meeting the needs of approximately one-third of the Church membership if necessary while level IV — the most ambitious — called for the Church to be able to take care of a full 40 percent of its members.

We do not know with certainty which level of the master plan was ultimately supported by all Church officials (if indeed there was unanimous agreement). The fact that the growing Church would have had to expand most of its facilities anyway, even if CMP's master plan had never been drawn up, complicates matters. However, after reviewing the massive effort to increase the welfare program, we can infer that one of the higher, more comprehensive assistance levels became the Church goal. Throughout the latter half of the 1970s the Church began pouring vast amounts of money and energy into meeting this challenge. The effort was clearly regarded by Church leaders as part of the Church's millennial mission. Marion G. Romney, first counselor to the Church president, declared in 1975:

> This is the forerunner of the United Order. We have to live the program . . . The Lord will bless us and the [Welfare] program will spread all over the world. This will be in preparation for the coming of the Lord Jesus Christ in the not too distant future![26]

Church publications and Gentile newspapers point to many of the ways this was being done. In 1975 Bishop Victor L. Brown, presiding bishop of the First Bishopric, according to one official report "spoke of the great growth of the Church and subsequent expansion of the Church welfare service." "Before we're through," Brown declared, "the welfare program will give help to everyone in the Church throughout the world."[27]

In 1975 there were only seventy-eight regional Bishops' Storehouses in the Church Welfare Program, but by 1979 the Church claimed to have built more than one hundred with half a dozen at the completion stage and more planned for 1980.[28] Beginning in 1979 welfare farms and factories to produce supplies for the program were launched in countries like Australia, England, South Korea, and Fiji and Samoa in the South Pacific. By 1979 there were thirty-two fruit and vegetable canneries in operation.[29] The farming projects alone jumped from approximately 475 in 1975 to about 600 in 1979.[30]

Our interviews with ranch foremen and managers, present and former stake presidents, and former stake welfare committee chairmen (usually also members of their stakes' High Councils) told a similar story. In late 1979 and throughout 1980 the Church searched to acquire more land to bring under farming production. It looked particularly in Montana and North Dakota for approximately 45,000 acres on which it could grow enough hard winter wheat and sunflower seeds to help care for the needs of its members at level IV, the most comprehensive, of the master plan. Plans were under way to eventually expand other projects as well, such as the honey project of the Rapid City, South Dakota, stake. That stake was to have increased its eighty honey-producing beehives to *one thousand*, according to master plan guidelines. That much production alone would have supplied the honey needs of between 30 and 40 percent of all Church members. In 1979 and the early 1980s the Church also constructed many new dairies, some of them costing millions of dollars. The ultra-modern dairies completed in 1981 at Fallon, Nevada, and Queen Creek, Arizona, for instance, cost the Church about $2.5 million each to build. They each had the capability of milking 700 cows or more if necessary.

In these ways, an estimated $200 million or more (using a variety of separate estimates on real estate, livestock, construction, and other values) was spent between 1975 and 1981 by Church officials to improve and expand the Welfare Program following the guidlines of the master plan. These efforts received media attention and earned the Church a good deal of favorable publicity. President Reagan went on record in late fall 1981 as praising the Mormon Welfare Program and encouraging other churches to adopt a similar "help-thy-neighbor policy" to replace federal government welfare programs.[31] In fact, Reagan was so impressed by what the LDS organization had accomplished that he personally visited Church leaders in September 1982. Escorted by Gordon B. Hinckley of the Church's First Presidency, Reagan toured a welfare cannery facility in Ogden, Utah. He said after the tour that having volunteer labor in the Mormon Welfare Program is "an idea that once characterized our nation...an ideal that should be reborn nationwide...it holds the key to the renewal of America and the years ahead.[32]

But in late 1980 something else was happening. Church accountants and financial administrators began to calculate the costs ultimately involved in implementing this master plan. The growing number of poor families being successfully missionized in Central and South America alone (once the Church opened its priesthood to nonwhites) was one important economic consideration. In many cases recent converts were among the "poorest of the poor."[33] Another factor was the many Mormons who had been hurt economically during the recession of the late 1970s. Some Accounting Department officials (among others) estimated enormous figures, such as $615 million as the start-up cost to implement the master plan. Eventually projected costs simply became more than Church leaders wanted to bear. One official in the Church Welfare Social Services explained that the political ramifications would have been of great magnitude. In European countries, for example, there are laws that prohibit the owning of land by any religious organization and the excess accumulation (or hoarding) of foodstuffs and other necessary supplies. He said, "There was a lot of discussion concerning the negative impact which such large land acquisitions might make. It was decided not to implement this aspect of the Master Plan."[34]

The result of the Church's reassessment was a little-publicized retreat from the optimistic promise of a truly meaningful Church welfare program. Gordon B. Hinckley told one large gathering of regional representatives, stake presidents, and ward bishops in spring 1981 that expenses had to be cut to the bone. He urged "leaders at all levels of Church administration to carefully examine the cost of Church activity to members and ensure that such costs are not unnecessarily burdensome." He stated that "requests for additional welfare production projects and storehouses should be made only if added financial demands on members are not excessive." As one first step in this austerity drive, Hinckley announced a moratorium on acquisition and development of distant recreation properties.[35]

The Church dissolved nearly all the welfare production committees which had previously been established in each stake. Church officials announced a new policy change in the Welfare Program at the April General Conference in 1983. Henceforth, all welfare properties of the Church, which had formerly been owned by the individual stakes, would now revert to the Church and be owned and controlled by the Salt Lake City headquarters. The Church Investment Department was one of the principal movers to urge Church leaders to reduce substantially its welfare properties. It wanted to sell off the land, buildings, and livestock and put the money into some of its more lucrative investment portfolios from which it could then draw substantial interest.[36] A number of canneries that processed Church-grown produce were closed.[37] Certain welfare dairies were shut down, their herds either transferred or sold, and the land and buildings disposed of for the highest market price. Even some profitable, well-managed dairies were shut down.[38] In 1982 the Church owned thirty-three operating dairy farms. One year later this number had been trimmed to twenty-seven, with more reductions planned. For example, the modern dairy facilities recently built at Fallon, Nevada, in 1981 for $2.5 million were scheduled to be auctioned off only two years later.[39] Meanwhile the Church was also consolidating its welfare farmland properties. In 1980 it owned more than 210,000 acres, but after the decision to retrench, Church officials immediately ordered the sale of land not then directly producing for the Welfare Program. By summer 1983, welfare land holdings were down to approximately 180,000 acres with a final level sought of only 100,000 to 125,000 acres.[40]

Much of this turnabout in welfare policy received no public notice, even from Church members. In 1981, when President Reagan first praised the Church's Welfare Program, the Church had already declared a moratorium on building. By 1982 Church projections for taking care of the needy began dropping, first from the master plan's ideal level of help for 30 to 40 percent of Church membership to 15 percent and then (by the time Reagan toured some of the Church's welfare projects during a political campaign in 1982) a dismal 7 percent. After Reagan left Utah that number was again readjusted to 3–4 percent. It presently stands at less than 1.5 percent of the entire Church membership.[41]

In the end, however, nothing else demonstrates the Church's evaporating welfare hopes as well as the shrinking number of regional Bishops' Storehouses around the country. These store and manage welfare goods and products for needy members. In 1979 there were close to 106 regional Bishops' Storehouses in the Church's welfare system.[42] Yet by mid-1983 the number had been reduced to 71, a loss of roughly three dozen storehouses and a good indication of the Church's shifting commitment away from its earlier welfare aspirations. As one official in the Church Welfare Department told us half-jokingly in summer 1983:

> Only the feeble, halt, dumb, and blind will qualify for Church welfare when we get done! . . . The days of Church doles are just about over! We simply can't afford to feed our members like we used to. Other things have taken greater priority.[43]

There were other reasons for halting the expansion of the Welfare Program besides the tremendous membership gains in poor Third World populations, however. By the early 1980s many American welfare farms operated in the red, in essence subsidized by the Church Welfare Department. Sometimes the losses were a matter of pure bad luck. A prime example is the Boulder Stake Farm in Plattsville-Mead, Colorado. Despite skilled management, that farm lost a total of over $265,000 over three straight years.[44] One LDS dairy farm in Gilbert, Arizona, suffered disaster after twenty years of successful operation when its entire herd of 400 cows contracted tuberculosis and had to be destroyed. In Woodcrest, California, Church-owned citrus groves lost $3.4 million over fifteen years, a loss shared by twenty-seven stakes. Droughts, freezes, water increases, and similar problems eventually made the enterprise prohibitively expensive to operate.[45]

Other losses can be explained by negligence. For instance, over half a million cans of corned beef had to be taken to the Los Angeles County dump in 1981 because welfare employees at the Church's cannery in west Los Angeles failed to keep the proper records required by the Food and Drug Administration and other government agencies. The irony was that the food was edible, safe, and unspoiled. It was simply a bureaucratic error that led to the massive throw-away.[46]

Other losses are the result of mismanagement. In many areas stake officials had authority over farm or ranch managers but no working knowledge of agriculture. This happened at the Stake Welfare and Dairy Farm in Fallon, Nevada, where a stake president with no agricultural expertise tried to dictate policy to the project manager. In such cases the Church's rigid hierarchy proves to be a detriment to efficient operation of farms.[47]

An official in the Church Welfare Social Services office in Colton, California, concurred:

> For every success we have a large number of miserable failures to go with it. I think part of the problem lies in poor management. The other problem is with some of the stake presidents. You can have an excellent manager on a welfare farm, but his superior is a stake president who doesn't know beans about farming.[48]

He gave the example of the Church's hay ranch in Bakersfield, California. Originally the ranch had 900 acres of alfalfa hay, but instead of laying tile pipes beneath the land to let the excess water run into sump holes, the Church tried to cut corners by doing without pipes. The soil turned alkaline as a result and required half a million dollars to reclaim.

The LDS Church Welfare Program is already beyond the crossroads. Since the early 1980s it appears to have taken a step backward — not only away from the real opportunity it had to become the only American religion capable of supporting all its needy members but also back toward its "paper" welfare system of the 1930s. The chance to establish a truly independent, comprehensive welfare system for its members has, for the time being, been stymied by Church leaders. They will have enormous difficulty recovering it.

CHURCH AUTHORITY AND CENSORSHIP

In mid-April 1983 a late, heavy snowfall in the Wasatch and Uinta Mountains, together with warm temperatures, resulted in the worst flooding in Utah's history. More than 2,000 people had to flee their homes. The floodwaters and mud slides caused more than $200 million in damage. In location after location, however, Mormon volunteers came forward to fill sandbags, build makeshift levees, remove mud, or help support the workers. Often they mustered in an incredibly short time.

It was a perfect public relations event for the LDS Church, and the media responded accordingly. *Time* magazine's admiring references to the Church's complex organizational pyramid and the popular stereotype of Mormon values noted:

Utah's ordeal has put the Mormon virtues of organization, self-reliance and unstinting community service to the test. So far, the mud is losing — without heavy involvement on the part of the Federal Government.

The article quoted Utah Governor Scott M. Matheson's boast:

The Mormon Church has the best grapevine in the world. One phone call to the church triggered the quickest network of activity I've ever seen. When you push the button, people come out in droves.[49]

But there is a price paid for such spectacular mobilization. It is the pressure to conform in other matters not so directly tied to survival. Strictly speaking, the LDS president, as the living prophet of God, works through his apostles and lesser authorities to administer the providence, or will, of God. Because revelations may cover any subject, there is in theory no corner of members' lives exempt from Church authority. That quickly becomes apparent to Mormons when they seek temple recommends, certification to go through formal temple rituals, and have the most intimate aspects of their lives examined by Church leaders. Nor is the prophet's authority (and by implication his apostles' and administrators' authority) to be questioned. One apostle, Ezra Taft Benson, has claimed that the living prophet's revelations can overrule even the Bible, the *Book of Mormon*, and *Doctrine and Covenants* scriptures.[50]

The Church was not always so undemocratic. Modern Mormon leaders do not like to recall the looser, more open style of earlier Church administration. It was formerly the custom to discuss openly the strengths and weaknesses of the brethren, that is, the twelve apostles, before the president called for the membership at General Conference to "recommend" and "sustain" them with a show of hands. At one General Conference in 1838 a speaker named D. W. Patten spoke in praise of six men in the apostleship whom he could recommend to the conference; but he criticized one other member and flatly said he could not recommend four others.[51]

Brigham Young, one of the six recommended apostles, encouraged such honest dissent and discussion. In 1860 he told Mormons at General Conference:

We will first present the authorities of the Church; and I sincerely request the members to act freely and independently in voting, — also in speaking, if it be necessary. There has been no instance in this Church of a person's being in the least curtailed in the privilege of speaking his honest sentiments.

And Young assured Conference participants:

When I present the authorities of this Church for the Conference to vote upon, if there is a member here who honestly and sincerely thinks that any person whose name is presented should not hold the office he is appointed to fill, let him speak. I will give full liberty, not to preach sermons, nor to degrade character, but to briefly state objections, and at the proper time I will hear the reasons for any objections that may be advanced.[52]

However, the leadership style became more authoritarian as the Church increased in size. By 1945 the current practice by which leaders announce a decision and rank-and-file members rubber-stamp it had become set. In the June 1945 issue of the *Ward Teacher's Message* (a now defunct publication), the following policy of unquestioning submission was unabashedly defended:

When our leaders speak, *the thinking has been done.* When they propose a plan — it is God's plan. When they point the way, there is no other which is safe. When they give direction it should mark the end of controversy. God works in no other way. To think otherwise, without immediate repentence, may cost one his faith, may destroy his testimony, and leave him a stranger to the Kingdom of God.[53]

Elder Marion G. Romney, first counselor to President Spencer W. Kimball in the early 1980s, recalled similar sentiments voiced by the late President Heber J. Grant about the same time as the preceding quote. Grant said to Romney:

My boy, you always keep your eye on the President of the Church, and if he tells you to do something wrong, and you do it, the Lord will bless you for it.[54]

Compare that modern-day exhortation to trust blindly in LDS leadership with the more cautious attitude of the first-generation Saints. The following excerpt from an editorial in the November 13,

1852, issue of the *Millennial Star* (an English Mormon periodical)
presents a more fallible picture of Mormon authority:

> the question is sometimes asked — to what extent is obedience
> to those who hold the Priesthood required? This is a very
> important question, and one which should be understood by all
> Saints. In attempting to answer this question, we would repeat,
> in short, what we have already written, that willing obedience
> to the laws of God, administered by the Priesthood, is indispen-
> sable to salvation; *but we would further add, that a proper
> conservative to this power exists for the benefit of all, and none are
> required to tamely and blindly submit to a man because he has a
> portion of the Priesthood.*[55] (Italics partially ours)

The *Millennial Star* editorial goes on to condemn the uncritical,
lemming-like loyalty that Grant later espoused:

> We have heard men who hold the Priesthood remark, that they
> would do any thing they were told to do by those who presided
> over them, *if they knew it was wrong*: but such obedience as this
> is worse than folly to us; it is slavery in the extreme; and the man
> who would thus willingly degrade himself, should not claim a
> rank among intelligent beings, unless he turns from his folly.
>
> When the Elders of Israel will so far indulge in these extreme
> notions of obedience, as to teach them to the people, it is generally
> because they have it in their hearts to do wrong themselves, and
> wish to pave the way to accomplish that wrong; or else because
> they have done wrong, and wish to use the cloak of their authority
> to cover it.[56]

Throughout this century various observers have concluded that
the Mormon Church has traveled far down the road to an
authoritarian, elitist style of governing itself where most members
have little if any input. For example, one writer in 1947 concluded
that the Church had long ago lost the democratic impulse it demonstrated in its early days:

> [The Church's] only democratic characteristic inheres in the right
> of the membership to accept or reject law or doctrine transmitted
> from on high. There is no provision in the Church for nominations
> by the membership of the governing authorities, and church
> elections have the doubtful status of oral plebiscites.[57]

Dean R. Brimhall, the Utah-born critic of Mormon propaganda, had some unflattering words about the Mormons' regular "oral plebiscites" at their General Conference votes. In a letter to a sociologist in 1939 he commented:

I am sorry that no one has even taken a picture of the [General Conference] audience voting to accept the Church leaders for a new period of office. Every hand in the audience goes up simultaneously. The question of voting "Yes" or "No" on a particular candidate is so mechanical that the hands go up in a unison that is most dramatic. No member is ever asked to choose between two individuals; he is asked to vote "Yes" or "No" on the official or on the policies of the Church, as the case may be . . . The officials would be highly indignant if there were any hands raised in opposition and there have been instances where one hand has gone up in opposition and the person attempted to explain the reason for his opposition but such a person is usually ejected.

Brimhall concluded: "I do not want to bother you with the story but I am sure that any student of Sociology who is interested in the problem of authoritarianism would find the Mormon Church a laboratory rich in material for his studies."[58]

In the 1980s the system of authority has become even more fossilized than in Brimhall's day. Church publications now routinely proclaim the inerrancy of Church presidents (and, by extension, their apostles and assistants). In late 1981 the *Church News* asserted:

God will do nothing regarding His work except through His own duly anointed prophets! They are His servants. They are the watchmen on the towers of Zion.

They will give us the Lord's word in no uncertain terms as God makes it known. That is why He has His prophets on earth. They are for the edification of the Saints and to protect us from every wind of doctrine. Let us follow them and avoid being led astray.[59]

There is not just a patriarchy in the modern LDS Church structure but also among many members a "patriolotry" of the brethren. Questioning revelations as well as doubting the more mundane secular policy statements given by the Mormon gerontocracy has become increasingly taboo. The late Apostle Bruce R. McConkie bluntly asserted that "Christ and his prophets go together...it is not possible to believe in one without believing in the other...by rejecting the prophets we reject Christ himself.''[60] The result is a cloning from the top, a pressuring of leaders at each lower level in the Church hierarchy to conform to the wishes and attitudes of the leaders above them. The most extreme example of this trend can be seen in a speech delivered to a Brigham Young University audience by Ezra Taft Benson, the apostle next in line to become Church president when Spencer W. Kimball dies. Benson proclaimed to BYU students fourteen "fundamental" statements about the relation of Mormon prophets to the Church and the LDS membership. He warned students: "our salvation hangs on them.''[61] They are worth listing to appreciate the centralization of power Church leaders now claim for themselves and the blind obedience they expect.

FIRST: The prophet is the only man who speaks for the Lord in everything.

SECOND: The living prophet is more vital to us than the standard [scriptural] works.

THIRD: The living prophet is more important to us than a dead prophet.

FOURTH: The prophet will never lead the Church astray.

FIFTH: The prophet is not required to have any particular earthly training or credentials to speak on any subject or act on any matter at any time.

SIXTH: The prophet does not have to say "Thus Saith the Lord," to give us scripture.

SEVENTH: The prophet tells us what we need to know, not always what we want to know.

EIGHTH: The prophet is not limited by men's reasoning.

NINTH: The prophet can receive revelation on any matter, temporal or spiritual.

TENTH: The prophet may be involved in civic matters.

ELEVENTH: The two groups who have the greatest difficulty in following the prophet are the proud who are learned and the proud who are rich.

TWELFTH: The prophet will not necessarily be popular with the world or the worldly.

THIRTEENTH: The prophet and his counselors make up the First Presidency — the highest quorum in the Church.

FOURTEENTH: The prophet and the presidency — the living prophet and the First Presidency — follow them and be blessed — reject them and suffer.

Consider the implications of Benson's claims. The LDS Church president can in theory make any pronouncement on any subject, regardless of his personal knowledge about it or experience, and have it regarded as "divine revelation." His authority is therefore not limited to theological or spiritual matters; it is essentially limitless. Moreover, he has greater authority than any previous Church leader or prophet, including Brigham Young and even founder Joseph Smith, or any Church scriptures. He is infallible in his decisions (or if he is only sometimes infallible, Benson implies that Mormons will never know when). The living prophet does not have to limit his involvement to Church affairs — he may become a statesman or develop any other role he chooses. And there is a strong anti-intellectual warning against "the proud who are learned" to remind those who question any Church doctrine or policy about the danger of their doubts, no matter how reasonable.

There is the real danger in such a rigid claim to absolute authority that revelation may lead to a self-righteous arrogance and an intolerance of honest dissent. It promotes the worst stifling characteristics of bureaucracy.

A good example of such stifling can be seen in the Church's ecclesiastical trial of Sonia Johnson in 1979. Johnson was a mother of four children and a former college instructor with a Ph.D. Active in her ward as a Church organist and as the teacher of a women's class, she was also an active feminist lobbying for the Equal Rights Amendment. Her outspoken stance and tactics (she once rented a plane to fly a MORMONS FOR ERA banner over Salt Lake City during a General Conference) plus her refusal to toe the mark on the Church's anti-ERA policy eventually brought charges that she had spread false doctrine and worked against Church leadership. Specifically, she was charged with defaming LDS Church leaders by accusing them of "savage misogny" (that is, woman-hating).

Sonia Johnson was tried on the charge of apostasy in late 1979. Because women cannot hold priesthood offices in the LDS Church, she was entitled only to a trial consisting of the bishopric of her ward (the bishop and his two counselors). The trial was conducted behind closed doors. She could not bring an attorney to defend her case. Witnesses were called in to testify *in secret*; she could not be present when they gave evidence against her. Ironically the Church forbade Sonia Johnson's bishop, Jeffrey Willis (the CIA's personnel director mentioned in the previous chapter), from even mentioning the Equal Rights Amendment during the trial or her efforts on its behalf. It is typical in such trials that the "defendent" is given only a vague idea of the charges, has no opportunity to hear any of the testimony given against him or her (much less any chance to challenge or cross-examine accusers), and can appeal the verdict only to the stake president and then the Church.

Sonia Johnson was excommunicated, which means that she can still attend Church services but can participate in no other congregational activities. She appealed her bishop's decision for excommunication but Church superiors upheld it. If she does not publicly repent and ask to be rebaptized, Church doctrine states that she will never be able to join her husband and children in the afterlife.[62]

Ecclesiastical courts have no jurisdiction outside their own internal affairs, of course, and are not obliged to uphold the standards of due process and civil liberties required of secular courts. When heresy, apostasy, or other evil is suspected by Mormon leaders, the accused is often presumed guilty until proven innocent. Under conditions such as those in which the Mormon Church tries its accused dissidents, the odds are indeed against fair play. The very knowledge of such Kafkaesque "star chamber" proceedings that can isolate an individual not just from Church, community, and friends but even from family members, can have a chilling effect on any will to express sincere, opposition to Church policies.

Censorship at BYU

Journalist Peter Bart described Brigham Young University in a *Rolling Stone* article as "the educational showpiece of the Mormon nation," a "perfect microcosm of the best and worst" of Mormonism. He says of this institution where 97 percent of the students are Mormons:

It's a place where no one is allowed to drink or smoke; where sex is outlawed for everyone but married couples; where public figures like Senator Edward Kennedy and former first lady Betty Ford have been prevented from speaking on campus and films like *The Godfather* deemed unfit for student viewing; where a boy was brought to trial for looking up a girl's skirt in the library stacks (the girl never noticed, but a security man did); and where gays are not only systematically expelled but, until recent years, were even subjected occasionally to electroshock therapy to treat their "affliction."[63]

BYU is an internationally respected university with an impressive record of inventions, research, and scholarly accomplishments. Its faculty members are prominent in their respective disciplines; many have served in high-level government positions as well. Compared with other schools of similar size and caliber, however, BYU emerges as not just conservative but at times repressive of students and faculty. As members of a religiously affiliated institution, BYU students are understandably required to earn a certain number of credit hours in Mormon religious instruction. But other unique characteristics and symptomatic events are not far to seek:

—Reminiscent of the 1950s, BYU retains a dress code for students (no tanktops, sweatsuits, and the like for males; modest-length skirts or slacks for women).

—The sexual violations section of the Student Code of Honor forbids masturbation. Journalist Peter Bart remarks: "Some bishops distribute a handbook that dispenses some unusual recommendations to male students on how to curb their onanistic urge: avoid spicy foods, keep your shower door slightly ajar, and if all else fails, tie your hand to the bedpost . . . when *Playboy* magazine declared recently that, based on its survey of major college campuses, BYU had the lowest sexual temperature, the news was greeted with a sense of relief on campus."[64]

—Politics play a definite role in determining the student extracurricular groups that may exist. As in the outside Mormon world conservatism reigns. For example, in 1982 Amnesty International was denied club status on campus.[65]

—Student dissent is closely monitored and narrowly interpreted. In spring 1982 four students who protested the campus visit of General William Westmoreland were subsequently called on the carpet by the University Standards office and threatened with suspension.[66]

—During the mid-1960s Ernest L. Wilkinson, the BYU president who ran unsuccessfully for a U.S. Senate seat, organized a special squad of students to "gather information about professors whose political views differed from his own." A university committee of three vice-presidents investigated charges of such a "spy ring" and concluded they were true.[67] Until 1981 there was even a program paying cash to students for informing on one another's violations of the student code.[68]

—Accused of singing some songs that were "hard acid rock" and possibly "satanic," the popular musical group Earth, Wind, and Fire was banned from performing on campus.[69]

Against considerable but futile Gentile opposition the largely Mormon Utah legislature in 1979 passed House Bill 80 giving BYU campus police (agents of a private parochial school) public powers of arrest and law enforcement *throughout Utah*. That is, campus police were given all the powers possessed by police in cities and by county sheriffs. This effectively created a private police force, hired by and accountable to BYU administrators but with statewide authority.[70] (The unfortunate male student caught sneaking a glance up the coed's skirt in the BYU library was arrested for public lewdness.) One attorney commented: "BYU police are more concerned with petty offenses than any university force I know of."[71]

BYU students remain relatively isolated from influences that might seem benign to outsiders but which disturb the Mormon trustees of the "Y," as BYU is called. School administrators apparently feel the need to protect students' ideological virtue as well as their celibacy. In March 1980 the student newspaper, the *Daily Universe*, learned that the Board of Trustees and school officials had barred a number of well-known, respected public figures from speaking to student assemblies. According to the *Salt Lake Tribune*:

> Some speakers were rejected because of their politics, in spite of university policies prohibiting politics as a criterion for selecting speakers, and others were rejected for their "reputation" or statements on moral issues.[72]

The list of banned speakers reads like a Who's Who of prominent personalities on the college lecture circuit: Senator Edward Kennedy, Betty Ford, Senator George McGovern, consumer advocate Ralph Nader (one university official said the school "should not pay for carping"), and former Secretary of State Henry Kissinger.

A three-part series on homosexuality in Utah to have been aired on KBYU, the school's own television station, was halted after only the first segment. School administrators claimed they did not directly stop the series, but they made their displeasure clearly known to KBYU's general manager. What irked them in particular were the interviews with homosexual students at BYU and the lighting effect used to darken their faces to protect their identities.[73] (Admitting to being a homosexual at BYU results in automatic dismissal from the university.)

However, nothing better illustrates the thin-skinned sensitivities of BYU administrators and their willingness to run off dissenters than the fate of the short-lived but controversial *Seventh East Press*. Begun in 1981, the *Seventh East Press* was an independent off-campus newspaper in Provo, Utah, staffed largely by BYU student volunteers. Unlike the much larger, official (Church-supported) university newspaper, the *Daily Universe*, which reached most of the school's 26,000 students, the *Seventh East Press* had a more modest circulation of 4,000. It specialized in the type of "critical" journalism eschewed by the more conservative school paper: stories on the history of dissent at BYU (and administrative intolerance of it), current student protests, homosexuals on campus, the BYU president's "spy ring," and similar exposés. About evenly dependent on readers' subscriptions/campus sales and local advertising, the *Seventh East Press* was the type of alternative newspaper common in large university communities but an anomaly in the rigidly controlled climate of BYU.

The beginning of the end for the *Seventh East Press* was an interview published in the January 11, 1983, issue with Dr. Sterling

McMurrin, a Mormon philosophy professor at the University of Utah and respected former U.S. commissioner of education. Quoted as saying that he did not believe the *Book of Mormon* to be an authentic historical record, McMurrin continued:

> I came to the conclusion at a very early age, earlier than I can remember, that you don't get books from angels and translate them by miracles; it is just that simple. So I simply don't believe the Book of Mormon to be authentic. I think that all of the hassling over the authenticity of the Book of Mormon is just a waste of time.

For good measure the interview threw in some of McMurrin's negative comments about the Church's presentation of its own history:

> Many things have been intentionally ignored and sometimes concealed or have been taken to have religious meanings or implications which, in my opinion, have no religious connections whatsoever. I believe that the Church has intentionally distorted its own history by dealing fast and loose with historical data and imposing theological and religious interpretations on the data that are entirely unwarranted.[74]

That interview began a controversy with revealing overtones. On February 9, 1983, the *Seventh East Press* was banned from BYU's Provo campus. The official statement of Public Relations Director Paul Richards read:

> BYU is withdrawing permission for the *7th East Press* to sell or distribute issues on campus. BYU is a private university, owned and operated by the Mormon Church and articles relating to the Church have caused the University to feel it has no obligation to provide facilities for the distribution of the paper.[75]

Dean Haffaker, age twenty-two, the *Press*'s editor, tried unsuccessfully to have the ban reversed through an attorney who met with school officials. Meanwhile, the school's announcement produced split reactions among students and faculty. For example, the BYU chapter of the Society of Professional Journalists sent a letter (despite divided opinion among its own members) to the school administrators asking for reconsideration of the ban. The letter proclaimed: "It seems to us this Church, which is founded on truth, should not be afraid to have its members exposed to a variety of ideas." The board of directors of the Utah Headliner's chapter of the same society unanimously approved a resolution commending the chapter's letter. Nelson Wadsworth, a BYU journalism professor, concurred: "This is a freedom of information issue, and the most important thing journalists do every day is to battle for that freedom."[76] That week 160 faculty members signed petitions opposing the ban.

The staff and volunteer student workers of the *Seventh East Press* did not personally suffer any direct recriminations from the university administration. Overall, however, respect for the First Amendment's free speech clause was set back, in the opinion of one BYU professor:

> Quite frankly I was extremely disappointed and very upset to see *Seventh East Press* dismissed from the campus...It stimulated thinking and livened up the mundane routine of things around here a lot more. I hate to see it go. I think a real injustice has been done.[77]

More fallout developed over the ban. Tim Kelly, managing editor of the *Denver Post*, was scheduled as a guest lecturer at BYU the following month. But in a statement issued over the wire services on February 16 Kelly said he would decline the invitation. Explained Kelly:

> My feeling is that while the newspaper is small, the issue is large. I can't in good conscience as a journalist and a representative of The Denver Post sanction an institution that is trampling on a freedom that's a cornerstone of my profession.[78]

The most disturbing fact about the *Seventh East Press* incident was that the order to banish the newspaper on BYU's campus came from Salt Lake City and the First Presidency. The university's press statement about the ban was the result of agonizing by low-level BYU officials caught between the First Presidency's directive to purge the campus of the type of criticism offered by the independent newspaper and their own respect for free speech. One informant in the Church Public Communications Department who worked closely with the BYU public communications director said candidly:

It still bothers those of us who work here and must constantly juggle what the brethren want and what we ourselves know is right. You really have to wrestle with your conscience sometimes in cases like this, because if you don't, you're going to be in deep trouble. There are no accolades for heroes here. You either keep your mouth shut and do what you're told, or take a stand for honesty and find yourself immediately unemployed. Those, I'm afraid, are the hard, cold facts of life when you decide to work up here.[79]

There is a revealing epilogue to the *Seventh East Press* incident. Just after the *Press* published its first issue following the BYU ban, the newspaper's three-member board of trustees appointed a new editor, a BYU senior journalism major who was formerly editorial page editor for the BYU *Daily Universe*. The new editor in turn shortly announced he would change the *Seventh East Press*'s name to (tentatively) the *University Post*. The *Post*, it was said, would have less essay and commentary and more "straightforward reporting." The *Seventh East Press*'s former editor, Dean Huffaker, meanwhile decided to transfer from BYU to a California university.[80]

But there is more. Several months later plans to inaugurate a new, "independent" newspaper on the BYU campus were announced. This newcomer — to be called the *Western Scholar* — was to have a much different perspective from the *Seventh East Press*'s. It had direct connections to Apostle Ezra Taft Benson (whom many persons suspected of having been instrumental in helping ban the *Seventh East Press*) and to Cleon Skousen's Freemen Institute, in addition to about $60,000 in start-up money. About the time the *Seventh East Press* was causing furor with the McMurrin interview, Flora Parker (a founder of the right-wing Common Sense Studies, Inc.) and niece of Mark Benson, Ezra Taft Benson's son, took BYU student Stephen Reiher and the local chapter of Young Americans for Freedom to meet with Mark Benson and Cleon Skousen at the Freemen Institute in Salt Lake City. Ezra Taft Benson was instrumental in putting editor-to-be Reiher in touch with several conservative foundations, including the Institute for Educational Affairs, a New York group specializing in support of conservative student newspapers, as well as several other right-wing groups. According to Reiher, during the discussion among Benson, Skousen, Reiher, and several others, the only time the subject of the *Seventh East Press* came up was when one of us expressed concern that the ban would apply to other student newspapers like ours as well. [Ezra Taft Benson] shook his head and told us not to worry.

Reiher met with BYU's executive vice-president and the dean of student life in 1983 and received their blessing on the new newspaper project. One of the conditions was that Reiher would not print anything against the Church or against Mormon doctrine. He was told by BYU officials to print several issues and submit them for the school administration to look over. If the administration found nothing that it considered damaging or that it disapproved of, then Reiher would be allowed to distribute the new newspaper on campus.[81]

The well-heeled editors of the *Western Scholar*, bankrolled by right-wing sources outside the Church, obviously could afford to print several issues of a newspaper without even selling them. By their own account, they also considered freedom of the press a privilege in Provo, not a right.

The LDS Church and Its History

A religion such as Mormonism, which knows its beginning and is timing its accomplishments toward a definite end, is preoccupied with history. History, properly interpreted, vindicates the Church's emphasis on investments and wealth, its political involvements, and its control over many aspects of its members' lives. But, as writer Fred Esplin has observed, "History is both a blessing and a curse to Mormons."[82] The sacred history of the *Book of Mormon* has lent the movement purpose, while the secular history created a pioneer legacy and spirit still vibrant today. Yet credible history shows the blemishes, not just the heroics; it records profanity as well as fine speeches. The human quality of many early Mormons is quickly credited in chronicles of their suffering and sacrifice. But other potentially embarrassing evidence of normal human failure is not welcomed into the Mormon annals.

Mormon history has posed a persistent problem for the Church. Veneration for its highest officials, which we have termed "patriolotry," builds a tension into any "Mormon" version of history. Can history be used both to promote the faith and to give an accurate, meaningful account of events? This tension can be clearly seen in how Church-sponsored and even independent Mormon historians have treated their leaders. Historian Davis Bitton, a Mormon, has recognized this as a problem virtually built into the faith.

> The idea that nothing negative should be said about past Church leaders was a natural consequence of the position that nothing negative should be said about present leaders. "Sustaining the authorities" includes the idea, for Mormons, that one does not tear down, criticize, or otherwise resist the decisions of the leadership.[83]

Bitton, a former Church-employed historian, as well as others have pointed out how the LDS Church has put pressures on Mormon writers to "sanitize" their interpretations of Church history. Just as important, however, have been the measures taken to restrict access to specific documents and sources that might contain less than flattering information about the earlier Church. For example, most persons who have controlled the Church's archives have also been members of the General Authorities, their orthodoxy and high office serving as guarantees of their discretion. "Nonapproved" historians, including many Mormons, have routinely been denied access to the archives. Besides scrutiny of the backgrounds of researchers, other safeguarding procedures include allowing historians free access to materials but censoring their research notes; controlling the publication of research if it is released through a Church press or Church magazine; pressuring other, non-Mormon publishers not to publish certain research; and, in the event the research still makes it to publication, making sure it is never reviewed or mentioned in any Church publication.[84]

Such protectiveness is understandable, if not intellectually honest. As Sterling McMurrin said:

> Honesty is not a particularly common virtue of churches, or of any other organizations. There is nothing new about churches perverting history...Most institutions, including churches, governments, and government agencies...often find it advantageous to ignore historical facts and do a little reconstructing here and there on their own history.[85]

Such restrictions as Davis Bitton describes and "selective reconstructions" as McMurrin suggests lead to another conclusion. As

McMurrin put it: "When the Church refuses its own historians access to the materials in its archives, it obviously has something to hide."[86]

For a time, in the 1970s, changes in this policy seemed imminent. Leonard J. Arrington was called to be Church Historian, and Davis Bitton became Assistant Church Historian. Arrington was the first and only Church Historian who was not also a General Authority. Against resistance from his superiors, he tried to open Church records not just to historians but also to the Church's lay membership. In May 1972 he inaugurated the Friends of Mormon History Association for just this purpose. More than 500 interested people unexpectedly appeared at its first and only meeting. Arrington said:

> I was thoroughly delighted by such a turnout, but other ecclesiastical officials above me were completely floored by the sudden interest shown. I guess they had developed a kind of paranoia about rummaging through our archives like they would at a bargain basement sale.[87]

The Friends of Mormon History Association was short-lived. Arrington and his research colleagues made numerous attempts to secure permission to establish the association and open up Church archives. But the First Presidency repeatedly put Arrington off. Indeed, it was Apostle Ezra Taft Benson who helped squash the promise of openness in the Church History Department in 1982. Benson had once told a BYU audience:

> There have been and continue to be attempts to bring a [humanistic] philosophy into our Church history . . . to underplay revelation and God's intervention in significant events, and to inordinately humanize the prophets of God so that their human frailties become more evident than their spiritual qualities.[88]

Benson accused the "Arrington team" of just such heresies. One of Arrington's coauthored books, *Building the City of God* (dealing with economic cooperation among early Mormon pioneers), along with another book, *The Story of the Latter-day Saints* by James B. Allen and Glen Leonard, sold out, but Church leaders decided they would not be reprinted. Along with other such examples of "humanistic" scholarship, both books were placed on a blacklist of sources that the Church would not permit Mormon scholars to quote or even refer to in footnotes in any Church publications.[89] In the early 1980s Arrington and his fellow researchers were removed from the Church Historical Department and transferred to Brigham Young University.

Not that BYU champions academic freedom any more than it prizes journalistic integrity. In 1983 (the same year the Church, via the university, closed down the *Seventh East Press*) the vise started tightening on historical scholarship. First affected were at least fourteen Mormon writers, three of them BYU faculty, who had contributed articles either to the respected bimonthly *Dialogue: A Journal of Mormon Thought* or to the *Seventh East Press*. They were approached and questioned by their local bishops or stake presidents "and told the Church was worried about their faithfulness."[90] Six writers and seven editors of Mormon-oriented (but non-Church sponsored) publications admitted that they knew of such pressures.[91] Scott Faulring, a writer for the now-defunct *Seventh East Press*, received a warning from his stake president to be cautious in what he wrote. (The stake president refused to tell Faulring who had sent him and admitted that *he* had never read any of Faulring's work.)[92] Gary Bergera, who had also published articles in both the *Seventh East Press* and *Dialogue*, was visited by his Provo stake president. He recalled the familiar "patriolotry" line of questioning:

> My stake president told me that if the prophet told me to do something wrong, I would be blessed if I obliged. He said what I had written was anti-Mormon because it wasn't uplifting.[93]

One freelance LDS history writer personally knew eight others who had been interrogated by their stake presidents.[94] Even D. Michael Quinn, associate professor of history at BYU, seemed to be falling from grace. In a 1981 lecture he criticized the Church leadership's narrow view of Mormon history before a BYU student history association. At one point in tears because Church leaders had labeled him subversive, Quinn said that to avoid unsavory or unpleasant facts simply because they did not match how the Church preferred its history to have been was of "questionable honesty" and would ultimately undermine the Church's mission.[95] During the tightening of control over Mormon writers in 1983 Quinn also was called in by Gordon B. Hinckley for a "discussion" of the new "faith-promoting" history advocated by Church leaders. When respected Mormon scholar Hugh Nibley ignored similar pressures and gave a speech at BYU condemning free enterprise, a number of businessmen who were known to be generous donors to the school threatened to withhold gifts if some "corrective measures" were not taken. Nibley's speech had been published in the *BYU Today* magazine. BYU administrators could not do much about someone of Nibley's status, so as a face-saving gesture they fired one of the people responsible for publishing Nibley's speech (then quietly rehired him later).[96]

The order for this crackdown on Mormon writers and scholars originated from the First Presidency and other top leaders in Salt Lake City. An informant in the Church Historical Department named Gordon B. Hinckley, second counselor to Church President Spencer W. Kimball, as one major advocate of such a censorship campaign.[97] Hinckley had indeed criticized free and open historical research by "so-called intellectuals" as negative and counterproductive. He warned graduates at a BYU-Hawaii campus commencement ceremony:

> Do not be trapped by the sophistry of the world that for the most part is negative and that seldom, if ever, bears good fruit. Do not be ensnared by those clever ones whose self-appointed mission it is to demean that which is sacred, to emphasize human weakness rather than inspired strength, and to undermine faith.[98]

There were other LDS leaders who shared Ezra Taft Benson's distaste for "humanistic" history. One of these was the late Apostle Bruce R. McConkie, a hard-line conservative like Benson who once cautioned BYU students to "please note that knowledge is gained by obedience." Apostle Mark E. Peterson was also actively involved in the history censorship campaign.[99]

During the time that such pressures were being applied, the Church issued contradictory statements as to what kind of "interrogations" were being conducted. Jerry Cahill, director of public communications for the LDS Church, stonewalled, saying: "I have no information on the matter." One former LDS bishop and BYU faculty member commented on such reports: "I sincerely doubt that pressure existed."[100] But some were less evasive. The dean of BYU's College of Humanities put the matter in more straightforward terms:

All good LDS [Mormons], including scholars, must accept the judg-
ment of the Church's General Authorities. If it is what the
brethren want, then good LDS must say it is appropriate. This
may be difficult for scholars, but obedience is an important concept of the Mormon Church.[101]

The Church's attempt to control the versions of its history that
are learned by its members recalls Sterling McMurrin's comment
on such squeamishness: "No church can stand a close scrutiny of
its origins and history without a good deal of moral and intellectual
cringing.[102]

New restrictions were foreshadowed in spring 1982 when the
word spread through the LDS Church Archives Department that
no manuscript materials, including papers, journals or diaries, or
record books of any General Authority member, past or present,
living or dead, could be researched by any Mormon scholar other
than those employed by the history division of the Church.
Biographies and histories of past Church leaders have increasingly
been sanitized by editors in Church-owned publishing enterprises.
As long ago as 1974, one BYU Press book (*The Golden Legacy: A
Folk History of J. Golden Kimball* by Thomas E. Cheney) had its
6,000-copy first edition shredded because of an anecdote in which
one departed Church leader boasted to LDS Church President Heber
J. Grant that were it not for prostate problems he could "piss clear
across" a canal Mormons were building.[103] In 1982 such an item
would never have been released to a researcher: the Church has
stepped up its efforts to guard the memoirs of its leaders lest some
enterprising graduate student or archivist of fragile faith stumble
upon them. It now maintains the unofficial policy of contacting
family members of past Church leaders to secure literary and
publishing rights to journals and diaries in the Church Historical
Department's possession.[104]

Church leaders do not like to be reminded that the reason
prophet Joseph Smith and his brother Hyrum were locked in the
Carthage, Illinois, jail in 1844, later to be killed there by a mob,
was that Joseph Smith had earlier ordered the destruction of the
office of a Nauvoo newspaper that had criticized him. One of the
dangers of the certainty of religious crusaders is arrogance.
"Historical truth" becomes a casualty of "sacred truth." One is re-

minded of the sobering line in George Orwell's novel *1984*: "Who controls the past controls the future; who controls the present controls the past."

BEYOND DÉTENTE: MORMONS PENETRATE COMMUNISM

Mormonism has the ability to adapt to various political systems and "render unto Caesar what is Caesar's" perhaps because it respects its own internal channels of authority so well. It flourishes best in liberal democracies, but it can also survive in dictatorships. For example, in Germany in the 1930s the Saints weathered the Nazi reich with mixed fortunes. Some rank-and-file members as well as Church leaders supported Hitler and even promoted Nazi ideology in meetinghouses. Two Mormon scholars have written:

> Hitler enjoyed at least as much popularity among German Saints as he did among the population in general . . . Moreover, as "good Germans," the Mormons were acutely aware that Hitler had risen to power through legal channels . . . Some Church members even saw Hitler as God's instrument, preparing the world for the millennium. Superficial parallels were drawn between the Church and the Nazi party with its emphasis on active involvement by every member . . . The vital importance of "Aryan" ancestry gave new significance to genealogical research. And the Führer himself, the non-smoking, non-drinking vegetarian who yielded to no one in his desire for absolute law and order, seemed to embody many of the most basic LDS virtues.[105]

Alfred C. Rees, president of the German LDS mission from 1937 to 1939, apparently "tried to win Nazi sympathy by professing admiration for the Party's accomplishment" with an article he wrote for the official Nazi newspaper *Völkische Beobachter*. In it he compared the strength of the German people after World War II with the Utah pioneers' tenacity. (Rees also praised the German government for its condemnation of the use of tobacco and alcohol by youth.) Rees's article was reprinted and distributed as a tract by Mormon missionaries, a large swastika printed on its front cover.[106] Other Mormons resisted the Nazis and were martyred, some excommunicated beforehand to distance them from more patriotic or fearful Saints.[107] But most Saints coped as best they could, not wishing to confront their government and certainly not flaunting their otherwise strong identity with the Israelites of the Old Testament. Solomon Schwarz, a Mormon of Jewish ancestry and a deacon in a branch church, did not hide his "racial" heritage. Forced to wear a star of David on his sleeve, he was later imprisoned in a concentration camp.[108] However, Schwarz was atypical. The average Mormon was also an average German, with the same national pride and misgivings that grew among them all as the war progressed.

Currently the LDS Church is aggressively seeking footholds in Communist countries. This development is particularly ironic since for years the Church's public posture has been vehemently anti-Communist. Post–World War II Church leaders have insistently equated communism with satanism. President David O. McKay and other members of the First Presidency declared at a session of General Conference in 1942:

> Communism destroys man's God-given free agency. . .Latter-day Saints cannot be true to their faith and lend aid, encouragement, or sympathy to any of these false philosophies. They will prove snares to their feet.[109]

One of McKay's counselors, J. Reuben Clark, Jr., reportedly stated that communism "would destroy our American Constitutional government" and that "to support Communism is treasonable to our free institutions." Church members were called upon to "completely eschew Communism in any shape or form."[110] Years later President Harold B. Lee warned against "false prophets and christs" deceiving people in countries like Russia "under the label of politicians or of social planners or so-called economists." More recently, Apostle Bruce R. McConkie wrote that communism "necessarily is a dictatorship of the severest and most ruthless type."[111] Apostle Ezra Taft Benson, the Church's premier anti-Communist, suggested in 1977 that not just the teachings but even the discussion of communism be banned at Brigham Young University.

Yet, over the past thirty years, behind the strident rhetoric, Mormon leaders have been gradually but steadily shifting their thinking about dealing realistically with communism, at least so far as future missionizing is concerned. As early as October 1945, Church President George Albert Smith stated:

> I look upon Russia as one of the most fruitful fields for the teaching of the gospel of Jesus Christ. And if I am not mistaken, it will not be long before the people who are there will desire to know something about this work which has reformed the lives of so many people.[112]

Despite their public condemnations of communism during the cold war of the 1950s, Mormon leaders were at the same time, without benefit of publicity, actually courting goodwill and concessions from Communist countries. Exemplifying this contradictory stance was President David O. McKay, the Church leader who requested that right-wing Cleon Skousen write the hostile *Naked Communist*[113] and who was repeatedly on record as denouncing any contact with Communists. Yet McKay hosted a Soviet delegation in Salt Lake City in 1955. One of the Soviet party, the son-in-law of USSR Premier Nikita Khrushchev, recalled McKay's persistent inquiries about purchasing land in the Soviet Union on which the Church could build a mission headquarters:

> The head of the [Mormon] church, its president Mr. McKay, kept on asking during our visit, "Isn't it at all possible to buy in the Soviet Union, at least five acres of land and begin preaching there our Mormonism?" Naturally we answered Mr. McKay that the land in the Soviet Union belongs to the people and is not for sale.[114]

But it was not until the late 1970s that the LDS Church began in earnest its campaign to open up Communist nations for missionizing and to extend its influence. On repeated occasions the Council of the Twelve met and discussed the best strategy for tackling this unique crusade. After some time they selected Brigham Young University, their "cultural and educational showpiece," as the vehicle to launch it. Specifically they worked through the school's music and dance groups that regularly perform internationally. BYU touring cultural groups became a valuable entrée for the Church to Communist countries, permitting various Church leaders and representatives to gain legitimate, cordial entrance into countries that would deny visas to such leaders if they tried to enter simply on their Church credentials. In 1982 the chairperson of the BYU

Dance Department told us that the Brethren are able to take advantage of BYU's status as an invited educational and cultural (not a religious) institution. By accompanying BYU folk song and dance groups, the Brethren can act as official representatives for the religious organization behind the school.[115]

There was initial opposition, not surprisingly, from that bastion of conservatism Ezra Taft Benson. Benson at first adamantly refused to send young Mormons to Communist nations, but he was outvoted and outnumbered in the Council. He was also finally attuned to the changing drift of his fellow apostles. In fact, according to the director of BYU's Office of Performance Scheduling, Benson had to do a lot of doctrinal fence-mending among Council members who no longer subscribed to his right-wing extremism.[116]

In the end, pragmatism won.

Mormons Penetrate the Iron Curtain

While many American Protestant denominations during the late 1970s and early 1980s had to be content with smuggling religious literature and other paraphernalia into Communist countries where their adherents existed underground, the LDS Church triumphantly strode through the front door and at the invitation of Communist officials. From 1977 to 1981 five touring groups from BYU performed in Poland. In August 1977 Church President Spencer W. Kimball himself visited Warsaw and dedicated Poland for the preaching of the gospel (an event downplayed by the local press). In 1979 alone, BYU's American Folk Dancers troupe performed before hundreds of thousands of spectators in Romania, Czechoslovakia, Hungary, Poland, and the Soviet Union. They spent two full days before television cameras in Bucharest and Moscow on ninety-minute specials for the national networks of both countries. Romania's special was aired three separate times on the same day (August 23, the Romanian equivalent of our Fourth of July). Central Soviet Television aired its documentary on the youthful dancing Mormons across eleven time zones to an estimated 150 million viewers.[117]

The Mormons took Eastern Bloc Communist countries by storm. Their success encouraged Church leaders to continue the momentum. In 1981 Gordon B. Hinckley accompanied the Young Ambassadors, a BYU music/dance group, to cities such as Bucharest

(Romania), Belgrade and Zagreb (Yugoslavia), and Moscow, Kiev, and Leningrad (USSR). Again, Central Soviet Television taped them, this time for a full half-hour program. They appeared on Young Communist Radio and Radio Moscow as well. In addition, *Soviet Life* magazine (a major English-language propaganda organ) ran a positive article on the group and on Brigham Young University. Douglas Tobler, a BYU history professor who acted as tour manager, said the students acted in "a John the Baptist function in preparing [these] nations for the message of the gospel."[118] At the same time, Hinckley went on to meet privately with several Soviet government officials, the first time ever that a Mormon leader had met with representatives of the USSR in that country. Out of that initial contact came a meeting one year later between LDS Apostle Thomas S. Monson and Communist leaders in East Germany (the Soviet Union's closest Communist bloc ally). The result: in May 1983 the LDS Church was permitted to conduct ground-breaking ceremonies for not only a stake center but also a temple in Freiberg, East Germany.[119] This event marked the first time that an American Protestant group had ever been allowed to build a religious house of worship in a Communist bloc country.

Mormons Penetrate the Bamboo Curtain

While Mormon public relations victories behind the Iron Curtain and even permission to begin constructing a temple in a Communist country are impressive, they may not be as significant in the years ahead as the bridges the Mormon Church is building to mainland China. What follows is a condensed chronology of events that have transpired between LDS leaders and political representatives of the People's Republic of China during the last decade (1976–1984).

1976: In the first part of September, Dr. Paul Hyer, professor of Chinese at BYU, was dispatched by Church and BYU officials to the People's Republic of China. Hyer had just finished important diplomatic work for the Church and the university in the Soviet Union and the People's Republic of Mongolia. In China he was to represent the LDS Church at the funeral of Chairman Mao Tse-tung. Hyer was given an official welcome and had the opportunity to confer with assorted dignitaries. Dr. Paul Hyer was the only representative from any American denomination present at Mao's funeral.[120]

1979: On January 1 the United States and the People's Republic of China officially reestablished diplomatic ties after several decades of hostile relations. On March 30 Church President Spencer W. Kimball told a group of regional representatives at a special closed session in the Church Office Building at Salt Lake City:

> We have been conducting Mandarin classes in every meetinghouse in Hong Kong since September 29, 1978. Chinese children should be taught to save and put aside funds to prepare to serve in China. The door to China is starting to open.[121]

About the same time, various Church leaders conferred privately with Idaho's Senator Frank Church, then chairman of the powerful Senate Foreign Relations Committee, for U.S. government permission to send a group of Mormon students from BYU to mainland China. Permission was granted. As a result, the Young Ambassadors troupe, accompanied by no less than an apostle from the Council of the Twelve, James E. Faust, was the first group from a major American university to be allowed to entertain inside China since 1949. The Chinese were impressed by the students' uniform, clean-cut appearance, enthusiasm, and statements that, like the Chinese, they had a tradition of strong family ties and respect for their ancestors. One Chinese official reportedly commented: "These students must be the finest in American youth."[122]

Apostle Faust's status in the LDS Church was downplayed to the Chinese, but he went along for a theologically important reason. In 1921 David O. McKay, then an apostle in the Council of the Twelve, and Apostle Hugh J. Cannon had also journeyed to China. Within the walls of the Forbidden City in Peking, in the Pavilion of a Thousand Springs, the two Mormon elders dedicated the entire country of China for the preaching of the Restored Gospel. On instructions from the First Presidency, Apostle Faust in 1979 conducted a special prophetic prayer (in the presence of his hosts and colleagues) on precisely the same spot, using vague religious allusions that confused Chinese interpreters but that were perfectly clear to Mormons: that the McKay mission's dedication to importing Mormonism to China was reaffirmed.[123]

1980: The Peking government invited the Young Ambassadors to return. This time they were accompanied by Gordon B. Hinckley, and he too visited the identical spot prayed over in the Forbidden City by both the 1921 mission elders and Apostle James E. Faust.[124]

1981: The BYU International Folk Dancers were received with the pomp and ceremony usually reserved for visiting political dignitaries. On this occasion Apostle Boyd K. Packer accompanied them. The students performed in China's most prestigious theater, the Red Tower Theater. A massive crowd, including hundreds of Communist officials, attended.[125]

By now such goodwill overtures began to show results. In early 1981 the ambassador of the People's Republic of China to the United States met with Church President Spencer W. Kimball during a two-day visit to Salt Lake City. He also addressed BYU faculty members and students, spoke with members of the Mormon Tabernacle Choir, visited the Granite Mountain genealogical vaults, and conferred with other Church leaders.[126]

1982: Apostle Neal Maxwell accompanied the Lamanite Generation, a BYU dance and music ensemble consisting of Native American LDS converts, to China.

1983: This year marked more serious efforts by Church leaders to expand relations with the Chinese government. The practice of having high-ranking Church officials traveling with the musical groups began to pay off. Two apostles, Howard W. Hunter and Bruce R. McConkie, went along with the BYU International Folk Dancers and the Young Ambassadors, respectively. They used the opportunity to continue discussions with Chinese leaders. Significantly, in 1983 relations between Peking and Washington had cooled after a U.S. decision to continue selling arms to Taiwan. Several U.S. government–sponsored tour groups involving college-age young adults from across the country were canceled by the Chinese in retaliation. But the Mormon tours were not canceled.

1984: In January Zhao Ziyang, the first Communist Chinese premier to visit American soil since 1949, stopped off in Hawaii on his way to Washington, D.C., to confer with President Reagan. After touring Pearl Harbor, he stopped at the Mormon-owned village of Laie on the island of Oahu. He met with Apostle Marvin J. Ashton and officials from BYU-Hawaii as well as the Mormon-owned Polynesian Cultural Center. Ashton raised several proposals for an educational-cultural exchange program coordinated by BYU. Ashton had previously instructed everyone present not to discuss any religious topics. By the end of the meeting a number of mutual compliments were exchanged, and Mormon prospects seemed brighter than ever.[127]

The Mormon mission to China is still just beginning. There is no way yet to know how the Peking government places the LDS Church within America's plurality of religions, or if the Communists know they are being subtly proselytized as they are being entertained. Perhaps they are using the Mormons in some way the Church is not yet aware of. But the Church is earnest about employing such future cultural trips as wedges to open the Chinese door (the Mormons' metaphor) to LDS missionary work. These visits permit Church representatives to lead Chinese officials into discussions about BYU, the Church, and Mormonism.[128]

Some Mormon leaders hold enormous hopes for a future Mormon-Chinese relationship. And various Mormons are working to keep a Mormon presence in U.S.-China relations. For example, LDS member Jon M. Huntsman, Jr., was press coordinator for President Reagan's April 1984 visit to China, according to a May 13, 1984, article in the *Deseret News*. That same month, Dr. Russell M. Nelson, the heart surgeon newly appointed to the Council of the Twelve, traveled to China for a two-month visit to teach Chinese medical authorities complex techniques of heart-bypass surgery. According to a reporter on Salt Lake City's KUTV television's "Newswatch" program on April 9, 1984, "His knowledge of world health conditions as well as his international travels will greatly contribute to his opening the bamboo curtain for future missionary work."

Just as European converts pumped fresh blood into the LDS Church after 1840 during the great immigration to Salt Lake City, so Church leaders have looked both to the Third World and to Chinese Asia in recent years for the souls to produce dramatic Church growth. Some call China an awesome "sleeping giant to the truth" and "the next great missionary harvest."[129]

MORMONS AND MINORITIES

Mormon leaders traditionally have regarded skin color as spiritually significant. Earlier in this century a "Mormon racial theory" was put forth that the more any group's skin color differed from the Caucasian ideal the more inferior it was. Similar judgments were made about the governments and cultures of nonwhites. Interracial marriage was viewed by Mormons as a source of contamination.

Historian B. Carmon Hardy said:

> Even before the migration to Mexico had begun, Apostle Brigham
> Young, Jr. had warned members of the Church living in Arizona
> "that the blood of Cain was more predominant in these Mexicans
> than that of Israel." For this reason he "condemned the mixing"
> of Mormons with "outsiders."[130]

Mormonism has progressed beyond such blatant racism. The
1978 revelation opening the LDS priesthood to blacks is proof of
that. Nevertheless, three prominent minorities still hold unresolved
positions in the Church's millennial plans: native Americans,
women, and Jews:

Native Americans

Native Americans hold a special status in Mormonism, for they
are considered the descendants of the Lamanites, an ancient
Palestinian tribe that sailed to North America, fought in civil war
with the more virtuous Nephites, and degenerated into barbarism.
Native Americans are to be reclaimed for Christianity, Mormon
doctrine says, before the millennium. To this end the LDS Church
invests a great deal of effort in missionizing various Indian tribes
in the southwestern United States. President Spencer W. Kimball
has been especially vigorous in promoting Indian missions and
fighting racial prejudice. At the October 5, 1980, General Conference
Kimball told the audience of the Lamanite mission program: "We
are greatly conscious of the fact that among the Lamanites — as
well as among all peoples of other countries — we have a responsibility to see that the gospel touches their hearts and minds and
that they understand it."[131]

Mormon dealings with Indians have changed in the same ways
that all white-Indian relations have. Though Mormons sometimes
got along better than other white groups with native Americans,
particularly in the early days when the Saints were outnumbered
in frontier settlements, there were still problems. In many cases
Mormons simply pushed the Indians out and took over their lands.
It happened gradually, the Indians yielding a foot, unaware that
they would be forced eventually to give a mile.

Like most whites, nineteenth-century Mormons regarded
Indians as stone age savages. Some Church members did take Indian

children into their homes and raised them, but in general the relations were strained and heavily laced with prejudice.

The modern Mormon view of Indians is not only more benevolent but more in line with an appreciation of their spiritual inheritance according to the *Book of Mormon.* A Navajo, Elder George P. Lee, is a member of the First Council of the Seventy. Mormon congressmen have even been active in seeking to restore, particularly to the Paiute tribe, traditional lands (along with oil and mineral rights) that had been taken by the federal government.[132]

Today Mormons most frequently relate to Indians through the Church's placement program for Lamanites, run by the LDS Relief Society. Under this program, Indian children from eight to eighteen years of age are transported off their tribal reservations to attend white schools and live with Mormon families for nine months out of every year. The Indian youths are often pressured into becoming baptized Mormons. They are frequently the most promising young people in their tribes (which naturally makes them the most likely candidates for the Mormon program). Likewise, the white Mormon host families are screened carefully by Church officials. In an article titled "The Kids Go Out Navaho, Come Back Donny and Marie," journalists Bob Gottlieb and Peter Wiley noted:

> Only a select group of the nearly 1 million Mormon families in California is carefully chosen by Church elders and then counseled on how to provide a home away from home and an avenue into the white world for their Indian wards.[133]

The native American portion of modern Mormonism is considerable. Church estimates say there are 30 stakes with predominantly native American members. There were approximately 350,000 such members, or 10 percent of the total LDS membership, in 1976 alone. Not all were North American Indians, however. Many were on various Pacific islands or in Central and South America. But even in the mid-1970s, 13,000 native Americans were enrolled in seminary classes in the United States and Canada. Fifteen hundred attended Brigham Young University at both the Provo and Hawaii campuses. Proclaimed one *Church News* editorial:

> The Book of Mormon prophecies are being fulfilled among those peoples. Advancement will continue. The day of the Lamanite

has dawned, and they are responding to the opportunities given them.[134]

Reaction to the LDS mission placement program is mixed. One study commissioned by the Church found that 90 percent of the program's former students, parents, and tribal leaders endorsed it. According to other inquiries, however,

> when non-Mormon Indians are asked about the program, their response is invariably bitter and hostile as they explain that many Indians view the program as a form of kidnaping that takes away the Indian community's most prized people, its youth.[135]

Our own investigation confirmed this darker side of the otherwise "noble" mission program. Interviews with Crow, Cherokee, Navajo, Shoshone-Bannock, and White Mountain Apache spokespersons revealed Indian resentment at Mormon "cultural imperialism" in Indian populations. The more assimilated tribes, such as the Cherokee nation (at 90,000 the second-largest in the United States) have fewer problems with Mormon missionaries. Parents in those tribes are more willing to encourage their children to seek white education. But in other tribes Mormon missionizing turns the Indians into marginal persons, educated in white culture but deprived of their grounding in native traditions. One Indian official claimed that the Mormon program does some good but also causes more problems than the Mormons admit. Identity problems for Indian youth were a prime example. It was this official's experience that youths in Indian placement programs are more likely to turn eventually to drugs and alcohol to relieve their frustrations than Indians raised on the reservation or those who had lived with their families continuously while growing up. The official cited the case of a man who was taken out of his Indian environment when he was ten years old and raised in a Mormon home. He graduated from Brigham Young University and today is a very successful administrator. The official admits the man could not have achieved as much if he had stayed on the reservation. Yet the man is also a very unhappy, personally frustrated individual. Having lost the ability to speak his native tongue, he also lost his tribal identity. He became in effect a non-Indian, unable to relate even to his relatives.[136]

One Shoshone-Bannock tribal leader bitterly summed up his feelings, saying he does not allow the Mormons to recruit for their program among his tribe members any longer. He said: "We resent their tactics of taking our kids away from us and thinking that they can make better kids out of them than we can."[137] Perhaps the most insightful analysis of the Mormon Placement Program, all anger removed, came from an Apache leader. His conclusion was that the LDS Church really wasn't taking the needy as prescribed in the policy statements of their program. Instead, the Church really recruited the most promising children, who already were equipped to succeed in white society. And like most Indians interviewed, he was angry at the Mormon missionizing that is so much a part of the program: "We don't want our children to be changed into believing that their old beliefs — the Apache traditions and values — are evil and superstitious."[138]

Not all Indian leaders are so negative. Some, who have been in placement programs themselves, see benefits. Peter McDonald, former tribal leader of the Navajo Tribal Council, praised the economic opportunities made available to Indian youth.[139]

AIM, the American Indian Movement, has been less kind. Vernon Bellecourt, AIM's national field director, bluntly warned the LDS Church to "recall all your missionaries from the reservations and the areas where native Americans frequent."[140]

Mormon missions have been criticized elsewhere for spreading Mormon religion at the expense of native cultures. There is a parochial strain in much Church thinking that believes that all Mormons should conform to the white, Anglo-Saxon Salt Lake City model. One Mormon musicologist who worked in Nigeria spoke of the Mormon missionaries' "cultural blinders": Mormons, he observed, were guilty of "cultural colonization," trying to implant the same Utah-specific hymns, musical forms, and even musical instruments into a radically different African culture.[141]

But there is one final issue, and it is purely economic. Many Indian lands have recently been found to hold valuable mineral, fossil fuel, water, and other deposits. What seemed barren and worthless regions to Mormon settlers when they helped drive the Indians into wastelands in Arizona, Colorado, New Mexico, and Utah during the nineteenth century now have taken on a new value. The newest generation of native Americans will wield a good deal of influence as to what becomes of the land. If the Church's practice of establishing generous contributions for itself through members' wills, tithings, and gifts and its penchant for diversifying its corporate investments through member-controlled companies are any indication, then the Lamanites had better seriously look to their stewardship of tribal properties and rights.

Women

Mormon women, slower than their Gentile sisters to rise together in protest against the constraints of male-oriented American culture, are still decidedly second-class in LDS Church doctrine. They may enter the highest heaven only if their husbands are members of the priesthood in good standing. Even then, though polygamy on earth was abandoned by the Church in 1890, a woman may well be one of many wives to her husband in the celestial realm. No one woman may enter the priesthood, which is an extremely important form of Church involvement for men.

Mormon women have a noticeably limited role in temporal Mormonism as well. Some Mormon leaders soft-pedal this point, extolling LDS women's freedom to pursue self-development while simultaneously and subtly dropping references to the Church's preferred homemaking role for them. For example, the *Salt Lake Tribune* published the following excerpt from an interview with Barbara Smith, Relief Society president and the highest-placed female official in the Church:

Q. If a couple believes that the needs of their children are being met, can a woman choose to pursue a career, even though the family doesn't need the money?

A. Yes. Each woman in the LDS Church is encouraged to use her agency, make her own decisions, and accept the responsibility of that choice. . . Those who lead the LDS Church will always give the membership the wise counsel, but they do not take away the responsibilities of each individual to be answerable for his or her own life. I feel confident that they will always counsel us to give the highest priority to the rearing of our children.[142]

It is true, as Smith says, that a Mormon woman *can* choose to pursue a career, but there is frequently in such answers a hint that the homemaking role is inherently the better. In the final analysis, any course of action othe than exclusive child-rearing and home-making is portrayed as inappropriate for a married woman.

Contrast Barbara Smith's moderate statement with what the probable next president-prophet of the LDS Church has to say about working women and mothers. ezra Taft Benson told the 152nd semi-annual General Conference participants that the major problems of American society — many of them sexual, such as promiscuity, pornography, and homosexuality, as well as drug abuse, alcoholism, vandalism, and violence — can be directly traced to the deterioration of the "traditional" family. Benson defined this vanishing species as "one which has a husband, a wife not working outside the home, and children."[143] Women who feel the allure of careers or outside employment, according to the elder, are choosing false goals and literally contributing to this society's ills. He claimed that "many parents have been enticed to abandon their responsibilities in the home to seek after an alusive 'self-fulfillment'" and that "it is time to awaken to the fact that there are deliberate efforts to restructure the family along the lines of humanistic values."[144]

Benson's condemnation of women working outside the home is ironic, given the history of Mormon women involved in com-munity affairs. For example, Martha Hughes Cannon, fourth wife of a polygamist Church leader and a mother, was also Utah's first woman state senator. Deseret Hospital, opened by the Women's Relief Society in 1882, was staffed entirely by female doctors, most of them also wives and mothers. The history of nineteenth-century Mormonism in Utah is replete with women whose efforts beyond their homemaking roles helped build the Church and the state of Utah. They would have scoffed at Apostle Benson's logic and his fears of "humanistic values." As one Baptist letterwriter told the *Salt Lake Tribune* in 1982:

the reason LDS youth organizations were reactivated in the later 1800s was that the LDS boys were running wild, doing mischief when they should have been attending church...

Surely most mothers at that time were at home with their fam-ilies...history makes it very plain that the majority of LDS women *were* at home, caring for their children, building and repairing their homes, running their farms. (Those out-of-classification jobs being put upon them by the frequent absences of husbands on Church missions)... Did [Benson] overlook the fact that the quality of time spent with anyone, child or adult, is far more important than just being with them 24 hours a day?[145]

There is no conclusive social scientific evidence that working mothers are less effective child-rearers or that their babies grow up to become "problem children" any more than full-time home-makers' infants. Indeed, research on family violence shows that many families with high rates of spousal violence and child abuse have full-time homemakers struggling to uphold the traditional female role.[146] Nevertheless the LDS Church has increasingly become interested in discouraging careerism among female members. Carrie A. Miles, a graduate student at the University of Chicago, in a study of Church-sponsored magazine articles found that articles encouraging women to stay at home in traditional home-making roles increased from thirty-three in the period 1940–1959 to seventy-four in the 1970s. During the 1940s only one article was published that claimed women should not work for pay. In the 1970s nine such articles were published.[147]

There is a concentrated effort among the Church patriarchy opposing what may ultimately be a rear-guard action stimulated by the inevitable forces of the economy. Mormon middle-class families have difficulty maintaining the lifestyle held out to them as a goal (particularly if they tithe) unless the woman works as well as the man. At a time when the Church still encourages large families and condemns birth control, both the demands on single-income families and the opportunities open to women are enormous. Yet the Church chooses to instill guilt and to blame all manner of social problems on working mothers instead of realistically dealing with the bind in which many Mormon families find themselves.

The Jews (and the Arabs)

The LDS Church is courting Jews. Like many millennial Christian groups, Mormons believe that the Jews will play a critical role in ushering in the millennium and Christ's return — when they convert to Christianity, in this case the Christianity of the Restored Gospel. In those crucial last days, no doubt, "good Jews" will all be Mormons. The late Apostle LeGrand Richards, who prepared a number of pamphlets and other materials aimed at building bridges between Judaism and Mormonism, wrote in *Israel! Do You Know?:*

> God is calling to the Jews. He invites them into the fold of Christ. He wants them to come and take their place in the Church of Jesus Christ of Latter-day Saints, the Kingdom of God which "shall stand forever." (Dan. 2:44)[148]

Mormons see themselves as Joseph and the Jews as Judah, two of the twelve sons of Jacob in Genesis. It is therefore inevitable, say Mormon leaders, that the two religions shall eventually unite. In a 1976 address to a mixed-faith audience in Calgary, Alberta, Ezra Taft Benson spoke of Old Testament prophecies predicting the "gathering" of Israel and the Jews and of three pre-millennial events that must happen (though he carefully avoided directly mentioning the millennium):

> This predicted gathering has three phases: the gathering of Israel to the land of Zion, the American hemisphere; the return of the Ten Tribes from the north countries; and the reestablishment of the Jews in Palestine which had been long ago predicted by the prophets.[149]

Steeped as they are in Old Testament imagery when thinking about their own history, the Mormons naturally see parallels between themselves and the Jews, such as the Israelites' special covenant with God, their years of travails in the wilderness, and their persecution. This commodity of experience is the central theme of Mormon messages to the Jews — as in a pamphlet by LeGrand Richards, "The Mormons and the Jewish People":

> You have been driven, robbed, and ravished — so have we. You have been persecuted, mistreated, misunderstood — so have we. Why? We were driven from our homes to desolation beyond the boundaries of the United States. You, too, have been driven. Why?
>
> What a power we could be in the world if we were united... The complete accomplishment of our mutual and heaven-assigned responsibilities involves our becoming united (as the descendents of Joseph) with the descendents of Judah (the Jewish people) in the fulfillment of the promises given by the Lord to Abraham

and renewed upon the heads of Isaac and Jacob, that through them and their seed all nations of the earth would be blessed.[150]

Just as Mormons believe they will be a bulwark of discipline in a coming time of chaos, stepping in to save the U.S. Constitution and restore order, so too they believe that when the country of Israel has its back to the wall in a final confrontation with its enemies, the Mormons will perform a similar rescue. They claim it was revealed to Joseph Smith that the Shiloh personage mentioned in Genesis — he who will gather the people together — is the messiah. And the Mormons, with their Restored Gospel and divine mandate, will act on behalf of Shiloh.[151]

This Mormon concern with Judaism is not new. In 1840, before Joseph Smith was killed, he sent Apostle Orson Hyde (of Jewish descent) to Palestine. There, much as twentieth-century Church leaders have already done in China, Hyde prayed and dedicated the Holy Land to Mormonism and the Lord. A number of Church leaders throughout the nineteenth century and in the early part of this century continued to prophesy about a future Mormon-Jewish conciliation and to make pilgrimages to Palestine. Since the establishment of the state of Israel in 1948, Mormons have been actively setting up mission work there. In 1972 Church President Harold B. Lee, accompanied by Gordon B. Hinckley, journeyed to Jerusalem. (*The Israel Light*, a newsletter of the Israel district of the LDS Church, called it "the first time a presiding Prophet of God had been here since the days of Peter, almost two thousand years ago.")[152] In 1979 President Spencer W. Kimball led a much grander entourage, including N. Eldon Tanner (his first counselor), Ezra Taft Benson, three other apostles from the Council of the Twelve, and almost 2,000 LDS members, to commemorate Orson Hyde's original visit and dedicate the Orson Hyde Memorial Garden on the Mount of Olives. At the same time, Mormon scholars from Brigham Young University, such as Truman G. Madsen, director of Judeo-Christian Studies in BYU's Religious Studies Center, and David B. Galbraith, resident director of BYU's Jerusalem Center for Travel Study, have held visiting lectureship positions or studied at prestigious institutions like the University of Haifa and Hebrew University. Galbraith helped organize the first Jerusalem branch of the LDS Church in

1972 (he became its president) and is now president of the Israel district of the Church's International Mission. Since 1972 more than 12,000 Mormons have participated in tours and studies in Israel.[153]

We do not know what the Israelis actually think about Mormon efforts to "build bridges" between the two faiths. Ezra Taft Benson, who has visited Israel a number of times, reported that once after spending an evening with David Ben-Gurion and his wife in their Tel Aviv apartment, Ben-Gurion remarked to him: "You know, there are no people in this world who understand the Jews like the Mormons." Benson had also had dinners held in his honor by other legendary Jewish figures such as Levi Eshkol and Moshe Dyan.[154]

Jewish Americans (among other Jewish nationalities) have had to contend with the smug confidence of ambitious Christian missionaries for centuries. To put it mildly, they do not appreciate proselytizers' assumption that the Jewish covenant with God has been supplanted by Christ's new covenant, Restored or otherwise. For many fundamentalists, in particular, "converting a Jew" seems a special achievement. In the United States "Jews for Jesus" is one aggressive, outspoken group of born-again Christian Jews (which mainline Jewish groups regard as an abhorrent cult). The Mormons have their own version in Salt Lake City, called B'nai Shalom, which encourages former Jews to contribute their "insider" knowledge of Judaism to the Church's Mission Training Center.[155]

Most Jews do not see an easy convergence of Judaism with any form of Christianity. Just as various national Jewish groups in the United States have denounced the alleged "compatibility" of traditional Judaism with a faith in Jesus of Nazareth as a divine messiah, they also resist embracing their "brother Joseph." Harry Howard, an elder of the Mormon Church and a converted Jew, protested to the B'nai B'rith Grand Lodge headquarters to prevent his expulsion in 1959, claiming he could still practice orthodox Judaism and be a Mormon:

> My tribe, the tribe of Judah, is so fraught with internal disorder that I merely decided to walk across the street and live with my in-laws — the tribe of Joseph. Mormonism is a continuation of Judaism; all Jews are Israelites, but not all Israelites are Jews. Mormons are Israelites, too.[156]

One Reform Judaic rabbi dismissed Howard's claim and stated

the major obstacle that all missionizing Christians, Mormons included, face when they propose rapprochement with the Jewish faith: "the fact remains that the Mormons give Jesus Christ divine status, and this destroys the indivisible status of God in which we Jews believe."[157]

Unknown to the Jews (and to most Mormons), however, the LDS Church at the same time has been gaining entry into Islam, the traditional sworn enemy of Christianity and current nemesis of Judaism. Such dual missionizing is not hypocritical because Mormons intend ultimately to convert everyone, not just Jews, to Mormonism. The brotherhood of Joseph and Judah provides the temporary grounds for establishing a dialogue with Israel that the LDS Church hopes will not have to continue for very long.

Mormon missionaries established a foothold in Saudi Arabia in 1980. But negotiations for something more substantial took three more years. The Saudi Arabian Peninsula stake is a growing outpost of the Church. In April 1983 Apostle Boyd K. Packer organized the first Saudi Arabian stake of approximately 1,600 members as well as wards in Dhahran, Ras Tanur, Al Khobar, and Riyadh. (Riyadh is incidentally the location of Mecca, the holy city of Islam.) That makes Mormonism the only major American religon permitted to have a geographical outpost in an Islamic country. This Saudi Arabian wing of the LDS Church has flourished. A good portion of its membership already belonged to the Church before moving to Saudi Arabia for employment opportunities, but through their quiet efforts the Church has made some missionary inroads in the local population. Christian missionizing is illegal in Saudi Arabia, and the fact that Mormons enjoy religious privileges there must be atrributed to the crucial link that exists between the highest LDS Church leadership and a family from Saudi Arabia now investing heavily in Salt Lake City.[158]

That family is the Khashoggis: specifically, the brothers Adnan and Essam Khashoggi. Their father, Mohammed, was personal physician to the king of Saudi Arabia and a man who cultivated many important contacts within the country. Adnan Khashoggi attended college in California, where he found he could receive sizable commissions by representing American companies' interests in his homeland. He later founded *Al Nasr* ("Victorious" in Arabic) to handle foreign requests to do business in "the Kingdom."

Journalists Bob Gottlieb and Peter Wiley, who thoroughly researched the intricate web of international interests surrounding
the Khashoggis, write:

> [Adnan] had the enormous advantage of close ties with several
> members of the royal family, most particularly with King Sultan,
> a half-brother of the King, who as minister of defense retained
> personal control over the armed forces.
>   American arms companies took note of Adnan's special rela-
> tionships to the prince and by the early 1960's, Adnan Khashoggi
> was rapidly becoming a significant figure in the Mideast arms
> trade. Lockheed retained him and Litton, Northrop, Raytheon,
> and dozens of other arms merchants in the U.S. and Europe
> followed suit.[159]

The Khashoggis' tie to the LDS Church is through Triad
America, a real estate holding company of the Saudi family. Initially
they were contacted by Bill Gay, a top Mormon in the corporate
empire of paranoid millionaire Howard Hughes, about jointly
financing a land deal to build industrial parks in Salt Lake City and
Houston. The "joint" part of the joint venture eventually fell
through, but when all was done the Khashoggis ended up with
hundreds of acres of land in the Southwest and a need to develop it.

It is a complex story, much of it detailed by Gottlieb and
Wiley,[160] of how the Khashoggis negotiated with Mormon leaders
to build the Triad Project, an ongoing investment program involving
restoration of historically valuable sites, office buildings, and
industrial complexes (including a nine-story building to accommo-
date Bonneville International, the broadcasting wing of the LDS
Church). The Khashoggis, through their Utah representatives in the
Church, arranged to obtain a federal HUD grant of $1.5 million with
the help of Utah Senator Jake Garn. Essam Khashoggi visited Salt
Lake City in spring 1982 for the ground-breaking ceremonies of the
Salt Lake International Center and met with LDS leaders Spencer
W. Kimball, Gordon B. Hinckley, N. Eldon Tanner, and Marion
Romney.

Emanual "Manny" Floor, general manager of the Khashoggis'
Salt Lake properties (and a non-Mormon) became a very useful go-
between with the LDS Church leadership: among his key contacts
were Gordon Hinckley, Marvin Ashton, and J. Howard Dunn, presi-

dent of Zion Securities Corporation, the Church's real estate arm. The Khashoggi connection, facilitated by Floor, may explain why the Mormons obtained their otherwise unaccountable welcome in Saudi Arabia and why in April 1983 Apostle Boyd K. Packer was able to fly to that country and quietly organize a stake. One informant in the Church's International Mission Office called that Church outpost one of the hardest areas of the world in which church doctrine are promulgated. Without the help of "some Arabs friendly to the Mormon cause," Mormons would have achieved little in that traditional Moslem country.[161]

LDS, INC., IN COURT

In a legalistic society such as ours it would be surprising if a corporate religion the size of the LDS Church was not entangled in a constant string of lawsuits. We surveyed numerous court cases involving the Church for the last thirteen years in eleven different states, interviewing various plaintiffs and defendants. Much of this research was laborious: the suit of Garn Baum against the Church over his cherry orchard and cannery, for example (reviewed in Chapter 2) consists of fifty-four volumes of court transcripts and depositions, totaling thousands of pages.

Most of the Church's legal fees are paid to the Utah law firm Kirton, McConkie and Bushnell. Oscar McConkie, a senior partner in the firm, is the brother of the late Apostle Bruce R. McConkie. He also married one of the daughters of the late LDS President Joseph Fielding Smith. Smith was instrumental in having Bruce R. McConkie "called" to the First Council of the Seventy and later to apostleship on the Council of Twelve as well as in arranging to have KM&B handle most of the Church's growing legal needs.

KM&B's forty-one attorneys[162] handle an estimated 3,000 lawsuits both in the United States and overseas. The lawsuits we reviewed fell into four categories, listed in order of relative frequency before 1980:

1. *Disaffected Members and Others.* These included members who voluntarily left the Church or were excommunicated for whatever reason as well as ordained ministers and others outside the Mormon faith.

2. *Business-Related.* Here we include suits both when the Church was a plaintiff and when it was defendant. On occasion the Church has also been a third party in a suit (such as a beneficiary to the estate of a deceased person).

3. *Discrimination.* The LDS Church has been involved in numerous cases involving alleged racial, religious, and sexual discrimination.

4. *Government Tax Status.* The Internal Revenue Service and state, county, and city governments have on occasion challenged the tax-exempt status of Church lands and enterprises.

Litigation by Disaffected Members and Others

Many of the suits involving the LDS Church are oddities. Consider, for instance, the case of Reverend Walter Martin, a fundamentalist author who has long accused the Church of being a non-Christian cult. Martin unsuccessfully tried to sue the Church for $11 million for the humiliation he claimed he had experienced "because a member of the Church publicly accused him of misrepresentation, fraud, libel, and character assassination" when in a speech he called Joseph Smith and Brigham Young "false prophets."[163] In 1975 a Mormon mental patient named Alvin Marc Cowden tried to sue the Church's former Health Services Corporation for releasing him from a psychiatric ward sooner than he felt he was ready. Later that year he tried to sue the Church again, singling out his local bishop and LDS President Harold B. Lee. Cowden accused the bishop of spreading rumors that Cowden, among other things, had evil spirits in his house and of encouraging Cowden's wife to leave him and take their ten children with her. (The judge in the case, known to have taken a tough anti-Church position in other rulings, listened for four days to Cowden's harangues and seemingly endless accusations before ruling in favor of the Church. He described Cowden as "a very sick and neurotic man" and Cowden's lawsuit as "the most outrageous case I have ever heard about.")[164] A Boise, Idaho, father sued the Church for $28 million in 1983, claiming the Church's strict moral teachings against masturbation had so depressed his adolescent son that the boy tried three times, with eventual success, to commit suicide.[165] One Douglas A. Wallace, a former Mormon high priest, was a thorn in the side of the Church

for years. Wallace first made headlines in April 1976 when he baptized a black man and then ordained him to the Aaronic Priesthood
in Portland, Oregon. Later that year the LDS Church responded
by excommunicating Wallace. (Ironically, the Church decided to
admit blacks to the Mormon priesthood just two years later.) Wallace
filed a succession of lawsuits against the Church and its leaders in
the next several years, alleging religious discrimination: all of the
suits were thrown out of court as frivolous. At the April 1976
General Conference, before an audience of 7,000 (plus hundreds
of thousands more via network television) Wallace and two
associates had to be physically ejected by Church security staff after
they stormed down the aisles yelling, "Make way for the Lord! Don't
touch the Lord!" Eventually the Church was successful in obtaining
an injunction barring Wallace from Temple Square.[166]

Business-Related Litigation

Business litigation runs the gamut of issues common to large
corporations: bad personal checks written to Church-owned businesses, occasional embezzlement by Church employees, foreclosures
on mortgages held by the Church, right-of-way and boundary dis-
putes over property, and even something as seemingly mundane
as the Church's failing to obtain a permit from Salt Lake City authorities to demolish some old apartment buildings. Though we have
in our files far too many cases to describe here, examining a few
briefly gives a flavor of LDS, Inc., as a corporate entity.

In 1981 the Salt Lake City Prosecutor's Office filed a criminal
complaint against Zion's Securities Corporation, the Church's real estate arm, stating that Zion's Securities "did unlawfully begin, through
its agent or agents, to alter, to remove portions of, or to begin salvage work in anticipation of demolition on said apartments without
obtaining the required permits."[167] The Canyon Road Apartments
were the target of demolition. Zion's Securities immediately deposited
the $150 for the necessary permit, and the criminal complaint was
dropped. But this was only the beginning of their problems. The
reason: the Canyon Road Apartments built at the beginning of this
century constituted a historical landmark in Salt Lake City. This
was repeatedly certified by the Utah State Historical Society, the
Utah Heritage Foundation, and the Historical Landmarks Committee
(the latter holding public hearings on the matter). Public outcries were

not far behind the news of the apartments' planned destruction.

However, the Church rejected numerous appeals from preservation groups and private citizens calling attention to the building's historical value.[168] Nor did similar attempts to stop the destruction of historic Eagle Gate Apartments succeed. Church profits rather than nostalgia or archaeological value prevailed. Wrote one reporter:

> Preservationists had lost a number of battles over the past year, including the confrontation with Zion's Securities over the Canyon Road Apartments. Gargoyled, turreted, and historically significant buildings were coming down with frightening regularity to be replaced with parking lots or monoliths of steel and glass.[169]

One lawsuit filed against the LDS Church and eventually appealed to the Utah Supreme Court illustrates the Church's ability to defend itself. Mormon Malcolm McKinnon, an owner and operator of coal-mining property in Emery County, Utah, claimed that in exchange for a $14,000 donation from him, the Church had agreed to give him a right-of-way across Church-controlled property. The right-of-way would enable McKinnon to bypass a fault running through his own property and to continue his coal-mining operations on the other side. According to McKinnon, his attorney had delivered his $14,000 to Henry D. Moyle, a counselor in the First Presidency, who had earlier confirmed that the Church would have no problem in giving McKinnon the right-of-way.

As McKinnon saw it, his mistake was in sending the check to the Church without a written agreement guaranteeing the right-of-way, for after the check was delivered, no right-of-way agreement was forthcoming. Nor was McKinnon's $14,000 payment. McKinnon claims that he repeatedly requested written confirmation of his right-of-way, to no avail. He then turned to informal channels, contacting his bishop, stake president, and influential friends. Meanwhile, Henry D. Moyle had died, to be replaced by N. Eldon Tanner, and eventually McKinnon (now with his lawyer) met with Tanner.[170]

In a recent interview, McKinnon's attorney recalled that meeting. One of the first questions Tanner raised was whether McKinnon was a good member of the Church. The attorney pointed out that McKinnon taught a priesthood class to young men in his ward. As the attorney put it, "I've never seen such arrogance in all my life. The man treated us like we were trying to cheat the Church or something, like we were ex-cons." Tanner told them that Henry Moyle was too good a businessman to have ever made the deal they described. Asked why the Church was holding McKinnon's $14,000, Tanner said he knew nothing about it. Greatly upset by what he saw as Tanner's callous attitude, McKinnon decided to do what for him was unthinkable — to sue the Church for "welching" on a "good faith" agreement.[171]

Church lawyers used two arguments in the attempt to have the suit dismissed. First, they argued that the Corporation of the President of the Church of Jesus Christ of Latter-day Saints was not the proper defendant for McKinnon's suit, identifying the proper defendant as Cooperative Security Corporation, a Utah business whose president had been the late Henry D. Moyle. Moyle "just happened" to be a member of the First Presidency during the period of the right-of-way negotiations, they said, but he was acting in his capacity as president of Cooperative Security Corporation and not as a Church official. Cooperative Security Corporation, not the Church, owned and held leases in coal interests in Emery County.[172] McKinnon's attorneys called this maneuver nothing more than a game of musical chairs.

Furthermore, the Church's attorneys argued to have the suit dismissed because McKinnon's legal action came too late under Utah's four-year statute of limitations. Even if he did have a solid enough case (which they contended he did not), he still would be unable to seek restitution because too many years had elapsed for him to begin legal action.

In response, McKinnon's lawyers pointed to his Mormon faith and his trust in his Church leaders:

[McKinnon] was a member in good standing of The Church of Jesus Christ of Latter-day Saints and as such had been taught that Henry D. Moyle, as a member of the First Presidency, was a person directly revelating with God on behalf of the Church and for the guidance and protection of all members of the Church, including [himself]. This special and unique relationship removed respondent's agents from the mundanities of every day business transactions and placed all of the dealings between [McKinnon] and the Church on a higher plane.[173]

McKinnon's lawyer also claimed that N. Eldon Tanner had

urged McKinnon to wait while Tanner had the Church check on the matter. Thus the Church had created a Catch-22 situation for McKinnon: first stalling him indefinitely and then claiming he had no suit because he had waited too long to file it. However, the court dismissed McKinnon's case on the grounds of insufficient evidence, and the Utah Supreme Court upheld that decision after a long appeals process.[174]

Discrimination

Discrimination suits against the LDS Church have involved its role as employer. In Chapter 3 we mentioned a suit brought against the Church in 1982 by five former employees of the Church-owned Beehive Clothing Mills and Deseret Gymnasium who claimed they were forced to tithe to the Church or be fired. Since Beehive Clothing employed non-Mormons who did not have similar pressures put on them, one plaintiff, Christine J. Amos, claimed she was the object of religious discrimination.[175]

The Church appeared in court and tried to have the lawsuit dismissed. It claimed that it had offered all five former employees ample opportunities to regain their religious worthiness but that all had rejected these opportunities. More important from a legal standpoint, its principal argument for dismissing the employees was that Beehive Clothing was a "religious activity." The Church's attorneys cited case after case, to prove the "religiousness" of the two companies, pointing to their tax-exempt status, Church-appointed boards of directors, and so forth. The Church even included as evidence a copy of the prayer of dedication given at the opening of the Deseret Gymnasium by a prominent Church leader. (The American Civil Liberties Union attorneys countered: "Surely, delivering a prayer is not enough to make Deseret a religious activity. If it did, every session of every legislature which opens with a prayer would be rendered thereby a religious activity.")[176] Church attorneys argued that

> it is a matter internal to the Church to set its membership standards. Government must remain neutral; the approach of the Supreme Court is simply to keep out of such religious affairs . . . *This is an internal matter exempt from sovereign interference.*[177] (Emphasis in the original document)

The workers' affidavits included the following points:

—Not all the former Beehive employees and Deseret Gymnasium employees had been given an adequate chance to meet the new strict Church "worthiness" requirements. One woman testified that she was being terminated because she was not "worthy" of a temple recommend two days before she was to arrange one with her bishop.[178]

—Workers felt that they had been used as examples in front of their fellow workers to humiliate them. For instance, envelopes containing notices for a final (termination) interview with company officials were delivered conspicuously to the "unworthies" on Beehive Clothing's sewing shop floor.[179] (This less than subtle tactic apparently had its intended effect. Since that time we learned from informants that Beehive Clothing Mills and Deseret Gymnasium have almost 100 percent regular Church attendance, full tithing, and current, active temple recommends from its Mormons employees.)

—The rules for members at the allegedly "religious" Deseret Gymnasium were much like those of any secular health club. The no-smoking rule was not enforced in the women's massage salon or in the beauty shop, and skimpy bathing suits on women proliferated.[180]

The decision by the U.S. District Judge (himself a Mormon) on the motion to dismiss the discrimination suit is one of the longest delivered in recent U.S. district court history for Utah (Central Division). He denied the Church's motion, and the five former Church employees were then permitted to continue their lawsuit against the Church. (As of this date, the workers have not pursued the case.)

This case may have set an important precedent in how religiously owned companies and businesses can treat their employees. At about the same time as the judge's decision in the Beehive case, Terence J. Moore, associate professor of law at California State University, wrote about the emerging legal basis for challenging such "business as usual" practice of huge corporate conglomerates:

There are large private corporations today that have more power and more employees than a number of countries. These corporations have tremendous economic and, at times, political power. Yet, because they are private organizations, they can violate a person's natural rights at will, and it does not constitute a violation of a person's constitutional rights because it is a "private action" as distinguished from a "state action." . . .

Large corporations have much power in our society and indeed throughout the world and, internally, are more powerful than many governmental administrative agencies. Based upon this premise, any action by a corporation that violates an employee's rights constitutes state action, for which the employees may seek redress.[181]

So far as we know only one plaintiff in a discrimination case filed against the LDS Church has petitioned for a hearing in the U.S. Supreme Court. Mary J. Larsen was hired by the LDS Business College during the school year 1971–72, but her reemployment for the following academic year was in doubt. Her "lack of Church activity," she was told, was one of her deficiencies. She threatened to file a civil rights action if she was not offered a contract renewal. Subsequently she was rehired (though on probationary status). The next year she was told she would not be rehired. On October 31, 1973, she filed through an attorney a charge of religious discrimination against the LDS Business College and the LDS Church with the Anti-Discrimination Division of the Utah State Industrial Commission. The Business College told the Anti-Discrimination Division only that her teaching abilities were mediocre and did not mention any religious criteria. When the State Industrial Commission and the federal Office of the Equal Employment Opportunity Commission in Denver did not help her, she took the matter to court.[182]

The lower court in which Larsen's suit was heard declared the Church within its rights not to rehire Larsen, and two higher courts supported that ruling. Her petition to have the case heard in the Supreme Court of the United States was denied.

Government Tax Status
On a number of occasions, the LDS Church has faced the unpleasant prospect of having to pay taxes on property that it wishes

to remain tax-exempt. General Authorities themselves or prominent Church attorneys have been known to visit an area where the tax issue has arisen and try to preserve the Church's tax-exempt status. In 1963, for instance, the Church sent Henry D. Moyle, first counselor to the Church president, with his wife to London to help the Church's legal counsel there appeal a taxation of the London temple.[183] Church attorney Oscar McConkie recalled with pride to a Brigham Young University audience how in the early 1970s he had met with state officials in Portland, Oregon, in an effort to persuade them not to pass a bill that would have eliminated the tax exemption on all Church properties. Jason Boe, an optometrist from Reed's Post, who was then president of the Oregon state senate, invited McConkie to a luncheon where, bragged McConkie, "it just so happened" that the head of the committee working on the taxation bill was seated across from him. "This is Oscar McConkie," said Boe, introducing his guest, "former president of the Utah state senate. I don't know what he wants with us, but whatever it is, you had better listen to him." McConkie was successful in convincing Oregon legislators to kill the proposed taxation bill.[184]

In 1982 the Church hoped to persuade county commissioners in Power County, Idaho, to reinstate the tax exemption of its profitable 6,742-acre welfare farm in Arban Valley. According to Ben Canvaness, deputy prosecuting attorney for Power County:

> The Church sent some of their real big shots up here to meet with the county commissioners. One of them was one of the McConkies and another big shot official from the Welfare Department. They laid the old routine on us of how much they've helped people in our county. They threw all kinds of figures around for us. We tried to explain to them that if we didn't tax their farm, which was making a profit anyway, that we'd have to close down our elementary school in Arban. Well, they didn't seem to care one way or the other. All they wanted was to try and get their tax-exemption status back for that damned farm of theirs! But we told them, Listen, we're prepared to take this thing to the courts if we have to. Right away they backed off and accepted the payment of the taxes.[185]

The prominent business journal *Nation's Business* has declared that the LDS Church "pays taxes on every cent" it earns.[186] Another important periodical echoed these sentiments: "The Church is proud that it pays full taxes — federal, state, local — on all these businesses and its commercial real estate holdings, even though it could often claim exemptions."[187] However, since 1970 the LDS Church has had at least two dozen major tax cases brought against it in the courts. (These were merely ones we learned of without great effort.) In some cases local communities have been reevaluating some of the Church's businesses and properties to determine whether these are business entities that should be taxed like any other privately held concern. For example, in Tacoma, Washington, all the property of the Church in Pierce County was placed on property tax rolls by the assessor's office in 1971 when Church leaders in Salt Lake City refused to turn over documents proving that their stakes were supported by donations.[188] Throughout Idaho numerous LDS welfare farms were placed on the tax rolls in counties like Bannock and Bingham despite the strong protests of LDS Church officials.[189]

The Church has had other tax status problems in Arizona. During 1969 in Maricopa County, 1,500 acres of welfare farmland was transferred into a nonexempt classification by the county assessor. He claimed that the LDS farms and dairies in the county were indeed very profitable and therefore taxable. He pointed out "that the Church admitted that income from the farms exceeded the expenses for any one year." The Church counterargued that its farms were exempt under the Arizona constitution, which provides that "property of educational, charitable and religious associations or institutions not used or held for profit may be exempt from taxation by law." Under protest the Church paid $21,275 in taxes and then took the county assessor to court. The Church attorney gave the court a glowing account of Mormon welfare programs. The county assessor and his attorney pointed out that the crops and milk produced on Church welfare farms were sold in the open market and in competition with other tax-paying farm producers. "They also noted that at least one of the Church welfare properties contained renters unrelated to the LDS welfare program. Though a Superior Court judge in Maricopa County ruled in favor of the Church, this decision was eventually reversed."[190]

The IRS and the Polynesian Cultural Center
A number of LDS Church enterprises have been very profitable

and have drawn the scrutiny of the Internal Revenue Service. Perhaps the most outstanding example is that of Brigham Young University's Polynesian Cultural Center in Hawaii. This tax case, in the U.S. District Court in Honolulu, continued for four years and at the time of this writing had not been settled.

The LDS Church established the Polynesian Cultural Center (PCC) in the town of Laie on the island of Oahu in 1963 as a way to provide employment for students at the nearby Hawaii extension campus of Brigham Young University. The plan was simple enough. Many of the students attending the university were converts from Pacific islands. They would work their way through school by demonstrating their particular island skills and cultures to tourists. The other students on campus could provide support for the PCC in jobs that would give them experience in business administration, the travel industry, and public relations as well as in teaching languages and Polynesian history.

According to a report in the *New York Times*, however, what started out as a sort of student welfare program, designed with good intentions, became a phenomenal Disneyland-like financial blockbuster grossing close to $23 million in 1981 alone, bringing it "a possible embarrassment of riches." The *New York Times* article continued:

> It worked, though perhaps too well. The Internal Revenue Service recently decided that the Polynesian Cultural Center, which has grossed more than $125 million since it opened in 1964, is too profitable and too professional to be tax-exempt. The Center is appealing the decision. If it should lose its appeal, the Polynesian Cultural Center could face a bill of $9 million for back taxes.
>
> Critics of the center have complained that the center exploits the students and underpays them. For foreign students without employment papers there is no other place to work except the cultural center. And, although some student performers make up to $6 an hour, others are paid the minimum wage, $3.35. If the center paid the students like the professionals they are, critics say, the center would not have such a problem with excess funds.[191]

On December 9, 1980, the PCC filed a "Complaint for Refund of Taxes" in the U.S. District Court of Hawaii against the Internal

Revenue Service for back tax refund. In its complaint it said:

—that PCC was a nonprofit corporation;

—that during the fiscal year ending September 30, 1980 it was a corporation organized *exclusively* for educational, charitable, and religious purposes;

—that it had not accumulated sizable reserves and that its practices as a corporation were distinguishable from regular commercial business practices; therefore it was not subject to the IRS's general corporate income tax; and

—that in June 1980 the IRS had illegally and erroneously assessed PCC for a federal income tax of $528,184 (plus $63,157.78 interest) and rejected the PCC's related claim for a refund.

The IRS countered that the facts did not support the PCC's claims, however.

As for being a corporation organized exclusively for educational, charitable, and religious purposes, the IRS cited Shop Polynesia (a gift shop in the PCC), stating:

Shop Polynesia sold some items directly related to its purposes. However, it also sold many items that can be found in commercial gift shops. There is no substantial causal relationship between the sale of film, commercially made candles, clothes, and jewelry, for example, and a purpose to teach about the cultures of Polynesia.[192]

In addition, the IRS questioned many of the PCC's attempts at "cultural education," such as the PCC's type of "Polynesian" food served daily to tourists. The IRS said:

The buffet is a smorgasbord type dinner, which initially featured Polynesian cuisine. However, within the past few years, the menu has been changed almost entirely to an American buffet, since many visitors disliked Polynesian food, and ate at the for-profit Lanilos Inn located immediately adjacent to the Center...During the time when Polynesian food was served, the buffet activity was itself one of the demonstrations of the culture and had a *substantial* causal relationship with *educating* the public within the meaning of [IRS regulations]. The question of a substantial rela-

tionship becomes more difficult in considering that the Polynesian menu was abandoned.[193]

Another example seized on by the IRS was the PCC's brochures
that emphasized glamour and exotic entertainment rather than education or cultural enrichment.

The IRS concluded that the PCC could not be distinguished from
regular commercial businesses. It found that PCC used extensive
commercial advertising, employed Hollywood professionals in pro-
ducing shows, sold souvenirs and other tourist items, priced tickets
to maximize profits, and paid minimum wages to student employees. Not only had PCC garnered large annual profits, but it had made
large expenditures for capital improvements without significant
outside contributions.[194] As for PCC's not accumulating sizable
resources, it *had* accumulated $10,172,766 as of the 1978 tax year.
In the words of the IRS, "the reserves were inconsistent with the
tax exempt purpose of the center since they were over and above
the amount necessary to continue operations, such as maintaining
or replacing equipment."[195]

Finally, PCC's general manager, William Cravens, told a reporter that "we put the money [earned by the PCC] right back into the
university or the center. Not even the Church gets it."[196] Yet documents received from the Polynesian Cultural Center clearly reveal
that as of September 30, 1972, the Corporation of the President of
the Church of Jesus Christ of Latter-day Saints held $3 million of
PCC funds that had been turned over to its Financial Department
in Salt Lake City for investment purposes. One year later the PCC
handed over another $1,100,000 to the Church administration in Salt
Lake City.[197] The IRS concluded in 1976 that the Polynesian Cultural Center was not eligible for further tax-exempt status and
recommended that revocation of its exemption be backdated to 1971.

The PCC-IRS controversy still rages. The trial date has been
repeatedly postponed and delayed years after the original date. The
irony is that the Church now has its back to the wall fighting an
IRS bid to reclaim $9 million in back taxes and interest penalties
from a very lucrative Church business, yet the furor originally began
when the LDS Church and PCC brought suit against the IRS for
a relatively insignificant $591,341.78. Had the Church left well
enough alone, that lawsuit would not have backfired.

In short, because the Church's millennial vision includes earthly economic and political power, it continues to establish and run profitable businesses while claiming the tax-exempt status accorded non-profit religious organizations. We are not the first to note this aspect of Mormonism, but it is a subject rarely dealt with by the national press.

6

Religious Liberty and the Kingdom of God

Journalist Paul Blanshard faced the same problem as we when he wrote his *American Freedom and Catholic Power* in the 1940s. He, too, examined an accepted, respected American religion that had once been the victim of prejudice and vicious repression. To ask certain questions about its motives and operations seemed to risk a return to an era before religious tolerance and ecumenical goodwill had become mainline American values. Accused of hate-mongering and bigotry, Blanshard raised such questions because the Roman Catholic presence in American society was not nearly so comfortable as many liked to think. In answer to critics of his project, he wrote, "The refusal to face unpleasant facts in the field of religious controversy frequently passes for 'tolerance' and 'broad-mindedness.'"[1] He suggested that a democratic society's accommodation of large, influential groups that repudiate democratic goals and may interfere with republican processes could ultimately endanger everyone's basic liberties. There may be times, he concluded, when "the highest duty of a citizen" is to increase social tension, no matter how unpleasant the task, to deal with the policies and impact of such groups honestly and fully.

In creating such a tension ourselves, some will say we have attacked the LDS faith, which was not our intention. We have attempted to deal strictly with secular, not religious, aspects of Mormonism, but the Mormon intertwining of secular and religious activity makes an unequivocal separation almost impossible. The facts presented here do indeed challenge the popularly accepted

249

image of Mormonism. Conservative politicians find in the Mormons an inspiring example of how some Americans are purportedly able to do without benefit of the liberal welfare state. Most journalists see Mormonism as a workable cooperative religion that epitomizes the American success story: efficient, thrifty, self-sufficient, brilliantly organized. Indeed, we wonder if the legacy of nineteenth-century discrimination against Mormons is a collective sense of guilt so that the Church must always be portrayed as conservative, industrious, and wholesome. The popular stereotype, in any case, has scant use for many of the other Mormon characteristics we discuss: antidemocratic authoritarianism, vast corporate wealth and partisan political influence, sexism, censorship, and bureaucratic insensitivity.

Inclusive views of the LDS Church do exist, to be sure. A prime example is the recent *America's Saints: The Rise of Mormon Power* by investigative reporters Robert Gottlieb and Peter Wiley[2] and newspaper and magazine articles by journalists such as Michael Parrish, Bill Beecham and Daniel Briscoe, Paul Swenson, and Fred C. Esplin. But these are exceptions. We have described how the LDS Church has clamped down on those of its own writers who stray too far from the orthodox fold.

Ironically, most of the trends, statistics, and interviews presented in this book are available to anyone with the curiosity and persistence to seek them out. Much of the information can be found in public libraries and courthouses. The LDS Church regularly publishes a great deal about itself for those willing to immerse themselves in the details of this sprawling corporate enterprise. In general, the media have not looked beyond the benign image that the LDS Church works hard to promote. Nevertheless, if journalism is meant to go beyond dutiful printing of apologetic press releases, then the fourth estate's treatment of the LDS Church has been woefully inadequate.

There are reasons to think free and open media coverage of the Mormon Church may face great obstacles in the future. The reactionary sentiments of some LDS leaders are stronger than ever. Ezra Taft Benson, the apostle next in line to become LDS Church president (and therefore a leader whose views must be taken seriously), is known for his extreme rightist attitudes. What we have seen of Benson's intolerance of journalistic freedom at Brigham Young University suggests that dissenters could become an endangered species throughout the Church during his administration.

Likewise, the Church bureaucracy is tightening up information leaks and its members' access to information. Even its own scholars are frequently barred from Church archives. From personal experience we know that Church security has been committing increasing energy to tracking down administrative information passed from one member to another. Any public discussion of the Church's full history is seen as a threat. Any reasonable attempt to examine the true extent of its economic and political activities is condemned as muckraking.

In 1983 nationally syndicated political columnist Jack Anderson, along with his assistant Dale Van Atta (former investigative reporter for the *Deseret News*) — both active Mormons — announced their intention to set up a tabloid (later reduced to a newsletter) called "For Mormons Only." The purpose of this publication is to report political information pertinent to the LDS Church (such as impending domestic legislation, political changes in foreign countries, and the like) and to cover the latest efforts of anti-Mormons (broadly defined) by maintaining contacts with sources such as the Church's Security Force in Salt Lake City, police departments in states like Washington and California, and right-wing information networks. In 1983 Anderson organized the Millennial Star Foundation to publish his newsletter. ("This will be my service to the Church," he was quoted as saying.[3]) He worked with two men, Neal Blair and Mark Stoddard, both active Mormons. Blair was an intimate associate of the late Congressman Larry McDonald, president of the John Birch Society. Stoddard is also executive director of a citizens' lobby called Free of the Eagle (a number of staff members of Free of the Eagle are also involved in Anderson's new publication). Free of the Eagle, as one might expect from its name, embraces traditional conservative positions, including a 10 percent reduction in taxes, strong national defense, international nuclear superiority, and reduced government spending on social programs. One Free of the Eagle staff person told us that LDS Church leaders in Salt Lake City are aware of the organization's activities but would not elaborate, saying he would be putting some of them "in a delicate position" if he divulged anything further.[4]

This network, with its loyalty to LDS leaders and its connections to sensitive information in virtually every corner of the federal government, lends the Millennial Star Foundation considerable influence in advancing Church interests on the national scene. Not just pending legislation but even research such as ours could become part of the foundation's watchdog agenda.

In late 1984 a series of events began that focused national attention on Salt Lake City. Facts and motivations are not yet sorted out, and the ramifications for Mormon theology and the Mormon public image may never be fully understood. An ambitious young Mormon, 30-year-old Mark Hofmann, had made a business of acquiring and selling historical documents, many of them related to Mormon history. The most controversial of the documents Hofmann discovered was the "Salamander Letter," which contradicts some central facts in the orthodox Mormon account of Joseph Smith's original revelation. In 1984 Hofmann sold the Salamander Letter to a Mormon stockbroker, Steven F. Christensen, who in turn donated the letter to Church leaders. In October 1985, Christensen and the wife of a business associate were killed in separate bomb blasts in Salt Lake City. A day later Hofmann himself was critically injured in a similar explosion. Both Christensen and Hofmann appear to have been in financial straits, and it is clear that the LDS Church's role in these headline-making incidents was only peripheral.[5] But the media's hungry coverage of the story and continuing public curiosity have invaded the Church's closely guarded privacy to an unprecedented extent. The Church's carefully constructed public image has undoubtedly suffered damage.

We believe that the LDS Church has an obligation to be more open in conducting its affairs. As journalist Richard N. Ostling wrote in *Secrecy and the Church: A Reporter's Case for the Christian's Right to Know*, any church organization owes such information first of all to its own members, who are expected to foot the bill for projects and priorities that may vitally affect them as individuals. Secrecy by any church's leaders promotes speculation and sometimes suspicion at lower levels. Fearful, inadequately informed religious administrators in turn dam the downward flow of information even further, which feeds paranoia in all camps. The result, which we have seen in the modern LDS Church's treatment of even its own in-house scholars, becomes what Roman Catholic philosopher Hans Küng, a critic of his own church's secrecy policies, described in his book *Truthfulness*:

Authority simply determines what is truth, and truth in authoritarianism is what suits authority: its organization, its regime, its system . . . People adapt themselves. They avoid telling the truth, contradicting authority: "This is dangerous. It is not true to the party-line, not according to the mind of the church."[6]

Moreover, the abuse of influence and authority, a problem in any large organization, flourishes when secrecy is entrenched. Ostling observed: "Secrecy can hardly be considered a Christian atmosphere for the conduct of human affairs in society, much less the church."[7]

The Church's empire benefits enormously from tax exemptions — essentially subsidies — granted by the federal government. In Richard Ostling's words, "a church which benefits from the society has responsibilities to it,"[8] and, we argue, should not claim "executive privilege" from serious inquiries into its resources and goals. In fact, Mormonism is an archetypal example of the dilemma the Internal Revenue Service has faced for years: when is a religious enterprise more business than religion? If every enterprise is motivated by some theological or spiritual imperative, where can a line be drawn? If a religion elevates material success to the status of a religious sign or reward, then what is not religious? The courts are still grappling with this issue, and the LDS Church may force them to resolve it — sooner than will the more visible millionaire evangelists and multi-limousined gurus now at large in America.

Likewise, church-state scholars need to define more clearly the distinction between a corporate religion and a religious corporation. As we see it, a religious corporation may have religious roots or sponsorship, but its daily operations and decision making do not revolve around the religion that began it. The LDS Church is a corporate religion which administers theologically determined decisions in the same manner as it does investment portfolios — and often mixes the two.

THE MATURING OF LDS, INC.

In his classic *Sociology of Religion*, the German sociologist Max Weber articulated a useful distinction between *prophetic* and *priestly* forms of religion. Prophetic religion, Weber said, is dynamic, even revolutionary, and it threatens those comfortable with the status quo because it uncompromisingly points out spiritual blemishes. Priestly religion, on the other hand, is at ease with establishment society in all its imperfection. It represents a matured, prosperous, nonradical, simmering version of the boiling tempest that originally inspired the religion. Weber saw all religions as cyclical, beginning as radical, innovative reforms led by charismatic leaders and eventually falling under the stewardship of cautious bureaucrats. These bureaucrats, as they consolidate power, worry more about protecting and extending their bureaucracies — concerns that soil their own limited charisma with political and economic realities — than about the spiritual implications of a large organization. Only a new prophet, unpleasant and unsettling to the entrenched priestly management as he or she may be, can revitalize the enterprise and perhaps start the cycle again.[9]

The LDS Church has tried its best to escape this cycle, but it has manifestly failed. Not even by staunchly maintaining that its president is not merely a temporal leader but a literal prophet and living vessel of ongoing revelation could the Church prevent the inevitable effects of mass bureaucracy. This is not to say that the Church has lost the capacity for bold innovations and pioneering accomplishments. Certainly its missionary efforts in Communist and Third World countries, its adoption of the latest communications technology, and its recent alignments with the political establishment and former sectarian enemies prove otherwise. But such achievements serve to build the LDS bureaucracy even larger and further the corporate religious worldview not just of the Church leadership but also of its followers.

As a corporate religion, the LDS Church is comparable to secular corporations. The secular equivalent of the prophetic/priestly distinction in religion is what business analysts call the leader-manager transition. Leaders, as Mormon scholar Hugh Nibley describes them, are "movers and shakers, original, inventive, unpredictable, imaginative, full of surprises that discomfit the enemy in war and the main office in peace." He contrasts the "prophetic" innovative leaders with the "priestly" managers: "the managers are safe, conservative, predictable, conforming, organizational men and team players dedicated to the establishment." Managers are merely the caretakers for what leaders built. But, as Nibley sadly observes (and he has the LDS Church clearly in mind), "the rise of management always marks the decline, alas, of culture."[10]

The Church practice of "patriolotry," tied as it is to the "gerontocracy" of the Council of the Twelve Apostles, is another handicap. Frank Goble, author of *Excellence in Leadership*, writes of top corporate management:

> In theory, boards of directors are elected by the organization's members or stockholders. In practice, boards tend to be self-perpetuating.
>
> Self-perpetuating boards have a tendency to gradually lose the energy and creativity that companies need to remain dynamic. The problem of aging boards develops so gradually that the problem is seldom recognized until it is almost too late. The best solution is to establish, as early as possible, policies and procedures to maintain a proper balance between youth and experience on the board.[11]

Nor do LDS Church leaders' attempts to assert control over rank-and-file members with threats of excommunication and ideological monitoring provide a sound long-run strategy for encouraging loyalty to the organization. Members of any corporate entity, as industrial social scientists have known for years, need to be positively motivated to stimulate enthusiasm for the organization's policies. Negative motives stemming from fear or intolerance erode morale (and, we would argue, religious faith as well). Says Frank Goble:

> Fear exerts a heavy price upon the institution, and upon the people within the institution. It reduces the freedom people feel to innovate, to be creative, to change and be responsive. It results in a rigidity of attitude, of structure and response, and, worst of all, it strips us of some of our humanness.[12]

At the end of his book, Goble presents an organizational checklist of 142 categories that can be used to evaluate the efficiency and effectiveness of any corporation. On some the Church does well. On other critical measures, it falls short. For example, its top leadership has a poor age balance and does little to rotate its leaders. Nor do the highest levels of the Church avoid involvement in the details of daily operation, despite the theory that the Council of the Seventy handles the actual administration of the Church while the apostles and the First Presidency simply dictate policy. In fact, the top-level leaders have often become embroiled in lesser controversies precisely because of their dealings in mundane affairs. In one case a member of the First Presidency almost resigned in the mid-1970s because of a persistent disagreement over who would direct the Mormon Tabernacle Choir;[13] in another the First Presidency had to be consulted about the propriety of the Budweiser Brewing Company's Clydesdale horses pulling a beer wagon in the annual Days of 47 parade.[14]

Goble suggests that in the case of a rigid pyramidal structure such as the LDS Church organization, leaders ought to "flatten the pyramid," that is, devise an organizational structure that resembles a short, squat pyramid rather than a tall, thin one. In concrete terms it entails decreasing the real number of people reporting to a single supervisor — in principle what the Church already practices with its apparent decentralization of authority but not in reality the way upper-administrative Church leaders run the enterprise.

THE LDS CHURCH AND RELIGIOUS PLURALISM

The LDS corporate bureaucracy still pursues the original millennial dictates of accruing economic and political influence in societies worldwide. LDS historian Hugh Nibley has criticized the economic motives that equate the kingdom of God on earth with personal prosperity:

> The Economy, once the most important thing in our materialistic lives, has become the *only* thing. We have been swept up in a total dedication to the Economy which, like the massive mudslides of our Wasatch Front, is rapidly engulfing and suffocating everything.[15]

Even more than its pro-profit orientation, the post-millennial political goals of Mormonism have brought it to a turning point in its own development. Given the already potent influence of the Church in national affairs, this may also be a turning point in the delicate, unfinished "experiment" of American religious pluralism. The Mormon Church is no longer simply "another" Christian sect or denomination with peculiar yet wholesome values that happens to possess extraordinary political and cultural influence in one regional area. As we have shown, its members influence the highest executive, legislative, regulatory, and military decisions that vitally affect this nation. Evidence shows that these faithful members play their roles while mindful of the Church's continuing emphasis on preparing for a post-millennial crisis that will propel the LDS Church into a special savior position. Many Mormons regard themselves as part of this preparatory process, happy to be of service to their Church in performing otherwise secular duties. In short, the modern LDS Church is making good on what must have seemed in the nineteenth century incredibly pretentious promises and ambitions.

The question left to be answered is apparent: What will those who value religious pluralism and democratic government, mindful of those traditions' tolerance even for fanatical and inimical groups, advocate about Mormonism? There are several possible alternatives. One that is clearly unacceptable is a return to the rabid fear-mongering and anti-Mormon hatred of the nineteenth century. To religious bigots we point out that persecution of and vicious propaganda about Mormons did nothing but ultimately strengthen the resourcefulness of the Church beyond its enemies' wildest imagination. The history of Christianity is full of similar examples.

Another alternative would be to dismiss this analysis as prejudice or eccentricity and leave well enough alone. In the short run this option would no doubt appease the mainstream middle-class American distaste for the uncomfortable "tension" Paul Blanshard raised when he proposed similar questions about Roman Catholicism in America. Yet in a practical sense that would be a head-in-the-sand solution. Disproportionate Mormon influence in government and economic institutions, wielded in the post-millennial cause of theocracy, is no fiction. The data presented here are real, can be independently confirmed, and must be faced.

A third alternative is to extend the same criticism, skepticism, and expectation of accountability to the LDS Church that Americans now eagerly employ when they examine post-Watergate public officials. No organization of any size, government or church, can operate itself in a completely charitable and forthright manner. That we have come to expect otherwise is as much the result of our own wishful thinking as the product of the Mormon Church's desire to manipulate its public image. An increased, honest flow of information from the LDS Church leadership, not just to outsiders who are affected by its goals and policies but most important to its own members as well, will make rational evaluation of the Church's activities possible.

Finally, the religion of the Restored Gospel is no more or less radical than many American variations of Christianity that envision this society as transient and in desperate need of redemption. LDS members have every right to damn, reject, and pray for this society's and this world's replacement. But when Mormons achieve enough acceptance to enter into society's foremost institutions and help steer national events in accordance with their post-societal beliefs, then the best interests of both the American pluralistic system and Mormons are served explicitly by entering into a dialogue. Privileges and freedoms are the contractual rewards of mutual respect and tolerance among American religions, however much a given religion sees these as costs.

Mormon observers have expressed concern over the Church's strong emphasis on material prosperity, including its simplistic tendency to vindicate faith and rationalize greed in the wake of economic success. But materialism is only symptomatic of a larger problem. There is a broader reason for concern, stated by the famous nineteenth-century French observer of America, Alexis de Tocqueville. Tocqueville probably never heard of Joseph Smith or the Restored Gospel (though he was a contemporary) as he traveled across our young nation. Nevertheless his analysis is applicable to modern Mormonism. He wrote:

> As long as a religion is sustained by those feelings, propensities, and passions which are found to occur under the same forms at all periods of history, it may defy the efforts of time; or at least it can be destroyed only by another religion. But when religion clings to the interests of the world, it becomes almost as fragile a thing as the powers of earth.[16]

Mormons would do well to contemplate how fragile their faith may have become in the midst of so many temporal accomplishments.

Notes

Chapter 1   The Emerging Kingdom of the Saints

1. Orson Pratt, *The Seer* (Washington, D.C., 1854), p. 215.
2. See Chapter 3 for a detailed discussion of estimates of LDS investments and property holdings.
3. See Chapter 4 for a discussion of the LDS Church's involvement in national politics.
4. Some would insist that the Mormons are really pre-millennialists because they believe Jesus Christ's return will *precede* a thousand-year reign of peace rather than follow it. This issue of labels is largely one of splitting hairs, since scholars agree that Mormon beliefs require establishing the Kingdom of God on earth before the Second Coming can occur.
5. Joe Edward Barnhart, "Post-Millennial Nationalism," *Proceedings of the Association for the Scientific Study of Religion: Southwest* (ASSR: SW: Dallas, 1983), pp. 2–3.
6. Leonard J. Arrington and Davis Bitton, *The Mormon Experience* (New York: Knopf, 1979), p. 46.
7. On LDS Church growth see Arrington and Bitton, *Mormon Experience*, pp. 22, 69.
8. Edwin Scott Gaustad, *Dissent in American Religion* (Chicago: University of Chicago Press, 1973), p. 2.
9. "A Personal Interview with Brigham Young, *New York Times*, 31 July 1858, p. 1.
10. Diary of Mary Haskin Parker Richards, typescript, Sunday, 14 May 1848, Marriott Library, University of Utah, Salt Lake City, p. 69.
11. Nineteenth-century writers portrayed Mormon men as satyrs and women as dupes or worse. Historians Arrington and Bitton correct this impression.

> The response of the men who were introduced into polygamy between 1841 and 1846 was anything but enthusiastic. The same was true of the women who were offered the chance of becoming plural wives. Apart from the fact that the new system collided with moral assumptions they had grown up with, there were practical difficulties that made polygamy less attractive. For the men to support additional wives was seldom easy. And for women to be married on this basis without being legally acknowledged as wives

259

can hardly have been reassuring. It was not the kind of scheme that aroused cheers and applause. (*Mormon Experience*, p. 197)

In one case they report: "One Mormon raised the question with his spouse, who minched no words in replying, 'All right Jody — you get another wife and I'll get another husband!'" (*Mormon Experience*, p. 200).

12. See Arrington and Bitton, *Mormon Experience*, Chapter 7, "Immigration and Diversity," for a comprehensive picture of the role immigration played in building the early LDS Church.

13. Chief Washakie told a large audience of about 3,000 Shoshone gathered at a special conference arranged by two Mormon elders representing President Brigham Young that the Mormons "are our good and true friends." See Charles E. Dibble, "The Mormon Mission to the Shoshoni Indians, Part II," *Utah Humanities Review* 1 (1947): 175.

14. A Salt Lake City ordinance providing for the arrest and detention in the county jail for up to ninety days of anyone fitting the description of a vagrant (that is, drunkard, beggar) exempted *only* Indians from such lockup (*Deseret News*, 25 April 1904).

15. Leonard J. Arrington, *From Quaker to Zion: Life of Edwin D. Wooley* (Salt Lake City: Deseret Book Co., 1976), pp. 421–22.

16. Mormon historian Juanita Brooks noted that "some of the early missionaries had seen the Indians as a possible ally in case of trouble with the Gentiles; one had even referred to them as 'the battle-ax of the Lord,' which they might learn to use with skill" (*The Mountain Meadows Massacre* [Norman: University of Oklahoma Press, 1970]), pp. 32–33.

17. Arrington and Bitton, *Mormon Experience*, p. 96.

18. Space limitations do not allow us to develop this argument regarding the Protestant millennialism of the early American colonists and later westward pioneers. Readers can, however, find a summary of it, with considerable supporting evidence in Martin E. Marty's *Righteous Empire: The Protestant Experience in America* (New York: Harper and Row, 1970).

19. *Doctrine and Covenants* (Salt Lake City: The Church of Jesus Christ of Latter-day Saints, 1969), p. 253, sec. 135, v. 7.

20. Joseph Fielding Smith, *Doctrines of Salvation* (Salt Lake City: Bookcraft, 1956), 1:135.

21. Brooks, *Mountain Meadows Massacre*, p. 56.

22. It is curious to note in connection with the doctrine of blood atonement that out of this country's fifty states Utah is alone in providing execution by firing squad as an alternative to hanging for those receiving the death penalty. According to the late LDS President Joseph Fielding Smith, this particular legislation was created by "the founders of Utah" to comply with the laws of the land and also the law of God with respect to blood atonement (*Doctrines of Salvation*, 1:136).

23. The hymn "O Ye Mountains High" (among many) has been considered a "serious battle song" by one Mormon historian. The hymn originally contained the threatening words "In thy mountain retreat, God will strengthen thy fee, On the necks of thy enemies thou shalt tread" but it was later changed to reflect a more moderate message. See Brooks, *Mountain Meadows Massacre*, p. 29.

24. *Journal History of the Church of Jesus Christ of Latter-day Saints*, 16 September

1868, p. 1; 3 October 1868, p. 1, Latter-day Saints Archives, Salt Lake City.

25. Joseph Heinerman, *Eternal Testimonies* (Manti, Utah: Mountain Valley Publisher, 1974), pp. 99–100.

26. David Croft, "A Weight on His Shoulders," *Church News* (8 November 1975), p. 7.

27. For example, David W. Patten, an early Mormon martyr, claimed to encounter Cain as follows: "As I was riding along the road on my mule I suddenly noticed a very strange personage walking beside me. He walked along beside me for about two miles. His head was about even with my shoulders as I sat in my saddle. He wore no clothing, but was covered with hair. His skin was very dark. I asked him where he dwelt and he replied that he had no home, that he was a wanderer in the earth, but that he could not die, and his mission was to destroy the souls of men. About the time he expressed himself thus, I rebuked him in the name of the Lord Jesus Christ and by virtue of the Holy Priesthood, and commanded him to go hence, and he immediately departed out of my sight." See Lycurgis A. Wilson, *Life of David W. Patten* (Salt Lake City: Deseret News, 1900), p. 50. An endorsement of the biography of Patten in which this account appeared was signed by Lorenzo Snow, fifth president of the LDS Church. See also John Heinerman, "The Concept of Cain in Mormon Theology" (paper delivered at the Creatures of Legendary Symposium, Omaha, Nebr., University of Nebraska, 29 September 1978).

28. See, for example, "History of Brigham Young," *Deseret News*, vol. 7, p. 402. Personal interview with Mrs. Werner (Mercedes) Kaiepe, a daughter of LeGrand Richards, 12 January 1983.

29. Both early and modern Church apostles, such as Orson Pratt and Rudgar Clawson, respectively, have been explicit in interpreting Nebuchadnezzar's vision to mean eventual Mormon theocratic control of the entire earth. See, for example, *Journal of Discourses*, vol. 7, Amasa Lyman, ed. (Liverpool, England: Amasa Lyman, 1860), pp. 217–20, and *Seventy-Fifth Annual Conference* (Salt Lake City: Deseret News, April 1905), pp. 35–36.

30. Joseph Smith, Jr., *History of the Church of Jesus Christ of Latter-day Saints* (Salt Lake City: Deseret Book Co., 1927), 6:290, 292.

31. D. Michael Quinn, "The Council of Fifty and Its Members, 1844 to 1945," *Brigham Young University Studies* 20 (Winter 1980): 183–91.

32. *Journal of William Clayton*, 11 April 1844, 1 January 1845, History Department Archives of the LDS Church, Salt Lake City.

33. Dale Morgan, "The State of Deseret," *Utah Historical Quarterly* 8 (1940): 139–40.

34. *Journal of Discourses*, vol. 18, Joseph F. Smith, ed. (Liverpool, England: Joseph F. Smith, 1877), p. 341.

35. Duane S. Crowther, *Prophecy: Key to the Future* (Salt Lake City: Brookcraft, 1967), pp. 65–66.

36. Klaus J. Hansen, "The Theory and Practice of the Political Kingdom of God in Mormon History, 1829–1890" (Master's thesis, Brigham Young University Department of History, Provo, Utah, 1959), pp. 15–16. See also Klaus J. Hansen, *Quest for Empire* (E. Lansing: Michigan State University Press, 1970).

37. Ezra Taft Benson, "Prepare Yourselves for the Great Day of the Lord" (address delivered to the Devotional Assembly, Ricks College, Idaho, 16 September 1980).

38. Hyrum L. Andrus, *Doctrines of the Kingdom* (Salt Lake City: Bookcraft, 1973), p. ix.

39. Andrus, *Doctrines*, pp. 40–60.
40. See *Journal of Discourses*, vol. 21, Albert Carrington (Liverpool, England, 1881), p. 31, and 7:218.
41. *Church News*, 12 April 1980, p. 19.
42. *Journal of Discourses*, vol. 7, Amasa Lymans (Liverpool: 1860), pp. 123–25.
43. Wilber G. Katz and Harold P. Southerland, "Religious Pluralism and the Supreme Court," in William G. McLoughlin and Robert N. Bellah, eds., *Religion in America* (Boston: Beacon, 1968), p. 269.
44. Katz and Southerland, "Religious Pluralism," p. 269.
45. For two recent books that demonstrate this fact, see David G. Bromley and Anson D. Shupe, Jr., *"Moonies" in America: Cult, Church and Crusade* (Beverly Hills, Calif.: Sage, 1979), and David G. Bromley and Anson D. Shupe, Jr., *Strange Gods: The Great American Cult Scare* (Boston: Beacon, 1981).
46. Paul Blanshard, *American Freedom and Catholic Power*, rev. ed. (Boston: Beacon, 1958), p. 1.

Chapter 2   From Telegraph to Satellite

1. *Federal Communications Commission Reports*, vol. 1, 2d ser. (February 1969): 464–65.
2. Kenneth L. Woodward, "Onward, Mormon Soldiers," *Newsweek*, 27 April 1981, pp. 87–88.
3. Woodward, "Onward, Mormon Soldiers," pp. 87–88.
4. Michael Parrish, "The Saints Among Us," *Rocky Mountain Magazine* (January/February 1980), p. 27.
5. Parrish, "Saints," pp. 28–30.
6. Rodney Stark and William Sims Bainbridge, "Networks of Faith: Interpersonal Bonds and Recruitment to Cults and Sects," *American Journal of Sociology* 85 (May 1980): 1386–87.
7. Stark and Bainbridge, "Networks," p. 1387.
8. For a description of similar tactics by this newer Christian sect, see David G. Bromley and Anson D. Shupe, Jr., *"Moonies" in America: Cult, Church, and Crusade* (Beverly Hills, Calif.: Sage, 1979), pp. 169–96; and David G. Bromley and Anson D. Shupe, Jr., *Strange Gods: The Great American Cult Scare* (Boston: Beacon, 1981), pp. 92–127. Actually, knowledge of the importance of personal relationships in the Mormon conversion process has been recognized for some time. See, for example, John Seggar and Philip Kuntz, "Conversion: Evaluation of a Step-like Process for Problem-Solving," *Review of Religious Research* 13 (Spring 1972): 178–84.
9. For a review of early efforts to spread copies of the *Book of Mormon*, see Gordon B. Hinckley, "Joseph Smith: His Short Life Changed the Future for Millions," *Church News*, 5 January 1980, p. 5, and Hal Knight, "Book of Mormon Is Woven into the Basic Threads of Restored Gospel," *Church News*, 5 January 1980, p. 6.
10. See Brigham Young's report in *Journal of Discourses* (Liverpool, England: F. D. Richards, Publisher, 1855), 2:245.
11. See, respectively, Perry Benjamin Pierce, "The Origin of the 'Book of Mormon,'" *American Anthropologist* 1 (1899): 694, and Theodore Schroeder, "Authorship of the Book of Mormon," *American Journal of Psychology* 30 (January 1919): 66.

12. For example, a popular debunking of Mormon pre-Columbian American history can be found in anthropologist Robert Wauchope's *Lost Tribes and Sunken Continents* (Chicago: University of Chicago Press, 1962), pp. 50–68.

13. Knight, "Book of Mormon," p. 6.

14. See, respectively, *Elders' Journal* (1837–38), p. 48; Oliver Cowdery, "Egyptian Mummies — Ancient Records," *Latter-day Saints' Messenger and Advocate* 2 (December 1835): 236; and *Times and Seasons* 5 (15 December 1844): 746–47.

15. W. W. Phelps, "Free People of Color," *Evening and the Morning Star* 2 (July 1833): 109; 2 (December 1833): 114.

16. David L. Brewer, "The Mormon," in Donald L. Cutler, ed., *The Religious Situation, 1968* (Boston: Beacon, 1968), pp. 521–52.

17. Sterling McMurrin, "The Mormon Doctrine and the Negro" (address delivered to the Salt Lake City Branch of the National Association for the Advancement of Colored People, March 1969).

18. Leonard J. Arrington, *Great Basin Kingdom* (Cambridge: Harvard University Press, 1958), pp. 114–16.

19. Paul Swenson, "Nostrums in the Newsroom," *Dialogue: A Journal of Mormon Thought* 10 (Spring 1977): 50.

20. Elaine Jarvik and George Buck, "Probing the Power Structure," *Utah Holiday* 5 (24 May 1976): 15.

21. These events are summarized in Wallace Turner, *The Mormon Establishment* (Boston: Houghton Mifflin, 1966).

22. D. Michael Quinn, *J. Reuben Clark: The Church Years* (Provo, Utah: Brigham Young University Press, 1983), p. 75. It is a well-established fact that the Mormon Church tried throughout the nineteenth and the first half of the twentieth century to gain control of nearly all the newspapers in the Salt Lake City and Ogden areas to sway votes and silence Gentile criticism of the Church among the *Deseret News'* competitors. During the 1890s the Church hierarchy was forced by the federal government to have its members join either the Republican or Democratic party as part of the massive "disenfranchisement" and reorganization of the Church. The Church purchased various local newspapers and declared them nominally either Republican or Democrat as it saw fit. In 1891, for example, the Church leadership decided to purchase secretly the *Salt Lake Times* and maintain the appearance of a non-Mormon Republican newspaper to counter the city's actual Gentile, moderate Republican *Salt Lake Tribune*. It did, and this strategy was repeated many times throughout Utah. In the final analysis, Mormon historian D. Michael Quinn wrote, "as the Mormons entered national politics the hierarchy either openly or privately controlled prominent Democratic, Republican, and politically independent newspapers of Utah's two most populous cities." See D. Michael Quinn, *The Mormon Hierarchy, 1832–1932: An American Elite* (Ph.D. diss., Yale University), 1976, pp. 241–42, 249.

23. Swenson, "Nostrums," p. 51.

24. Bob Gottlieb and Peter Wiley, "Static in Zion," *Columbia Journalism Review* (July/August 1979), pp. 59–60.

25. Interview with Robert Mullins, *Deseret News* investigative reporter, 19 April 1982.

26. Interview with William B. Smart, editor of the *Deseret News*, 19 April 1982.

27. Swenson, "Nostrums," p. 52.

28. Paul Swenson, "Nostrums," p. 52.

29. Interview with Robert Mullins, April 19, 1982.
30. See Edward Geary, "The Last Days of the Coalville Tabernacle," *Dialogue: A Journal of Mormon Thought* (Winter 1970): 42–49, and Swenson, "Nostrums," p. 53.
31. Interview with William B. Smart, editor of the *Deseret News*, 2 March 1982.
32. Interview with anonymous staff member of the *Church News*, 1983.
33. The *Deseret News* is not held in high esteem by its counterparts. In the process of seeking estimates of the *Deseret News'* dollar value we encountered some very unflattering descriptions of it by other newspaper publishers in Utah and surrounding states.
34. See, for example, Jeffrey Kaye, "An Invisible Empire: Mormon Money in California," *Newsweek*, 8 May 1978, p. 37; and Russell Chandler, "Mormons: Change Is in the Wind," *Los Angeles Times*, 26 June 1983, p. 26.
35. Interview with Rosel H. Hyde, 6 February 1982.
36. The significance of this "electronic church" for national politics and for the average American is outlined in two recent studies. See Jeffrey K. Hadden and Charles K. Swann, *Prime Time Preachers: The Rising Power of Televangelism* (Reading, Mass.: Addison-Wesley, 1981), and William A. Stacey and Anson Shupe, "Correlates of Support for the Electronic Church," *Journal for the Scientific Study of Religion* 21 (December 1982): 291–303.
37. Richard Barnum-Reece, "Arch Madsen," *This People* 2, no. 6 (1981): 46.
38. See Arrington, *Great Basin Kingdom*, pp. 228–31, and Leonard J. Arrington, "The Deseret Telegraph: A Church-Owned Public Utility," *Journal of Economic History* 11 (Spring 1951): 117–37.
39. Fred C. Esplin, "The Church as Broadcaster," *Dialogue: A Journal of Mormon Thought* 10 (Spring 1977): 28–29.
40. *Federal Communications Commission Reports*, vol. 62, 2d ser. (1976): 255.
41. Esplin, "Church as Broadcaster," p. 25.
42. This is public information, and it is available from the other *Federal Communications Commission Reports* cited in this chapter. For a Mormon analysis of such media holdings, see Esplin, "Church as Broadcaster."
43. See *Broadcasting* (12 January 1981): 26; and (25 April 1981): 26.
44. Bob Gottlieb and Peter Wiley, "Mormonism, Inc.," *The Nation*, 16–23 August 1980, p. 15.
45. Telephone interview with Don Cavaleri, sales manager for First Media Corporation, at station WPGC-AM, Morningside, Md., 21 January 1982.
46. See *Federal Communications Commission Reports*, vol. 16, 2d ser. (1969): 345–55, 458–66.
47. *Federal Communications Commission Reports*, vol. 16, 2d ser. (1969): 460.
48. *Federal Communications Commission Reports*, vol. 16, 2d ser. (1969): 460.
49. *Broadcasting* (16 May 1966): 52.
50. *Federal Communications Commission Reports*, vol. 7, 2d ser. (1966): 844.
51. See "Networks, Others Attack DPA Plan to Lengthen Hours for Daytimes," *Broadcasting* (21 March 1983): 130; and "Open Mike," *Broadcasting* (4 April 1983): 23.
52. Petition of the Department of Justice to Deny Renewal Applications, in the Matter of KSL, Inc., Federal Communications Commission, Washington, D.C., 3 September 1974.
53. Esplin, "Church as Broadcaster," pp. 34–35.
54. Interview with Rosel H. Hyde, 6 February 1982.

55. Interview with James Conkling, 10 February 1982. The "Homefront Series" is the group of thirty- and sixty-second spots on radio and television for which the Mormons are well known.

56. John Dart, "Mormon Planning Satellite TV System," *Los Angeles Times*, 10 October 1981, I-A, p. 4.

57. Interview with Bruce Hough, 12 February 1982. Hough was correct when he said other religious groups were consulting with Mormons about electronic media usage. In fall 1982, the Catholic Telecommunications Network of America began leasing time from Bonneville Satellite Corporation and broadcasting to seven Roman Catholic archdioceses and dioceses with receiving equipment in place. See "Catholic TV Network Begins to Broadcast," *Salt Lake Tribune*, 1 October 1982.

58. Interview with Bruce Hough, 5 July 1983.

59. *Church News*, 3 October 1983, p. 16.

60. Rachel Wrege, "The Human Roll Call," *Personal Computing* (December 1982): p. 55.

61. Hal Knight, "Satellite to Beam Cabin Rites," *Church News*, 5 April 1983, p. 7.

62. "They're Coming!" *Latter-day Sentinel*, 13 November 1981, p. 4.

63. "Youths' Fireside to Be Beamed over Satellite Network," *Church News*, 13 November 1982, p. 3.

64. Interview with Mike Hannon, 18 July 1983.

65. Interview with Mike Hannon, 18 July 1983.

66. Richard Alan Nelson, "From Antagonism to Acceptance: Mormons and the Silver Screen," *Dialogue: A Journal of Mormon Thought* 10 (Spring 1977): p. 59.

67. Nelson, "Antagonism," p. 65.

68. James V. D'Arc, "When Hollywood & Vine Met at Temple Square," *Mountainwest* (April 1979): 35.

69. Interview with James Conkling, 10 February 1982.

70. Interview with Wetzel O. Whitaker, 8 February 1982.

71. Interview with G. Judy, 8 February 1982.

72. Steve Preston, "Mormon Ideas Alive in ABC's 'Galactica.'" *Daily Universe*, 9 February 1979, p. 10.

73. Advertisement in *TV Guide*, 4 November 1978, p. A-23.

74. Stephen W. Stathis and Dennis L. Lythgoe, "Mormonism in the Nineteen-Seventies: The Popular Perception," *Dialogue: A Journal of Mormon Thought* 10 (Spring 1977): 95.

75. Kenneth C. Danforth, "The Cult of Mormonism," *Harper's* (May 1980): 71.

76. Dennis L. Lythgoe, "Marketing the Mormon Image: An Interview with Wendall J. Ashton," *Dialogue: A Journal of Mormon Thought* 10 (Spring 1977): 15.

77. Frank Rigby, "Church Evaluates Image," *Daily Universe*, 15 November 1978, p. 12.

78. "Church Inserts to Be Featured in Reader's Digest," *Daily Universe*, 28 February 1978, p. 1.

79. "Packaging Mormonism in Digestible Form," *Christianity Today* (4 May 1979), pp. 50–51.

80. Interview with Norman R. Bowen, director of International Public Communications, 16 February 1983.

81. "Marketing," p. 19.

82. Phyllis Starr Wilson, "Hearts and Minds," *Self* (February 1983), p. 56.

83. Further details of the case can be found in numerous local newspapers and

other media accounts, such as "Farmer Files Suit Against LDS Church," *Salt Lake Tribune*, 2 May 1979, and Gary M. Smith, "Strange Harvest," *Utah Holiday* (24 May 1976), pp. 16ff.

84. Interview with Reed Irvine, president of Accuracy in the Media, Inc., 22 January 1982; also interview with Jerry Cahill, LDS Church Public Communications Department, 12 January 1982.

85. John Weisman, "'60 Minutes': How Good Is It?" *TV Guide*, 16 April 1983, p. 5.

86. Personal correspondence with Richard Clark, 15 January 1982.

87. Interview with Richard Clark, 13 January 1982.

88. O. Kendall White, Jr., and Daryl White, "Abandoning an Unpopular Policy: An Analysis of the Decision Granting the Mormon Priesthood to Blacks," *Sociological Analysis* 41 (Fall 1980): 233.

89. See Armand L. Mauss, a well-known Mormon sociologist of religion, who has supported this general argument in "Comments: White on Black Among the Mormons; A Critique of White & White," *Sociological Analysis* 42 (Fall 1981): 277–82.

90. Information on the Church's consultation with public relations firms concerning its internal affairs was obtained from interviews with Church officials and with various informants in both Salt Lake City and New York City whose identities must remain anonymous to protect their present positions of employment.

91. See, for example, Janet Brigham, "To Every Worthy Member," *Sunstone* (July–August 1978): 5. See also Brigham, "Warm Responses to Priesthood Announcement," *Ensign* (August 1978): 78, and Brigham, "Ordination Revelation A Momentous One," *Daily Universe*, 15 June 1978, p. 16.

92. Several dozen pages of original notes used to determine the approximate wealth of LDS Church–owned communications have been reproduced and placed in the archives of the Institute for the Study of American Religion (University of California, Santa Barbara, CA 93106). These materials contain not only details such as dollar estimates for the items discussed in the final section of this chapter but also the sources of such information, including notes from interviews with informants. Any specific estimate will be open to some modification when compared with actual figures, of course, but our intent is to let others see how we arrived at them.

Much of the background research in forming these estimates was done using available publications, such as the yearly *Broadcasting Yearbook-Marketbook*, the professional trade journal *Broadcasting*, the *Federal Communications Commission Reports* series (which is public information), and even Mormon publications, such as *Dialogue: A Journal of Mormon Thought*. We also interviewed academic and commercial experts on the broadcasting industry and used the known figures of comparable non-Mormon holdings in the estimating process.

The example of KSL-TV (Channel 5) in Salt Lake City may provide a sense of the research behind many estimates. WTAR-TV in Norfolk, Virginia, sold for $48 million in 1982, according to *Broadcasting* (11 January 1982), p. 38. The Norfolk area is forty-seventh in size in the national rankings of ADIs (Area of Dominant Influence, a Federal Communications Commission measure), just two ranks above the Salt Lake area. Comparing WTAR-TV and KSL-TV to learn what each station receives for a half-minute of advertising (information available in the *1981 Broadcasting Yearbook*, p. B-137), we see:

	Prime Time	Early Fringe	Daytime
WTAR-TV (Norfolk)	$ 750	$350	$120
KSL-TV (Salt Lake)	$1500	$600	$125

At first glance it would seem unlikely that KSL-TV's market value would be *less* than the approximately $50 million that WTAR-TV sold for and could be worth considerably more. One of us contacted Dr. Timothy Larson, professor of mass communications at the University of Utah in Salt Lake City. Dr. Larson had done previous appraisals for other television stations. Using an estimate of KSL-TV's yearly advertising revenue, he estimated that KSL-TV was worth approximately $52 million. Another University of Utah professor in the same department, a former news anchor for KSL-TV's chief rival, KCPX-TV (Channel 4), concurred. However, at a later interview, Dr. Larson raised his estimate to "a more realistic price at today's fair market value" of a little over $70 million (interview with Dr. Timothy Larson, Salt Lake City, 19 January 1982). In addition, we contacted Ward Quaal, head of the Ward L. Quaal Company (offices in Los Angeles and Chicago). The Quaal Company is a consulting firm to the broadcasting industry and does frequent appraisals of stations' market values. Emphasizing the Salt Lake area's growth and the ultramodern equipment of KSL-TV, Quaal appraised the station at an upper value of $80 million (cautioning that his estimate was conservative) (interview with Ward Quaal, Los Angeles, 8 January 1982).

Thus, with a range of $50 million to $80 million, we chose $71 million as a reasonable estimated value for KSL-TV. This was typical of the process we used to construct each estimate.

Chapter 3 LDS, Incorporated

1. David Briscoe and Bill Beecham, "Mormon Church Controls Extensive National Business Interests," *Post-Register* (Idaho Falls), 21 September 1975, p. A-11.
2. See, respectively, Ken Wells, "The Mormon Church Is Rich, Rapidly Growing and Very Controversial," *Wall Street Journal*, 9 November 1983, p. 1, and Clayton Jones, "A Passive Role in Business Adopted by Mormon Church," *Christian Science Monitor*, 28 April 1982, p. B-4.
3. Jeffrey Kaye, "An Invisible Empire: Mormon Money in California," *New West*, 8 May 1978, p. 39.
4. Leonard J. Arrington, "Zion's Board of Trade: A Third United Order," *Western Humanities Review* 5 (Winter 1950–51): 1. For a similar conclusion by the same expert on Mormon economic history, see "Objectives of Mormon Economic Policy," *Western Humanities Review* 10 (Spring 1956): 180.
5. Dean D. McBrien, "The Economic Content of Early Mormon Doctrine," *Southwestern Political and Social Science Quarterly* 6 (1925): 180.
6. Parley P. Pratt, *The Autobiography of Parley Parker Pratt* (New York: Russell Bros., 1874), pp. 99, 102–3, 112.
7. Leonard J. Arrington, *From Wilderness to Empire: The Role of Utah in Western Economic History*, monograph no. 1 (University of Utah Institute of American Studies, Salt Lake City, 1961), p. 16.
8. Briscoe and Beecham, "Mormon Church," p. A-11.

9. Cited in Stephen W. Stathis, "Mormonism and the Periodical Press: A Change Is Underway," *Dialogue: A Journal of Mormon Thought* 14 (Summer 1981): 66.
10. Kenneth C. Danforth, "The Cult of Mormonism," *Harper's* (May 1980): 68.
11. John Dalrymple, "Church Statistics Show Growth," *Daily Universe*, 30 March 1983, p. 17.
12. Gene R. Cook, "Miracles Among the Lamanites," *Ensign* (November 1980): 68.
13. Donald R. Snow, "Models Used in Projecting Mormon Growth" (extemporaneous address presented at the annual meeting of the Mormon History Association, Weber State College, Ogden, Utah, May 1982).
14. Neal A. Maxwell, "The Church Now Can Be Universal with Priesthood Revelation of 1978," *Church News*, 5 January 1980, p. 20.
15. Garth N. Jones, "Expanding LDS Church Abroad: Old Realities Compounded," *Dialogue: A Journal of Mormon Thought* 13 (Spring 1980): 10.
16. Interviews with anonymous informants in the Church's Confidential Records Department, 1982 and 1983.
17. Cited in Nels L. Nelson, *Scientific Aspects of Mormonism* (New York: Putnam's, 1904), p. 1.
18. Information about LDS Church leaders' salaries was obtained from interviews with an anonymous informant in the LDS Church Finance Office.
19. *Deseret News*, 19 May 1982, p. A-10.
20. *Salt Lake Tribune*, 5 April 1982, p. B-9.
21. *Time*, 7 June 1982, p. 69.
22. Interview with anonymous informant in Church Finance Department, 1983.
23. Interviews with anonymous informants in the LDS Church Finance Office, 1983.
24. Top LDS leaders' marginal health is an easily documented pattern. For example, see the following sample: "Pres. Kimball Feeling Better, Still Showing Effects of Age," *Church News*, 29 May 1983, p. 14; "Marion Romney in Serious Condition," *Salt Lake Tribune*, 23 June 1983; "LDS Leader's Health Improves," *Deseret News*, 23–24 May 1983. One Mormon colleague at Brigham Young University casually mentioned during a telephone conversation that the apostles' health concerns are frequent topics of conversation, sometimes on a par with sports scores and political election results.
25. Leonard J. Arrington and Davis Bitton, *The Mormon Experience* (New York: Knopf, 1979), p. 292.
26. "Planning for the Future Boom," *Nation's Business* 63 (June 1975): p. 58.
27. Interviews with LDS Church administration personnel, June 1982. See also Fred C. Esplin, "The Saints Go Marching On," *Utah Holiday* (June 1981): 48.
28. Esplin, "Saints," p. 48.
29. Arrington and Bitton, *Mormon Experience*, p. 290.
30. Hal Knight, "His Life's Work: Telling Church Story," *Church News*, 12 September 1981, p. 4.
31. See Dennis L. Lythgoe, "Battling the Bureaucracy: Building a Mormon Chapel," *Dialogue: A Journal of Mormon Thought* 15 (Winter 1982): 76. Lythgoe has written a detailed account of the obstacles and pitfalls in the Mormon bureaucratic maze that he encountered as a bishop trying to arrange for a new chapel to be built in his Massachusetts ward. Frequently the various departments and divisions of the Church failed to communicate with one another during the approval process and were ignorant of Lythgoe's ward's particular needs. In many ways the chapel was built in spite of, not on account of, the Church bureaucracy.

32. Quinn, *J. Reuben Clark*, pp. 106–7.
33. See, for example, David G. Bromley and Anson D. Shupe, Jr., "Financing the New Religions," *Journal for the Scientific Study of Religion* 19 (September 1980): 227–39.
34. See Nadine Scott, "College Opportunity — But Low Pay Scale," *Honolulu Star-Bulletin*, 23 July 1974, p. A-10; and Nadine Scott, "Four Students Exploited — BYU Faculty Questions Center's Labor Policy," *Honolulu Star-Bulletin*, 24 July 1974, p. D-2.
35. Evelyn Twigg-Smith, "Fijian Pickets Fear Church," *Honolulu Advertiser*, 26 July 1974, p. A-4.
36. Mark P. Leone, "The Mormon Temple Experience," *Sunstone Review* (September–October 1978): 10.
37. "Using Our Temples," *Church News*, 19 June 1983, p. 16.
38. See Paul McGrath, "Cities Pull Welcome Mat from Mormon Temples," *USA Today*, 3 May 1983, p. A-3, and Beth Frerking, "Convert Controversy: Mormons' Growing Ranks Worry Dallas Baptists," *Dallas Times Herald*, 17 April 1983, p. B-3.
39. Ray Ruppert, "Mormons Now Have a World Church, Says Leader," *Seattle Times*, 28 July 1979, p. B-9.
40. Interview with Emil B. Fetzer, retired Church architect, Salt Lake City, 8 April 1982.
41. See *Journal of Discourses*, vol. 10, Daniel H. Wells (Liverpool, England, 1865), p. 254.
42. "SBC: Southern Baptist Convention to Top 14 Million; Baptisms Decline," *Baptist Standard* 95 (21 December 1983): 4.
43. Excerpt from an article from the *Dallas Morning News*, reprinted as "Southern Baptists Brace for Invasion of Mormons," *Church News*, 24 May 1982, p. 10.
44. See Frerking, "Convert Controversy," p. 4.
45. See "Rowdy Scenes over Mormon Temple Go-Ahead," *Church News*, 24 May 1982, p. 10.
46. See, for example, "Church to Persist on Denver Temple," *Church News*, 21–22 December 1982, p. 10-D; "Mormons Give Up Temple Site Because of Neighbors' Gripes," *Salt Lake Tribune*, 20 August 1982, p. C-1; and "Bid Denied on Site of Temple," *Salt Lake Tribune*, 19 December 1982, p. B-2.
47. "Environmentalists Fight Temple," *Salt Lake Tribune*, 6 December 1982, p. A-3.
48. "Chicago Temple on 'Go': Suit Settled," *Deseret News*, 5–6 May 1983, p. Z-5.
49. "Mormon Temple Construction Begins," *Dallas Morning News*, 25 January 1983.
50. Interview with R. David McDougal, mission president of the Georgia-Atlanta Mission, 1 May 1982.
51. Susan Oman, "East German Communists Welcome Mormon Temple," *Sunstone Review* (November 1982): 28.
52. See "Short Subjects," *Sunstone Review* (July 1982): 21.
53. Arrington and Bitton, *Mormon Experience*, p. 283.
54. See Jay W. DeGraff, "An Investigation of the System of Church Finances, 1834–1842," unpublished manuscript, Lee Library, Joseph K. Nicholas Collection, Box 31, Folder 8, Brigham Young University, Provo, Utah.
55. Donald W. Cannon and Lyndon W. Cook, eds., *Far West Record* (Salt Lake City: Deseret Book Company, 1983), pp. 128, 132n. 4.

56. See, for example, J. H. Beadle, *Western Wilds and the Men Who Redeem Them* (Philadelphia, 1879), p. 96.

57. Russell Chandler, "Mormon Change Is in the Wind," *Los Angeles Times*, 26 June 1983, p. 25.

58. See Robert O'Brien, *Marriott: The J. Willard Marriott Story* (Salt Lake City: Deseret Book Company, 1981), p. 295; and, as one example of a Church leader's similar over-tithing, personal papers relating to George Albert Smith (letter of Emily Smith Stewart to Dr. Earl Pardoe at Brigham Young University, 12 May 1948, George Albert Smith Papers, Box 96, Folder 1, University of Utah Library, Salt Lake City.

59. Ernest L. Wilkinson and Leonard J. Arrington, *Brigham Young University: The First One Hundred Years* (Provo, Utah: Brigham Young University Press, 1976), 2:216, 218, 383–84, 414.

60. Dean R. Brimhall, letter to Henry D. Moyle, 20 June 1938, Dean R. Brimhall Papers, Box 26, Folder 19, University of Utah Library, Salt Lake City.

61. Wells, "Mormon Church," p. 20.

62. See Christine J. Amos et al. v. The Corp. of the Presiding Bishopric of the Church of Jesus Christ of Latter-day Saints and the Corp. of the President of the Church of Jesus Christ of Latter-day Saints, Civil No. C-83-0492W, U.S. District Court for the District of Utah, Central Division, Salt Lake City.

63. Interview with official in the Treasury Division of the Church, 1982.

64. Peter Bart, "Prigging Out," *Rolling Stone*, 14 April 1983, p. 91.

65. Wilkinson and Arrington, *Brigham Young University*, 3:258.

66. The foregoing information was obtained from interviews with personnel in Brigham Young University's Development Office and in the LDS Foundation during 1981–1983.

67. "Y Funding Campaign Is 'Virtually On Track,'" *Church News*, 18 September 1983, p. 13.

68. "Fund-Raising Office Now Called the LDS Foundation," *Church News*, 13 November 1982, p. 5.

69. Interview with Scott Barrett, an assistant director for the LDS Church Development Office, 7 January 1982, and interview with James Olson, assistant legal counsel for the LDS Church Development Office, 7 January 1982.

70. Interview with Carl Bacon, former director of Church Development at Brigham Young University, 5 November 1981.

71. Christy Custer, "'Ring, Ring' It's Telefund," *Daily Universe*, 5 November 1981, p. 1, and Christy Custer, "'Telefund Supports Y Projects," *Daily Universe*, 6 November 1981, p. 2.

72. "Attention: All BYU Students," *Daily Universe*, 2 November 1981, p. 5.

73. *Daily Universe*, 6 November 1981, p. 8.

74. *Daily Universe*, 5 November 1981, p. 3.

75. Readers wishing to obtain more detailed information on the wealth of the LDS Church as found in our research notes should contact Dr. J. Gordon Melton, director, the Institute for the Study of American Religion, P.O. Box 1311, Evanston, IL 60201.

76. Arrington and Bitton, *Mormon Experience*, p. 282.

77. Wallace Turner, *The Mormon Establishment* (Boston: Houghton Mifflin, 1966), p. 105.

78. Interview with an official of the LDS Church Investment Department, Salt Lake City, 1982.

79. See "Latter-Day Profits," *Newsweek*, 22 January 1962, p. 68, and Jeffrey Kaye, "An Invisible Empire: Mormon Money in California," *New West*, 8 May 1978, p. 41.

80. Jim Morris, "Utilities Say Setbacks Cut Nuclear Plants' Appeal," *Forth Worth Star Telegram*, 2 January 1984, p. 1-A.

81. Information on nuclear power plants was obtained in interview with Susan Phelps, nuclear program director, Edison Electric Institute, Washington, D.C., 12 December 1982, and from numerous annual reports from companies to the Federal Energy Regulatory Commission.

82. Data were taken from numerous Federal Energy Regulatory Commission annual reports submitted by utility companies and provided in an interview with Paul Shepherd, account executive, Dean Whitter Company, Fort Worth, Tex., 12 December 1983.

83. "Business Portrait: Alan Blodgett Is LDS Church's Wise Investment," *Salt Lake Tribune*, 7 December 1980, p. B-20.

84. Interview, 1982.

85. Estimates of earned income on "all other business investments" in 1982 and 1983 were obtained from personnel in the LDS Church Investment Department. Approximate average yield percentages were suggested by Paul Shepherd, account executive, Dean Whitter Company, Fort Worth, Tex., 13 December 1983.

86. We based our 1982 and 1983 estimates on two types of sources: previously published estimates that we judged reasonable and many formal and informal conversations with various LDS Church Investment Department personnel. Our 1962 estimate of Church income comes from Neil Morgan, "Utah: How Much Money Hath the Mormon Church?" *Esquire* (August 1962): 90. The 1976 estimate can be found in Samuel W. Taylor, *Rocky Mountain Empire* (New York: Macmillan, 1978), p. 142. The 1978 estimate comes from award-winning journalists Bill Beecham and David Briscoe, "Mormon Money and How It's Made," *Utah Holiday* (22 March 1976): 4.

87. See *Deseret News 1983 Church Almanac* (Salt Lake City: Deseret News, 1982), pp. 265, 269.

88. Elder Mark E. Petersen, "The Church 'Grows' Around the Globe," *Church News*, 5 January 1980, p. 4.

89. We relied particularly on the five-volume *The College Blue Book*, 18th ed. (New York: Macmillan, 1981), 1:715; *The Real Estate Atlas of State of Hawaii: 1st Tax Division City & County of Honolulu Real Estate Handbook*, 15th ed. (Miami: Real Estate Data, Inc., 1981), vol. 2, zone 5, p. 3357; and interviews with Scott Lyman, Century 21–John West Associates, Provo, Utah, 29 September 1983, and with Vicki Davidson, Century 21–Hathaway-Genta, Rexburg, Idaho, 29 September 1983.

90. See James H. McClintock, *Mormon Settlement in Arizona* (Phoenix: State of Arizona, 1921), pp. 50–51.

91. Table 3–8, Approximate Acreage in LDS Church Farm-Ranch System, is the summation of numerous interviews, consultations, and discussions with close to two dozen persons knowledgeable about the LDS Church and/or its specific farm-ranch properties. For example, the 316,000 acres of the Deseret Ranch of Florida include acreage owned by Zion's Security, an LDS Church com-

mercial real estate subsidiary, and its total estimated wealth (not presented in Table 3–8) is a straight $2,475 per acre, or $782,100,000. These figures are based on interviews with Harvey Dahl, former manager of the Deseret Ranch of Florida (8 February 1982) as well as with real estate experts in that area, among them Virginia P. Clement, Century 21–C & D Realty, Inc., St. Cloud, Fla. (25 January 1982), and Dave Ryan, Narcoosee Realty, Inc., Narcoosee, Fla. (27 January 1982). In other instances we obtained more "official" figures. For example, in the case of U&I, Inc., 109,000 acres can be said to be owned by the LDS Church since it owns two-thirds of the voting stock in U&I, Inc., or about 1.8 million shares. Moreover, officials of the Church Investment Department and Deseret Farms meet with U&I officials on occasion. In addition, lesser amounts of stock (not counted here) are owned by prominent Mormons. Our source was an interview with Darwin Packer, associate vice-president, U&I, Inc. (2 February 1982). Sometimes we found such information in publications. The 201,000 acres listed for Deseret Livestock Ranch comes from the article "LDS Church Negotiating on Deseret Ranch Buy," *Deseret News*, 26 October 1983, p. B-1.

As can be seen, the methods used to assemble such a composite picture in the absence of disclosure of information by the Church have to be eclectic. As is the case with our original notes and a good deal of detail that could not be included in this book, we have placed such materials on file with the Institute for the Study of American Religion (Box 1311, Evanston, IL 60201).

92. Jeffrey Kaye, "An Invisible Empire: Mormon Money in California," *New West*, 8 May 1978, 41.

93. Replacement cost data and estimates of building values supplied by Don Hunt, sales manager, Borton, Inc., Hutchison, Kans., 30 September 1983. Borton, Inc., is one of the nation's largest builders of grain elevators and grain annexes. Borton built an annex at Elberta, Utah, and the grain and bean storage facilities in Burley, Idaho, for the LDS Church several years ago.

94. Based on interviews with Salt Lake City realtors.

95. See Russell Chandler, "Mormons: Change Is in the Wind," *Los Angeles Times*, 26 June 1983, p. 1.

96. Estimates of the value of various LDS historical properties were obtained from knowledgeable real estate professionals and local officials (either LDS-connected or outside the Church). For example, the value of LDS sites in Palmyra and Fayette, N.Y., were provided by Charlie Stewart, Century 21 Realty, Palmyra, N.Y., 7 and 16 July 1983. Estimates of the Joseph Smith memorial in Sharon, Vt., were provided by Willis Stoddard, Century 21–Millstone Agency, Bethel, Vt., 7 July 1983. Carl Bainter, county assessor for Hancock County, Ill., supplied data on the Nauvoo Restoration, Inc., site (11 July 1983). All were interviewed by telephone.

97. See, for example, Rachael Wrege, "The Human Call," *Popular Computing* (December 1982): 48–50.

98. The estimated value of LDS Church archival and library holdings was assessed in the following way:

Book value was computed from several different sets of figures. An average of $30 per book was assigned to the volumes in general circulation (1,150,000 volumes worth approximately $34,500,000). About 20 percent of the books (especially in the general literature) are worth an average of $3 per volume. About 55 percent consist of good books in art, history, American, and so forth worth approximately $50 each. The remaining 25 percent are largely genealogical books such as old county and city histories, which average $75 and up per volume. About $30 per volume for a straight-run estimate is fairly conservative, based on today's book values (interview with Sam Weller, proprietor of Zion's Bookstore, Salt Lake City, Utah, 29 September 1983, several other book appraisers, and Brigham Young University library personnel).

About 150,000 volumes are kept in a restricted area known as Special Collections. Of these, about 14,000 are secured in a vault. Volumes here range in price, but an average of $3,000 per volume is assigned (for a total of $42,000,000). Estimates were obtained from the above-mentioned book appraiser and BYU library personnel, *College Blue Book*, 151, 156, 715, and "Vault Holds University's 'Treasurer,'" *BYU Today* (December 1978): 1, 5.

99. Interview with Ralph Pearson, legal counsel for Beneficial Life Insurance Company and secretary of Continental Life Insurance Company of Iowa, Salt Lake City, 29 January 1982.

100. Total life insurance in force for all members of the Beneficial Life Group were obtained from the company's annual statements for 31 December 1982, which are on file with the Utah State Insurance Division, Salt Lake City. Robert Brian of Conning & Company in Hartford, Conn., provided us with some complicated but thorough guidelines for estimating the book value of each of these companies. Conning & Company employs recognized specialists in investment securities, including the appraisal of insurance companies throughout North America.

101. The uniqueness of the Mormon experience in American religion is stressed in Rodney Stark's seminal essay "How New Religions Succeed: A Theoretical Model," in David G. Bromley and Phillip Hammond, eds., "The Future of New Religious Movements" (unpublished manuscript, 1985).

102. See Jeffrey K. Hadden and Charles K. Swann, *Prime Time Preachers: The Rising Power of Televangelism* (Reading, Mass.: Addison-Wesley, 1981). Hadden and Swann discuss the fund-raising tactics and results of many major television preachers.

103. See David G. Bromley, "Financing the Millennium: The Economic Structure of the Unification Church," in James T. Richardson, ed., "Economic Policies and Practices of the New Religions" (unpublished manuscript, 1985).

104. Marden Clark, "Whose Yoke Is Easy?" *Sunstone Review* (November–December 1982): 43.

Chapter 4   Political and Military Power of the Latter-day Saints

1. "Pres. Reagan Writes to Elder," *Church News*, 22 August 1981, p. 11.

2. Cited in Gerry Avant, "Poll Reflects Views Toward LDS," *Church News*, 30 October 1983, p. 3.

3. A Discourse by President Heber C. Kimball, August 2, 1857, in *Journal of Discourses*, vol. 5 (Liverpool: Asa Calkin, 42, Islington 1858), p. 133.

4. "Preserving Our Loyalties," *Church News*, 6 November 1982, p. 16.

5. An excellent analysis of this issue of church versus state and Mormonism's role in American politics can be found in Therald N. Jensen, "Mormon Theory of Church and State" (Ph.D. diss., University of Chicago, 1938). A copy is available at the Special Collections, Marriott Library, University of Utah, Salt Lake City.

6. J. D. Williams, "Separation of Church and State in Mormon Theory and Practice," *Dialogue: A Journal of Mormon Thought* 1 (Summer 1966): 52.
7. Williams, "Separation," pp. 30–31.
8. "The Certain Sounds," *Church News*, 9 October 1983, p. 24.
9. Williams, "Separation," p. 40.
10. This theory was proposed most recently in the *Wall Street Journal*, 26 October 1979, p. 18. In "The Crash and Classical Economics," Jude Wanniski saw a direct connection between the Smoot-Hawley Tariff Act and Wall Street's woes: "The market crashed in the last week of October 1929 as it absorbed the hard news that there would almost certainly be a tariff act passed into law the following year."
11. LDS President Heber J. Grant, letter to Hon. Reed Smoot, 26 August 1922, Reed Smoot Collection, Box 48, Folder 10, Brigham Young University Library, Provo, Utah.
12. LDS President Heber J. Grant, letter to Hon. Reed Smoot, 20 October 1921, Reed Smoot Collection, Box 48, Folder 10, Brigham Young University Library, Provo, Utah.
13. See *Deseret News 1983 Church Almanac* (Salt Lake City: Deseret News, 1982), pp. 283–84.
14. Interview with Curt Burnett, press secretary for U.S. Senator Jake Garn (R-Utah), Washington, D.C., 18 March 1982.
15. H. George Frederickson and Aldeen J. Stevens, "The Mormon Congressman and the Line Between Church and State," *Dialogue: A Journal of Mormon Thought* 3 (Summer 1968): 121–29.
16. Dorothy Stowe, "Ex-Missionary Makes Transition From 'Finlandia' to Finland," *Church News*, 20 November 1982, p. 4.
17. "Hatch's Carrying the Flag on Conservative Issues," *Salt Lake Tribune*, 25 November 1981, editorial page, p. A-9.
18. Glen Warchol, "Nader Says Hatch, Garn Not Telling Whole Story on How They Really Vote," *Deseret News*, 2 February 1983, p. D-6.
19. "Politics and Piety: An Interview with Senator Orrin Hatch," *Sunstone Review* (September–October 1980): 54–55.
20. Interview, 1982.
21. Williams, "Separation," p. 47.
22. Williams, "Separation," p. 47.
23. Wendy Ogata, "Be Agents of Lord in Politics," *Daily Universe*, 12 October 1978, p. 13.
24. "Mormons? 'Many Liberals,'" *Salt Lake Tribune*, 26 February 1974, p. 24.
25. LaVarr Webb, "Mormon Vote Makes Democrats Shiver," *Deseret News*, 5 June 1983, p. B-1.
26. Williams, "Separation," p. 49.
27. LaVarr Webb, "Mormon Vote," p. B-8.
28. See "2-Party System Decayed by Mormondom?" *Salt Lake Tribune*, 21 June 1983, p. B-1, B-8.
29. Armand Mauss, "Moderation in All Things: Political and Social Outlooks of Modern Urban Mormons," *Dialogue: A Journal of Mormon Thought* 7 (Spring 1972): 58.
30. William F. Buckley, "Senate ERA Testimony Is Revealing," *Salt Lake Tribune*, 21 June 1983, p. A-13.

31. See Mary L. Bradford, "The Odyssey of Sonia Johnson," *Dialogue: A Journal of Mormon Thought* 14 (Summer 1981): 14–26, and Sonia Johnson, *From Housewife to Heretic* (Garden City, N.Y.: Doubleday, 1981).

32. Dixie Snow Huefner, "Church and Politics at the Utah IWY Conference," *Dialogue: A Journal of Mormon Thought* 11 (Spring 1978): 58.

33. Huefner, "Church and Politics," p. 61. Indeed, Huefner found that most of the women she contacted in her ward had never heard of the conference and only half were willing or able to attend.

34. Huefner, "Church and Politics," p. 64.

35. Huefner, "Church and Politics," p. 64.

36. Huefner, "Church and Politics," p. 63.

37. Passages and details taken from Richardson's study of the Nevada election and connected Mormon influence can be located in James T. Richardson, "The 'Old Right' in Action: Mormon and Catholic Involvement in an Equal Rights Amendment Referendum," in David G. Bromley and Anson Shupe, eds., *New Christian Politics* (Macon, Ga.: Mercer University Press, 1984), pp. 213–33.

38. Richardson, "'Old Right,'" pp. 21–22.

39. Richardson, "'Old Right,'" pp. 222–23.

40. Linda Cicero, "State Plans to Investigate Mormon Political Donations," *Miami Herald*, 22 April 1980, p. A-16.

41. Cicero, "State Plans," p. A-16.

42. Linda Cicero, "Mormon Money Worked Against Florida's ERA," *Miami Herald*, 20 April 1980, p. A-1.

43. Linda Cicero, "How the Mormons Helped Scuttle ERA," *Miami Herald*, 20 April 1980, p. 33-A.

44. "The Freemen Institute: A Decade of Progress" (brochure), Freemen Institute, Salt Lake City, n.d. (c. 1981), p. 2.

45. "The Freemen Institute: A Decade of Progress," p. 7.

46. "The Freemen Institute" (pamphlet), Freemen Institute, Salt Lake City, n.d. (c. 1981).

47. Interview with anonymous official, Freemen Institute, Salt Lake City, 1983.

48. W. Cleon Skousen, *"Miracle of America": Study Guide Appendix* (Salt Lake City: Freemen Institute, n.d. [c. 1981]), p. 170.

49. W. Cleon Skousen, *Behind the Scenes* (March 1980), p. 169.

50. Murray Dubin, "Probing Too Far? Anti-Communist Group's Data Gathering Questioned," *Dallas Times Herald*, 29 September 1983, p. A-2.

51. Dubin, "Probing," p. A-2.

52. Interview with administrative assistant, Western Goals, Alexandria, Va., 1983.

53. Ezra Taft Benson, *Civil Rights: Tool of Communist Deception* (Salt Lake City: Deseret Book Company, 1968), p. 3.

54. See "Politics and Piety," pp. 55–56.

55. Skousen, *"Miracle of America."*

56. Interview with vice-president, Freemen Institute, Salt Lake City, 16 December 1983.

57. Newspaper article reprinted in "Freemen Institute: A Decade of Progress," p. 11.

58. "Freemen Institute: A Decade of Progress," p. 18.

59. Interview with Cal Thomas, secretary, Moral Majority, Inc., Lynchburg, Va., 19 December 1983.

60. For Tim LaHaye, see a broadcast of a dialogue among Tim LaHaye, Jerry Falwell, and Cleon Skousen, KWJS-FM 95, 26 June 1982, Arlington, Tex.

61. William E. Burrows, "Skywalking with Reagan," *Harper's* (January 1984): 51.
62. Interview with Cleo Carley, secretary to the president, Eyring Research Center, Provo, Utah, 8 February 1982; also George Day, vice-president, Eyring Research Center, Provo, Utah, 5 January 1984.
63. "Hill AFB Is an Important Cog for Air Force, Utah," *Salt Lake Tribune*, 21 February 1982, p. K-3.
64. Borrows, "Skywalking," p. 54.
65. From an interview with an anonymous official, Automated Language Processing Systems, Salt Lake City, 20 December 1983; and Robert H. Woody, "Computer-Assisted Translations: Language Solution of the Future?" *Salt Lake Tribune*, 23 November 1983, p. B-4.
66. Frank Church, "Cold War Tactics Gain Renewed U.S. in U.S.," *Salt Lake Tribune*, 19 June 1983, p. A-1.
67. "CIA Now a 'Growth' Industry," *Salt Lake Tribune*, 25 June 1983, p. B-3.
68. David Shribman, "It's No Secret . . . The CIA Is Knee-Deep in Resumes," *Register* (Orange County, Calif.), 20 February 1982, p. 1.
69. "What the CIA Knew," *Newsweek*, 15 July 1974, p. 29.
70. See *Report to the President by the Commission on CIA Activities Within the United States* (Washington, D.C.: U.S. Government Printing Office, June 1975), pp. 173–76, 193–97.
71. *Report to the President.*
72. Kenneth C. Danforth, "The Cult of Mormonism," *Harper's* (May 1980): 72. For another popular source on the CIA and Mormonism, see Frances Lang, "The Mormon Empire," *Ramparts* 10 (September 1971): 37.
73. Donna Anderson, "Missionaries Mistaken for CIA Officers," *Los Angeles Times*, 26 November 1981, p. 15.
74. Cited in "Missionaries and the CIA," *Sunstone Review* (November–December 1981): 9.
75. Interview with Stan A. Taylor, director, Center for International and Area Study, Brigham Young University, Provo, Utah, 3 April 1982.
76. Anderson, "Missionaries," p. 15.
77. See Patrick J. McGarvey, *C.I.A.: The Myth and the Madness* (Baltimore: Penguin, 1974), p. 57.
78. Interview with (Bishop) Jeffrey Willis, personnel director, Central Intelligence Agency, Sterling, Va., 1 April 1982.
79. Interview with (Mormon) Jack Hansen, recruiting officer, Central Intelligence Agency, Denver, Colo., 13 April 1982.
80. See Dale Van Atta, "News, Y. Turn Up in Files of FBI," *Salt Lake Tribune*, 25 January 1981, p. 10-A, and Dale Van Atta, "Mutual Esteem Marked," *Salt Lake Tribune*, 25 January 1981, p. 10-A.
81. For a brief sampling of newspaper articles that appeared at the time of Miller's arrest, see "FBI Arrests Own Agent for Spying," *Salt Lake Tribune*, 4 October 1984, pp. 1–2; "Arrested Agent Attended Y in Early '60s," *Salt Lake Tribune*, 4 October 1984, p. 2; "FBI Veteran and Soviet Spy: Amateurs Out of Their Depth," *Fort Worth Star-Telegram*, 5 October 1984, p. 4A; and "'Ex-Agent Had Problems,' Officials Say," *Dallas Morning News*, 5 October 1984, p. 3A.
82. "Files Show LDS Supervisor Urged an Alleged FBI Spy to 'Repent,'" *Salt Lake Tribune*, 1 January 1985, p. A-6.
83. "FBI Agent to Tell Court He's No Spy," *USA Today*, 9 January 1985, p. A-3.
84. "FBI to Evaluate Its L.A. Office in Wake of Espionage Arrest," *Deseret News*, 18 October 1984, p. A-3.

85. "U.S. Agent Accused of Espionage Reportedly Had Work Problems," *New York Times*, 5 October 1985, p. 1.
86. "FBI Slips into a More Comfortable Image," *Deseret News*, 23 December 1984, p. B-1.
87. "FBI Names Ex-Bishop as Office Head," *Church News*, 22 May 1982, p. 11.
88. Based on the authors' personal observations of Church Security offices and interviews with anonymous informants.
89. Lang, "Mormon Empire," p. 43.
90. See Hubert Howe Bancroft, *History of Utah* (Salt Lake City: Bookcraft, 1964), p. 107.
91. Andrew Jensen, *The Historical Record* (Salt Lake City: Andrew Jensen, 1886), p. 690.
92. Bancroft, *History*, pp. 146–47.
93. John Henry Evans, *Joseph Smith: An American Prophet* (New York: Macmillan, 1938), p. 177.
94. Interview with Brigham Young University professor, Provo, Utah, 1983.
95. Golden A. Buchmiller, " 'You Provide an Anchor,' " *Church News*, 9 October 1983, p. 23.
96. " 'Research' General Promoted," *Church News*, 23 January 1982, p. 11.
97. Interview with anonymous informant, Department of Defense, Washington, D.C., 1983.
98. Interview, Washington, D.C., 1983.
99. Interview, Washington, D.C., 1983.
100. Dale L. Morgan, *The Great Salt Lake* (New York; Bobbs-Merrill, 1947), p. 398.
101. "Nix to MX," *Time*, 18 May 1981, p. 28.
102. Scott Davidson, "Waiting for Armageddon," *Utah Holiday* (June 1983): 24.
103. See excerpts of the statement in Constance Holden, "Mormons Rebel on MX," *Science* (22 May 1981): 904.
104. Carl T. Rowan, "Mormon MX Stand Looks 'Convenient,' " *Salt Lake City Tribune*, 13 May 1981, p. A-15.
105. See "MX Fallout in Zion," *Sunstone Review* (July–August 1981) for these and additional reviews of the LDS Church's MX policy statement.
106. Interview with anonymous informant, Department of Defense, 1983.
107. Interview, 1983.

Chapter 5 The Darker Side of Mormonism

1. John Sabini and Maury Silver, *Moralities of Everyday Life*, cited in David Gelman, "The Morality of Muddle," *Newsweek*, 29 March 1982, p. 69.
2. Cited in "Columnist Says LDS Welfare Plan Won't Work," *Sunstone Review* (November 1982): 9.
3. "3 on White House Task Force," *Church News*, 3 December 1981, p. 4.
4. Marc A. Rose, "The Mormons March Off Relief," *Reader's Digest* (June 1937): 43–44.
5. See Leonard J. Arrington and Wayne K. Hinton, "Origin of the Welfare Plan of the Church of Jesus Christ of Latter-day Saints," *Brigham Young University Studies* 5 (Winter 1964), particularly pp. 67–82.
6. Arrington and Hinton, "Origin," p. 77.
7. Arrington and Hinton, "Origin," p. 81.
8. Dean R. Brimhall, letter to Mr. Harold B. Lee, LDS president, 7 August 1936,

Dean R. Brimhall Papers, Box 22, Folder 5, University of Utah Library, Salt Lake City.

9. Kate Williams, acting director, Social Service Division, Salt Lake County Emergency Relief Administration, letter to Bishop Sylvester Q. Cannon, 6 December 1935, Dean R. Brimhall Papers, Box 26, Folder 10, University of Utah Library, Salt Lake City.

10. Dean R. Brimhall, letter to Charles Mottashed, 18 December 1937, Dean R. Brimhall Papers, Box 26, Folder 12, University of Utah Library, Salt Lake City.

11. Dean R. Brimhall, letter to E. A. Rusk, 20 August 1938, Dean R. Brimhall Papers, Box 26, Folder 14, University of Utah Library, Salt Lake City.

12. Dean R. Brimhall, letter to E. A. Rusk, 20 August 1938, Dean R. Brimhall Papers, Box 26, Folder 14, University of Utah Library, Salt Lake City.

13. Dean R. Brimhall, "The Myth of Mormon Work Relief," January 1938, unpublished manuscript, Dean R. Brimhall Papers, Box 26, Folder 1, p. 1, University of Utah Library, Salt Lake City.

14. Brimhall, "Myth," p. 3.

15. Brimhall, "Myth," p. 4.

16. Brimhall, "Myth," pp. 9–10.

17. Dean R. Brimhall, letter to John Franklin Carter, 26 November 1937, Dean R. Brimhall Papers, Box 26, Folder 12, University of Utah Library, Salt Lake City.

18. Dean R. Brimhall, letter to R. A. Wilkinson, 6 January 1939, Dean R. Brimhall Papers, Box 26, Folder 15, University of Utah Library, Salt Lake City.

19. George S. Ballif, letter to Nels Anderson, WPA Labor Relations, 16 February 1938, Dean R. Brimhall Papers, Box 19, Folder 1, University of Utah Library, Salt Lake City. See also Anderson's reply of 19 February 1938 in the same source. At a meeting at Brigham Young University in January 1938 that Ballif attended, he reports: "Dr. John A. Widstoe [an apostle] frankly admitted that the plan was an ideal which had not yet been put into operation. Incidentally, he was the only one of the speakers who admitted this. Harold B. Lee, administrator of the plan [before his later ordination as an apostle] evaluated it in terms of several millions of dollars' worth of publicity received in leading newspapers and periodicals."

20. Bishop Gordon Taylor Hyde, letter to President Franklin S. Harris, 25 October 1938, Dean R. Brimhall Papers, Box 19, Folder 2, University of Utah Library, Salt Lake City.

21. D. Michael Quinn, *J. Reuben Clark: The Church Years* (Provo, Utah: Brigham Young University Press, 1983), p. 278.

22. Quinn, *J. Reuben Clark*, p. 278.

23. Leonard J. Arrington, Feramorz Y. Fox, and Dean L. May, *Building the City of God* (Salt Lake City: Deseret Book Company, 1976), p. 353.

24. Cited in Stephen W. Stathis and Dennis L. Lythgoe, "Mormonism in the Nineteen Seventies: The Popular Perception," *Dialogue: A Journal of Mormon Thought* 10 (Spring 1977): 105.

25. Dean R. Brimhall, "Welfare Figures Revealing," Letter to Editor, *Salt Lake Tribune*, 3 July 1966, p. A-12.

26. "Welfare Building Planned," *Church News*, 21 June 1975, p. 3.

27. "Storehouse Is Dedicated," *Church News*, 4 October 1975, p. 4.

28. Remarks made at the Welfare Session of General Conference, 4 October 1975. See *Church News*, 11 October 1975, pp. 11–18, and "Storehouse System Being

Developed," *Church News*, 11 August 1979, p. 7.

29. Leonard J. Arrington and Davis Bitton, *The Mormon Experience* (New York: Vintage, 1979), p. 276.

30. David Briscoe and Bill Beecham, "Mormon Church Controls Excessive National Business Interests," *Post-Register* (Idaho Falls), 21 September 1975, p. A-11.

31. See George Raine, "Mormons Provide Welfare Example," *New York Times*, 25 October 1981, p. 37.

32. See *Deseret News 1983 Church Almanac* (Salt Lake City: Deseret News, 1982), p. 33.

33. See Garth N. Jones, "Expanding LDS Church Abroad: Old Realities Compounded," *Dialogue: A Journal of Mormon Thought* 13 (Spring 1980): 10.

34. Interview with official, Church Welfare Social Services office, Colton, Calif., 1981.

35. "Manage Resources Efficiently, Church Officers Counseled," *Ensign* (May 1981): 97.

36. Interview, Las Vegas, 1983.

37. See, for example, "Mormon Church to Close 38 Year-Old Cannery," *Salt Lake Tribune*, 4 February 1982, p. B-4.

38. An excellent example was the profitable Portland East Stake Dairy and Welfare Farm on Sauvie Island, Portland, Oreg., which one of us visited in April 1982.

39. Interview, Fallon, Nev., 1983.

40. Interviews with an agricultural representative, Church Welfare Department, 1983, 1985.

41. Interview with official, LDS Church Welfare Department, 1982.

42. This figure is mentioned in *Church News*, 11 August 1979, p. 7.

43. Interview with official, LDS Church Welfare Department, 1983.

44. Interview, Plattville-Mead, Colo., 1982.

45. Interviews, Gilbert, Ariz., 1983, and Riverside, Calif., 1981.

46. Interview with an official in the Church Welfare Social Services, Colton, Calif., 1981, and with an officer of the Los Angeles LDS Cannery, 1982.

47. Interview, Fallon, Nev., 1983.

48. Interview, Colton, Calif., 1981.

49. Robert T. Grieves, "An Inspired Clean-Up Campaign," *Time*, 20 June 1983, p. 25.

50. Ezra Taft Benson, "Fourteen Fundamentals in Following the Prophets," typed transcript of address presented to a Brigham Young University Devotional Assembly, 26 February 1980.

51. Donald Q. Cannon and Lyndon W. Cook, eds., *Far West Record* (Salt Lake City: Deseret Book Company, 1983), p. 160.

52. Brigham Young, "Remark Delivered in the Tabernacle, Great Salt Lake City, April 7, 1960," *Journal of Discourses*, vol. 7 (Liverpool, England: Amasa Lyman, 1860), pp. 227–28.

53. See "Sustaining the General Authorities," *Ward Teacher's Message* (Salt Lake City: Church of Jesus Christ of Latter-day Saints, June 1945). This source is also quoted in a typed copy of a manuscript entitled "Obedience and the Problem of Agency" by Harald E. Singer (Logan, Utah, n.d.) in the authors' possession.

54. Marion G. Romney, "The Covenant of the Priesthood," *Ensign* 2 (July 1972): 98.

55. "Priesthood," in *The Millennial Star* (Liverpool, England: S. W. Richards, 1852).

56. "Priesthood."
57. Dale L. Morgan, *The Great Salt Lake* (Indianapolis: Bobbs-Merrill, 1947), p. 403.
58. Dean R. Brimhall, letter to Miss Dorothy Kahn, 17 April 1939, Dean R. Brimhall Papers, Box 26, Folder 15, University of Utah Library, Salt Lake City.
59. Written by the late Apostle Mark E. Peterson (who regularly penned editorials for the *Church News*) in "When Shall It Be?" *Church News*, 12 December 1981, p. 16.
60. Cited in *1978 Devotional Speeches of the Year: BYU Devotional and Addresses* (Provo, Utah: Brigham Young University Press, 1978), p. 118.
61. Benson, "Fourteen Fundamentals," p. 9.
62. See, for a brief account of the Sonia Johnson affair, "A Savage Misogyny," *Time*, 17 December 1974, p. 80. When a man who holds the LDS priesthood is charged, the trial is more complicated.
63. Peter Bart, "Prigging Out," *Rolling Stone*, 14 April 1983, p. 89.
64. Bart, "Prigging Out," p. 92.
65. "Amnesty International Denied Club Status," *Seventh East Press*, 12 April 1982, p. 1.
66. "Westmoreland Demonstrators Interrogated," *Seventh East Press*, 14 March 1982, p. 1.
67. Ron Priddis, "BYU Spy Case Unshelved," *Seventh East Press*, 14 March 1982, p. 1.
68. Bart, "Prigging Out," p. 94.
69. Stephen Barnes, "BYU Says No to Earth, Wind and Fire," *Seventh East Press*, 18 January 1982, pp. 1, 7.
70. See, for example, David Long, "Oaks Supports Security's Police Powers," *Daily Universe*, 18 September 1979, p. 1.
71. Bart, "Prigging Out," p. 94.
72. "BYU Rejected Speakers for Morals, Politics," *Salt Lake Tribune*, 10 April 1980, p. B-4.
73. "KBYU Cancels Gay Documentary," *Sunstone Review* (September 1982): 8.
74. Blake Ostler, "7EP Interview: Sterling M. McMurrin," *Seventh East Press*, 11 January 1983, p. 1.
75. "BYU Bans Paper: Academic Freedom Too?" *Chronical* (University of Utah student newspaper), 27 July 1983, p. 1.
76. Kris Radish, "Y. Society Divided over Press Letter," *Deseret News*, 25 February 1983, p. B-1.
77. Interview with Brigham Young University professor, Provo, Utah, 15 February 1983.
78. See "Editor Cancels Visit to Y. over Paper Ban Issue," *Deseret News*, 17 February 1983, p. E-1; Con Psarra, "Journalist Cancels BYU Lecture over Paper's Ban," *Salt Lake Tribune*, 17 February 1983, p. B-1; and original wire service copy.
79. Interview with anonymous informant, LDS Church Public Communications Department, Salt Lake City, 1983.
80. "A New Paper Rises from the Ashes of the *7th East Press* Ban," *Utah Holiday* (April 1983): 3.
81. Sources on the *Western Scholar* include "Right-Wing Students Plan to Establish newspaper at BYU," *Salt Lake Tribune*, 21 July 1983, and interview with Stephen Reiher, Provo, Utah, 24 January 1984.
82. Fred Esplin, "The Saints Go Marching On," *Utah Holiday* (June 1981): 47.

83. Davis Bitton, "Like the Tigers of Old Time," *Sunstone Review* (September–October 1982): 7:47, no. 5.

84. Bitton, "Like the Tigers," p. 48.

85. Ostler, "7EP Interviews," p. 2.

86. Ostler, "7EP Interviews," p. 2.

87. Interview with Leonard J. Arrington, former LDS Church Historian, now at the Joseph Fielding Smith Historical Institute, Brigham Young University, Provo, Utah, by a University of California, Los Angeles, graduate student, 19 January 1984.

88. Cited in Bob Gottlieb and Peter Wiley, "Mormon Infighting Intensifies as Theologians Vie for Power," *Daily Californian* (Berkeley), 6 April 1982, p. 20.

89. See Gottlieb and Wiley, "Mormon Infighting," and Esplin, "Saints," p. 47.

90. "Mormon Brethren Silencing Scholars?" *Salt Lake Tribune*, 26 May 1983, p. B-4

91. "Several LDS Writers Say Officials Caution Them to Promote the Faith," *Deseret News*, 23 May 1983, p. B-2.

92. "Several LDS Writers."

93. Dawn Tracy, "LDS Bishops Want 'Faith-Promoting' Articles," *Herald* (Provo, Utah), 22 May 1983, p. 3.

94. Tracy, "LDS Bishops."

95. "Historian Responds to Apostle," *Seventh East Press*, 18 November 1981, pp. 1–2.

96. Interview with George Boy, former seminary and institute instructor, Church Education System, Provo, Utah, 2 March 1983.

97. Interview with anonymous informant, Acquisitions Division, LDS Church Historical Department, Salt Lake City, 1983. See also Gottlieb and Wiley, "Mormon Infighting," p. 20.

98. Gordon B. Hinckley, "'Stop Looking for Storms and Enjoy the Sunlight,'" *Church News*, 3 July 1983, p. 11.

99. See Gottlieb and Wiley, "Mormon Infighting," p. 20.

100. Connie Thornton, "Y Historians, Writers Claim No Pressures from LDS Authorities," *Daily Universe*, 26 May 1983, p. 2.

101. "Mormon Brethren Silencing Scholars?" p. B-4.

102. Ostler, "7EP Interview," p. 3.

103. Interview with Thomas E. Cheney, professor emeritus of English and folklore, Brigham Young University, Provo, Utah, and author of *The Golden Legacy: A Folk History of J. Golden Kimball* (Provo, Utah: Brigham Young University Press, 1973), 5 March 1982, and 22 May 1985.

104. Interview with Scott G. Kenney, owner, Signature Books, Midvale, Utah, 22 May 1983.

105. Alan F. Keele and Douglas F. Tobler, "The Fuhrer's New Clothes: Helmuth Hubener and the Mormons in the Third Reich," *Sunstone Review* 5 (November–December 1980): 27. There is a shred of evidence that at least a few LDS leaders admired Benito Mussolini during the 1920s, not because the Church had made great inroads in Italy but because Mussolini made much of his own abstinence from alcohol and coffee. See "Editorial: A Prime Minister's Diet," *The Millennial Star* (published by the Church in Great Britain) 89 (10 February 1927): 88–90.

106. Joseph M. Dixon, "Mormons in the Third Reich: 1933–45," *Dialogue: A Journal of Mormon Thought* 7 (Spring 1972), pp. 70–78. Nazis stopped the dis-

tribution of this tract, "resenting the implication that the party sanctioned any American religious sect."

107. Keele and Tobler, "The Fuhrer's New Clothes," p. 23.
108. Dixon, "Mormons in the Third Reich," p. 74.
109. See R. Clayton Brough, *His Servants Speak* (Bountiful, Utah: Horizon, 1975), p. 77.
110. Brough, *His Servants*, pp. 75–76.
111. Bruce R. McConkie, *Mormon Doctrine* (Salt Lake City: Bookcraft, 1966), p. 151.
112. *My Kingdom Shall Roll Forth* (Salt Lake City: Church of Jesus Christ of Latter-day Saints, 1980), p. 108.
113. John R. Iler, "Cleon Skousen Retires, Reviews Many Careers," *Monday Magazine* (17 April 1978): 26.
114. Alexv Adjoubey, *The Silver Cat, or Travels in America* (Moscow, USSR, 1956), portion of an English translation discovered in the Frank Moss Papers, Box 245, Folder 22, Western Americana Section, Marriott Library, University of Utah Library, Salt Lake City.
115. Interview with chairperson, Brigham Young University Dance Department, Provo, Utah, 16 January 1982.
116. Interview with the director, Office of Performance Scheduling, Brigham Young University, Provo, Utah, 16 January 1984.
117. "Y Dancers Honored," *Church News*, 6 October 1979, p. 13.
118. "Touring Groups Touch Hearts," *Church News*, 20 June 1981, p. 4.
119. Interview with the director, Office of Performance Scheduling, Brigham Young University, Provo, Utah, 16 January 1984.
120. Interviews with Paul Hyer, Salt Lake City, 1980, and with Professor Spencer J. Palmer, Department of Languages, University of Utah, Salt Lake City, 18 January 1984.
121. "Door to China May Be Opening," *Church News*, 7 April 1979, p. 3.
122. Lynne Hollstein Housen, "Y. Students a Success in China," *Daily Universe*, 11 August 1979, p. 10.
123. Interview with Professor Spencer J. Palmer, Department of Languages, University of Utah, Salt Lake City, 18 January 1984.
124. Gordon B. Hinckley, "China Hosts BYU Performing Group," *Church News*, 23 August 1980, p. 4.
125. "Touring Groups Touch Hearts," *Church News*, 20 June 1981, p. 4.
126. "Chinese Ambassador Visits Utah," *Church News*, 17 January 1981, p. 5.
127. See Doug Curran, Mike Foley, and Reg Schwenke, "Through Open Doors . . .," *Church News*, 15 January 1984, pp. 8–10; interview with Dr. J. Elliot Cameron, president, Brigham Young University–Hawaii, Laie, Oahu, 16 January 1984; and Sheri L. Dew, "As Elder Statesman," *This People* (March–April 1984): 22–29.
128. Interview with director, Office of Performance Scheduling, Brigham Young University, Provo, Utah, 16 January 1984.
129. These are metaphors suggested to us by various Church representatives who have visited the People's Republic of China since 1979.
130. B. Carmon Hardy, "Cultural 'Encystment' as a Cause of the Exodus from Mexico in 1912," *Pacific Historical Review* 34 (1965): 447.
131. *Ensign* (November 1980): 76.
132. See, for example, George Raine, "Paiute Tribe's 3rd Gathering Holds Hope,"

Salt Lake Tribune, 2 April 1983, p. B-3.

133. Bob Gottlieb and Peter Wiley, "The Kids Go Out Navaho, Come Back Donny and Marie," *Los Angeles Magazine* (December 1979): 140.

134. "Prophecy Fulfilled," *Church News,* 17 April 1976, p. 16.

135. Gottlieb and Wiley, "The Kids Go Out," p. 140.

136. Interview with Courtney Reddoor, director, Indian Walk-in Center, Salt Lake City, Utah, 22 December 1981.

137. Interview with Kesley Edmo, tribal chairman, Shoshone-Bannock Nation, Fort Hall, Idaho, 8 January 1982.

138. Interview with Ronnie Lupe, chairman, White Mountain Apache Tribe, White River, Ariz., 1 February 1982.

139. Interview with Peter McDonald, tribal chairman, Navajo Tribal Council, Window Rock, Ariz., 23 December 1981.

140. Frank Brunsman, "AIM Blasts LDS Church, Demands Missionary Recall," *Salt Lake Tribune,* 12 April 1974, p. 6-B.

141. Murray Boren, "Worship Through Music Nigerian Style," *Sunstone Review* (November–December 1980): 42.

142. "LDS Relief Society President Talks About Women," *Salt Lake Tribune,* 4 September 1983, p. 4-W.

143. "Social Ills Created at Home," *Salt Lake Tribune,* 4 September 1983, p. 1.

144. "Social Ills."

145. Verna F. Willson, "Quality Counts," *Salt Lake Tribune,* 13 October 1982, p. A-13.

146. William A. Stacey and Anson Shupe, *The Family Secret: Domestic Violence in America* (Boston: Beacon, 1983), pp. 26–60.

147. Dawn Tracy, "A Dilemma for Working Mormon Women," *Salt Lake Tribune,* 14 September 1983, p. 1.

148. LeGrand Richards, *Israel! Do You Know?* (Salt Lake City: Deseret Book Company, 1954), p. 209.

149. Ezra Taft Benson, "Speaking Today: 'A Message to Judah from Joseph,'" *Ensign* (December 1976): 70.

150. LeGrand Richards, "The Mormons and the Jewish People" (pamphlet) (Salt Lake City: Deseret Press, n.d.), p. 1.

151. See Benson, "Speaking Today," p. 71.

152. "A Message from the District Presidency," *Israel Light* (September 1980): 1.

153. See Kathleen Lubeck, "David B. Galbraith: Teacher on the Mount," *This People* (October–November 1982): 31–34, and "Truman G. Madsen Teaches at Haifa University," *Israel Light* (September 1980): 2.

154. Benson, "Speaking Today," p. 67.

155. See, for example, "The Shofar," a mimeographed newsletter of B'nai Shalom, Salt Lake City, September 1981.

156. "Jew or Mormon," *Time,* 16 November 1959, p. 60.

157. "Jew or Mormon."

158. Interview with an anonymous informant, LDS Church International Mission Office, Salt Lake City, 19 January 1984; also personal correspondence with Jan Krancher, 29 July 1983, from Madinat Al-Jubail Al-Sinaiyah, Saudi Arabia.

159. Bob Gottlieb and Peter Wiley, "Triad Utah: Angels or Flying Carpetbaggers?" *Utah Holiday* (March 1983): 45.

160. Robert Gottlieb and Peter Wiley, *America's Saints: The Rise of Mormon Power*

(New York: Putnam, 1984), pp. 115–17.

161. Interview with an anonymous informant, LDS Church International Mission Office, Salt Lake City.

162. The number employed by the law firm as of 1983, according to interviews with anonymous KM&B personnel throughout 1982.

163. See Nadine W. Scott, "Mormon Sued for Slander," *Honolulu Star-Bulletin*, 3 April 1976, p. A-5.

164. See "Ex-Patient Asks for Damages," *Salt Lake Tribune*, 30 May 1973, p. B-5; "Rule Delay Okayed in LDS Suit," *Salt Lake Tribune*, 15 September 1973, p. 34; "Testimony Begins in Alienation Suit," *Salt Lake Tribune*, 11 October 1973, p. B-2; "Divorced Plaintiff Cites 'Devil Worship' in Case," *Salt Lake Tribune*, 12 October 1973, p. B-1; and "Ruling Exonerates Former Bishop," *Salt Lake Tribune*, 16 October 1973, p. 14.

165. "Father's Lawsuit Blames LDS for Son's Suicide," *Salt Lake Tribune*, 4 March 1983, p. C-2.

166. See "Corp. of the President of the Church of Jesus Christ of Latter-day Saints v. Douglas A. Wallace," *Pacific Reporter*, vol. 573, 2d ser. (St. Paul, Minn.: West), pp. 285–88.

167. Salt Lake City v. Zion's Security Corporation, summons 81CR005582, Circuit Court, Salt Lake City, 7 August 1981.

168. See, for example, "Mormons Reject Pleas to Save Buildings," *New York Times*, 30 November 1980, p. 26.

169. Margaret St. Claire, "A Compromise for the Eagle Gate Apartments: The Result of Concern for *That* Building on *That* Corner," *Utah Holiday* (February 1982): 12.

170. For further details on the case and our sources, see Malcolm N. McKinnon v. The Corp. of The President of The Church of Jesus Christ of Latter-day Saints, case no. 13553, 3rd Judicial District Court, Salt Lake County, Salt Lake City, appealed to the Supreme Court of the state of Utah.

171. Interview with attorney Frank Armstrong, Salt Lake City, 10 December 1981, and interview with Mrs. Malcolm McKinnon, Salt Lake City, 9 December 1981.

172. "Malcolm N. McKinnon v. The Corp. of The President of The Church of Jesus Christ of Latter-day Saints," case no. 13553, brief of cross-appellant and respondent (The Church); *Supreme Court of Utah Abstracts & Briefs*, 13551–13565, vol. 892, pp. 14–18.

173. *Supreme Court of Utah*, pp. 14–15.

174. *Supreme Court of Utah*, pp. 23–28.

175. Christine J. Amos, et al. v. The Corporation of The Presiding Bishopric of The Church of Jesus Christ of Latter-day Saints and The Corporation of The President of The Church of Jesus Christ of Latter-day Saints, civil no. C-83-0492W, filed in the U.S. District Court, District of Utah, Central Division, Salt Lake City.

176. Christine J. Amos, et al., "Memorandum in Opposition to Defendants' Motions to Dismiss or for Summary Judgement," pp. 61–62.

177. Christine J. Amos, et al., "Motion to Dismiss or for Summary Judgement, Memorandum in Support of Defendants' Motion to Dismiss This Action, Affidavits and Index," civil no. C-83-0492W, pp. 47, 50.

178. Christine J. Amos, et al., "Affidavit of Lorene Kite," p. 2.

179. Christine J. Amos, et al., "Affadavit of Deniece Kanon," p. 3.

180. Christine J. Amos, et al., "Affidavit of Arthur Frank Mayson," p. 3.
181. Terence J. Moore, "Individual Rights of Employees Within the Corporation," *The Corporation Law Review* 6 (Winter 1983): 39–40.
182. Mary J. Larsen v. R. Ferris Kirkham, Neal A. Maxwell, LDS Business College, et al., civil no. C-74-287, filed in the U.S. District Court, District of Utah (but kept in the Federal Records Center in Denver, Colo.). See particularly "Memorandum in Support of Motion to Dismiss & in Opposition to Motion of Plaintiff to Compel Discovery," pp. 1–3, and "Plaintiff's Answer to Defendants' First Set of Interrogatories," p. 10.
183. "England Bound," *Church News*, 23 March 1963, p. 3.
184. Wendy Ogata, "Be Agents of the Lord in Politics," *Daily Universe*, 12 October 1978, p. 13.
185. Interview with Ben Cavaness, deputy prosecuting attorney, Power County, Idaho, 31 December 1982.
186. "Planning for the Future Boom," *Nation's Business* (June 1975): 58.
187. "Change Comes to Zion's Empire," *Business Week*, 23 November 1957, p. 110.
188. See "LDS Placed on Area Tax Roster," *Salt Lake Tribune*, 11 July 1970, p. 19, and "LDS Tax Denial Not Universal, Official Reports," *Salt Lake Tribune*, 2 July 1971, p. 20.
189. See "LDS Loses Tax Break Bid," *Salt Lake Tribune*, 11 July 1970, p. 19.
190. See John L. Schwartz, "County and Church Continue Battle over Farmlands Taxes," *Arizona Republic*, 12 March 1972, p. A-1, and "Court Says Church Has Taxable Land," *Arizona Republic*, 30 June 1972, p. 32.
191. Pamela G. Hollis, "Cultural Center in Hawaii Fights I.R.S. Tax Ruling," *New York Times*, 26 March 1981, p. A-16.
192. Internal Revenue Service's National Office Technical Advice Memorandum Prepared September 24, 1976, pp. 13, 15. Exhibit A in civil no. 80-0636 filed in the U.S. District Court of Hawaii.
193. Internal Revenue Service's, pp. 3, 14.
194. See "Interrogatories of the Defendant," filed 8 May 1981, civil no. 80-0636, U.S. District Court of Hawaii, pp. 1–2.
195. "Interrogatories," p. 7.
196. Hollis, "Cultural Center," p. A-16.
197. Exhibits 81 and 85 accompanying defendants' (USA/IRS) interrogatories, civil no. 80-0636, filed 8 May 1981, in U.S. District Court of Hawaii.

Chapter 6   Religious Liberty and the Kingdom of God

1. Paul Blanshard, *American Freedom and Catholic Power*, 2d ed. (Boston: Beacon, 1958), p. 337.
2. Robert Gottlieb and Peter Wiley, *America's Saints: The Rise of Mormon Power* (New York: Putnam's, 1984).
3. "Anderson to Watchdog," *Sunstone Review* (June 1983): 3.
4. Interviews with staff members, Free of the Eagle, Centerville, Va., 25 January 1984.
5. "Bomb Injures Mormon Linked to Letter on Church," *New York Times*, 17 October 1985, p. A-17; "1980 Discovery of Anthon Letter Launched Hofmann's Career," *Deseret News*, 17-18 October 1985, p. A-3.
6. Cited in Richard N. Ostling, *Secrecy in the Church: A Reporter's Case for the Right to Know* (New York: Harper and Row, 1974), pp. 107–8.

7. Ostling, *Secrecy*, p. 162.

8. Ostling, *Secrecy*, p. 6.

9. Max Weber, *The Sociology of Religion*, trans. Ephrain Fischoff (Boston: Beacon, 1956), pp. 20–31, 46–59.

10. Hugh Nibley, "Leaders to Managers: The Fatal Shift," *Dialogue: A Journal of Mormon Thought* 16 (Winter 1983): 15.

11. Frank Goble, *Excellence in Leadership* (New York: American Management Association, 1972), p. 8.

12. Goble, *Excellence*, p. 106. Goble also notes: "The best way to kill creativity is to select suspicious, critical, insecure, defensive people as supervisors at every level." Fear has a gravity that drives out the nonfearful and courageous at each succeeding lower level in a pyramidal structure, leaving only the functionaries who treat the straight and narrow as their guide to moral certainty.

13. Interview with Jay E. Welch, former Mormon Tabernacle Choir conductor, 1984.

14. Interview with Dennis Drake, cochairman for the Days of 47 Parade Committee, Salt Lake City, 7 February 1984.

15. Hugh Nibley, "Leaders to Managers," p. 21.

16. Alexis de Tocqueville, "Principal Causes Which Render Religion Powerful in America" (1835), in Fred Krinsky, ed., *The Politics of Religion in America* (Beverly Hills, Calif.: Glencoe, 1968), p. 38.

Index

The Authors

John Heinerman is a medical anthropologist residing in Salt Lake City, Utah. He is the author of numerous books and professional as well as popular articles on herbal folk medicine. He has traveled extensively throughout the United States and South America, China, southern Asia, and Eastern Europe for his research and speaks frequently before various audiences. He has devoted much of the past several years' travels to investigating the wealth and influence of the Church of Jesus Christ of Latter-day Saints.

Anson Shupe is associate director of the Center for Social Research at the University of Texas at Arlington and professor of sociology there. His research specialties include the sociology of religious movements, politics, and family violence. He has coauthored two Beacon Press books: *Strange Gods: The Great American Cult Scare* (with David G. Bromley, 1981) and *The Family Secret: Domestic Violence in America* (with William A. Stacey, 1983).